FOR GOD'S GLORY ALONE

FOR GOD'S GLORY ALONE

A *festschrift* in recognition of
the service of Bob Penhearow

Biblical, Theological, Historical, Biographical and Pastoral Essays

Dr. Ron Barnes / Dr. Jonathan Bayes, editor / Dr. Tim Beavis
Dr. Gareth Crossley / Dr. Perry Edwards / Dr. Paul Engle
Dr. Michael Haykin / Dr. Ray Martin / Rev. Carl Muller
Dr. Glendon Thompson / Rev. Ray Tibs
Rev. Gang Wang / Dr. Steve West

CAREY
PRINTING PRESS

BOB PENHEAROW was born in Tottenham, London, England, on March 25, 1953. His early education suffered due to asthma, an eye injury and a radical change in the British school system. Bob eventually dropped out of school at age 15, having completed only seven years.

Looking for meaning in life, Bob joined a spiritualist church and trained for five years in a closed circle to become a psychic medium. Dorothy, his then-fiancée, desired a church wedding which, by God's grace, led to their conversion to Christianity at the age of 25. Bob was later set aside and sponsored by Broadmead Baptist Church, Woodford Green, UK, to study theology in Toronto, Canada. On completing his M.Div., Bob returned to London to be ordained in May 1986, returning to Canada to answer a church call. Bob pastored a total of three churches (Sudbury, New Dundee, Guelph) over the next thirty years.

By God's grace, Bob founded two ministries to train indigenous pastors globally: Carey Outreach Ministry (1997, Canada) and Carey International University of Theology (2005, USA). Today, Carey serves 13–15 Bible schools in 11 countries across three continents. As a humanitarian sister to Carey, Glory Grace International Ministries was founded in 2005 to serve indigenous churches globally, focusing on orphans, widows and the poor.

Realizing his lack of education, Bob studied part-time over a twenty-five-year period. He currently holds two Doctor of Ministry degrees (Faith, Knox) and is currently completing his third, a Doctor of Theology (Evangelical).

Bob is married to Dorothy and they have four children and three grandchildren. He enjoys scuba diving, motorcycling, chess (usually losing) and science fiction.

Bob & Dorothy Penhearow

CAREY
PRINTING PRESS

Published by
Carey International University of Theology Inc., The Villages, Florida, USA
www.careyuniversity.org

About us
Carey Printing Press is the publishing arm of Carey International University of Theology, an international Christian organization that provides theological training to spiritual leaders to shape the church and influence the nations.

First published in 2021 by Carey Outreach Ministries U.K. (ISBN 978-0-6071-869-7)

Cover design: Janice Van Eck

For God's Glory Alone: A Festschrift In Recognition of the Service of Bob Penhearow
Editor: Jonathan Bayes

ISBN **978-1-990586-01-9** (paperback)

Contents

List of Contributors

Ronald C. BARNES holds a D.Min. from Southern Baptist Theological Seminary. He is the Lead Pastor of Grand River Community Church, Elora, Ontario, Canada. He has been serving with *Carey* for 23 years as a lecturer and as secretary of the Board of Directors.

Jonathan F. BAYES holds a Ph.D. from the University of Sunderland. He is Pastor of Stanton Lees Chapel in Derbyshire, England, and *Carey*'s U.K. Director. He has been serving with *Carey* for 17 years as a lecturer and writer.

Timothy K. BEAVIS holds a D.Min. from Gordon-Conwell Theological Seminary. Based in the U.S.A., he has served as *Carey*'s Vice President of International Operations since 2018.

Gareth CROSSLEY holds a Ph.D. from the University of Birmingham. He is an itinerant preacher and trainer, counsellor and author, based in England. He has been serving with *Carey* for 8 years as a lecturer and writer.

Perry EDWARDS holds a D.A.R. from Whitefield Theological Seminary. He is Pastor of Sovereign Grace Baptist Church in Oromocto, New Brunswick, Canada. He has been serving with *Carey* for 16 years as a lecturer.

Paul E. ENGLE holds a D.Min. from Westminster Theological Seminary, Philadelphia. After serving in pastoral ministry and as a publisher with Zondervan, he is now a visiting professor at several schools in the U.S.A. He has been serving with *Carey* as a senior lecturer for a number of years.

Michael A. G. HAYKIN holds a Th.D. from Wycliffe College and the University of Toronto. He is Professor of Church History and Biblical Spirituality and Director of the Andrew Fuller Center for Baptist Studies at the Southern Baptist Theological Seminary in

Louisville, Kentucky, U.S.A., Professor of Church History at Heritage Seminary in Cambridge, Ontario, Canada, and Director of Newton House Theological Research Centre in Oxford, England. He served on *Carey*'s Board of Directors in its early years.

Raymond L. MARTIN holds a Th.D. from the University of Zululand. Now retired, he was previously Pastor of Trinity Baptist Church in Allentown, Pennsylvania, U.S.A. He has been serving with *Carey* as a lecturer since 2011.

Carl MULLER holds a B.Th. from Ontario Bible College. He is Pastor of Providence Baptist Church in Burlington, Ontario, Canada, and lectures in Homiletics at Toronto Baptist Seminary. He has served with *Carey* for some years as a lecturer.

Glendon G. THOMPSON holds a Ph.D. from the University of Potchefstroom. He is Senior Pastor of Jarvis Street Baptist Church in Toronto, Canada, and President of Toronto Baptist Seminary. He served for several years as a member of *Carey*'s Board of Directors and as a lecturer.

Raymond J. TIBBS holds an M.A. from Liverpool University. Now retired, he was previously Editorial Director of Go Teach Publications in the U.K. He has served with *Carey* as a lecturer since 1998, and was for several years the U.K. Coordinator; he has also been involved in providing libraries at some of *Carey*'s overseas teaching venues.

Gang WANG holds an M.Div. from Toronto Baptist Seminary, Canada, where he currently works as Registrar. He served with *Carey* as Resource Development Manager from 2007 to 2015, and is now a member of the Board of Directors.

Steven D. WEST holds a Ph.D. from Northwest University. He is Pastor of Madoc Baptist Church in Ontario, Canada, and a professor at Heritage College and Seminary. He serves with *Carey* as a lecturer and writer.

Preface

I first came across the name of Bob Penhearow when I read an article which he had written in *Evangelical Times* some time in 2001. The article concerned *Carey*'s work in the Philippines. This was also the first time that I had ever heard of *Carey Outreach Ministries* (as it was known internationally in those days[1]), but having relatively recently returned after teaching for the year 2000 summer semester at Grace Ministerial Academy in Manila, the reference to the Philippines caught my attention. I decided that I wanted to learn more about *Carey*'s work, and, with the help of *Evangelical Times*, I was put in touch with Ray Tibbs, *Carey*'s U.K. Coordinator at that time.

Having introduced me to the work, Ray then suggested that I might become involved, a suggestion to which I was very pleased to make a positive response. Ray passed my details on to Bob, whom he had known personally for many years, long before the birth of *Carey*. My first direct contact with Bob occurred a little while later when he phoned me, and gave me a further briefing on the vision and the work. That proved to be the first of many phone calls which I have since received from him, and how graciously he comes across, what encouragements he passes on, and what a blessing it has been so many times to share prayer together across the Atlantic, over the phone (and, more recently, via Zoom).

My first overseas trip for *Carey* took place in 2004, and, not surprisingly, given the source of my initial contact, took me back to the Philippines. On that first trip with *Carey*, I was accompanied by my wife and daughter. En route we stopped over in Manila to visit the friends we had made there, by now four years previously, before flying on to Panay Island and *Carey*'s base at Iloilo.

I shall always remember breakfast in the hotel on the first morning that we were there. I overheard a conversation across the dining room, and picked up references to *Carey*. I quickly realised that one of those present was Bob, so I went over to introduce myself.

---

[1] In 2019, *Carey*'s North American branches opted to rename the work *Carey International Pastoral Training*. The U.K. branch chose not to adopt the new title because of its similarity to the name of another U.K. ministry, and the need to avoid confusion.

And what a pleasant first meeting with him that was. I discovered that he had just flown into the Philippines from another Far Eastern country, though I had no inkling at that moment how significant that other country would become for me and my involvement with *Carey* in the years to come.

Since that first meeting with Bob, it has continued to be a sheer joy to work with him over 17 years so far. I count it a great privilege to have been asked by *Carey*'s Board of Directors to edit this Festschrift in recognition of his service for the Lord over many years. Although he has now entered into (semi) retirement, I have no doubt that he will remain busy about the Lord's work.

The title of the Festschrift, *For God's Glory Alone*, is based on the introduction to *Carey*'s stated philosophy of education: *Carey* "seeks to train leaders, who desire to shape their own local churches and influence the nations <u>for the glory of God</u>." The first of *Carey*'s seven principles, entitled 'Theology→Doxology,' emphasises this point. It reads: "All teaching must be exegetically based on Scripture with the goal of bringing <u>glory to God</u>."[2]

As I have re-read this entire book for its final edit, I have been freshly struck by the number of references to the glory of God that permeate these papers. It seems that this overarching goal, which, thanks to Bob, shapes *Carey*'s identity, has become deeply impressed upon all of us who have had the privilege of involvement with *Carey*.

In editing this work, I have tried to group the papers thematically, resulting in four sections. There are some papers which could have fitted perfectly into more than one section. I trust that the contributors will be satisfied with my decisions about allocation!

And so, as Bob himself would most definitely say, *soli Deo gloria*, to God alone be all the glory.

Jonathan Bayes
(Director, Carey-U.K.)

---

[2] www.careyoutreach.org/about-us/history-distinctives.

Biblical Papers

God's Blessing and his Glory

Tim Beavis

It is not uncommon, whether inside of the church or out of it, to hear people speaking of God's blessing. Many believers, unsure of what to pray for, may ask, "God, would you bless Aunt Sally today...." A sneeze, likewise, is routinely followed by the bestowal of "God bless you," from someone sat nearby. Furthermore, for those in the United States, we have grown accustomed to hearing whoever the sitting President is (regardless of political party), conclude his speeches with the words, "and may God bless these United States of America." It seems that the blessing of God is a recurring thought on the minds of people, even when they do not give any particular thought as to its meaning or significance.

Tragically, God's blessing has also become the central focus of false teachers and other preachers who distort the pure gospel for the purpose of personal gain. The so called 'prosperity gospel' seems to have spread like wildfire in many regions of the world. It is, however, a distortion of God's word, a near rejection of the sinfulness of man, and a departure from the substitutionary atonement of Christ and of the need of salvation through him alone. It is a man-focused rather than God-focused message. At its heart it is a doctrine of works, with the false promise of material blessing and the divine recompense for obedience to whatever the preacher may be advocating. Jones and Woodbridge summarise the problem of this "blessing-focused" teaching saying, "The prosperity gospel has an appealing but fatal message: accept God and he will bless you—because you deserve it." They go on to explain something of the extent of this destructive teaching which reaches far beyond the realm of the polished North American television evangelists:

> The appeal of this teaching crosses racial, gender, denominational, and international boundaries. The prosperity gospel is on the rise not only in the United States but also in Africa, South America, India, and Korea, among many other places. In 2006, the Pew Forum conducted an international

survey of Pentecostals and other like-minded Christians. The
results of this survey were staggering. In Nigeria, 96 percent
of those who professed belief in God either completely agreed
or mostly agreed that God will grant material riches if one has
enough faith. Believers in the countries of India (82 percent)
and Guatemala (71 percent) gave similar responses. Likewise,
a significant number of those surveyed asserted their belief that
God will grant good health and relief from sickness to believers
who have enough faith.[1]

The need has never been greater for faithful men, who know how
rightly to divide the word of truth,[2] to be trained up in order to
shepherd the church, expose falsehood, and winsomely declare the
pure and glorious message of Christ. While such training is often
widely available in westernised countries (a fact that we might rightly
refer to as a blessing), that is often not the case throughout much of
the rest of the world, where nearly 9 out of every 10 churches are led
by pastors who have never had the opportunity to receive any kind of
formal training. For this reason, the work of *Carey International
Pastoral Training* (formerly *Carey Outreach Ministries*), and other
ministries like it, is so strategic and so needed for the strengthening of
the church today.

Yet, while an unhealthy focus on God's blessing has caused great
harm, the answer is not to ignore it completely. Rather, there is a great
need to restore a proper biblical understanding of the blessing of God,
and with it the implications for those who, by grace, are recipients of
his blessings.

A survey of the biblical text reveals that Scripture has a lot to say
about the blessing of God, and certainly his blessings are many and
varied. While a full treatment of the theology of God's blessing is
beyond the scope of this work, it is believed that Psalm 67 has much
to say on the matter. As such, the following discussion will be rooted
in an exposition of this passage. Within the Psalm's seven verses
(eight in the Hebrew text), the observant reader finds answers to

---

[1] D. W. Jones & R. S. Woodbridge, *Health, Wealth & Happiness: Has the Prosperity
Gospel Overshadowed the Gospel of Christ?* (Grand Rapids: Kregel, 2011), 3.
[2] Cf. 2 Tim. 2:15 (NKJV).

important questions like, these: (1) Is it right for someone to seek God's blessing? (2) Why does God bless his people? (3) What is the purpose of God's blessing? (4) How are we as a blessed people to live? Rather than press the Psalm into these categories, the answers to these questions will unfold through the study of the text itself.

God blesses his people for the sake of the nations

Psalm 67 is a song of praise and of petition to God. Verse 6 has led some to believe that this was perhaps a harvest time song for the people of Israel. However, the prevalence of the blessing motif, combined with the missional focus of the nations, leads VanGemeren to conclude that any particular association with the Feast of Tabernacles and the harvest festival is unlikely.[3] The Psalm's title does little to aid in identifying either an author or setting, simply indicating "To the Choirmaster: with stringed instruments. A Psalm. A Song." Nevertheless, this lack of a clear historical setting does nothing to obscure the meaning or significance of the Psalm or its obvious rootedness in the Abrahamic Covenant—so much so that Kidner observes,

> If a Psalm was ever written round the promises to Abraham, that he would be both blessed and made a blessing, it could well have been such as this.[4]

Beginning with a petition to God in verse 1, it is clear that one of the questions already posited is answered in the affirmative, 'Is it right to seek or to pray for God's blessing?' The Psalmist, through his own petition, reveals to the reader a resounding 'yes!' Nevertheless, he goes on to demonstrate what the purpose of God's blessing is, and as he does so the attentive reader will discover the important corrective, that our God-given blessings are not primarily for ourselves.

---

[3] W. A. VanGemeren, 'Psalms,' in F. E. Gaebelein (ed.), *Expositor's Bible Commentary, Vol. 5* (Grand Rapids: Zondervan, 1991), 439.
[4] F. D. Kidner, *Psalms 1-72* (Downers Grove: IVP, 2014), 254.

One can hardly read verse 1 without hearing the echo of the Aaronic blessing from Numbers 6:24-26. It was almost certainly in the mind of the biblical author. While in Numbers the passage takes the form of a declaration of blessing, utilising the divine name *Yahweh*, here in the sixty-seventh Psalm it is a petition addressed, using the more general title for God, to *'Elōhîm*. Both the declaration and the petition, however, are concerned with the bestowal of divine favour. To be "gracious" and "make his face to shine upon us," both have the sense of appealing to God to 'look kindly on his people.' Both here and in Numbers 6 the word "bless" is from the Hebrew *bārak*. Although having at its root the sense of 'kneeling,' the context of its use as in these two passages is clearly that of bestowing a blessing (probably connected to this idea of the kneeling posture of the one who is being blessed). *Bārak* is commonly found in the Hebrew (occurring 3 times in this Psalm alone), and frequently gives the sense of

> invoking divine favor: the intent [is] that the object will have favorable circumstances or state at a future time.[5]

It is notably a 'blessing' that is particularly directed or bestowed from God toward people. This is in contrast to *'ašrê,* which generally denotes a state of blessedness or of enviable standing before God or others. As such, the petition of the Psalmist is that he, as well as all in the congregation, might enjoy the grace, presence, and divine favour of God, along with all of its accompanying privileges and bounty. Such blessing for Old Testament Israel was frequently synonymous with, but not limited to, material prosperity (see Deuteronomy 28:1-14). This is perhaps even somewhat implied in the bountiful harvest of verse 6.

Following verse 1, and again at the end of verse 4, *Selāh* is employed, perhaps denoting a rest or musical break before the purpose for the Psalmist's petition is disclosed in verse 2. This blessing of God that he and the people are seeking is not simply for themselves, but in order that the nations might come to know the God

---

[5] J. Swanson, *Dictionary of Biblical Languages with Semantic Domains: Hebrew (Old Testament)* (Oak Harbor: Logos Research Systems, 1997), # 1384.

of Israel. It is at this point that the connection with the Abrahamic Covenant becomes clear. In Genesis 12:1-3 God calls Abram saying,

> Go from your country and your kindred and your father's house to the land that I will show you. And I will make of you a great nation, and I will bless you and make your name great, so that you will be a blessing. I will bless those who bless you, and him who dishonours you I will curse, and in you all the families of the earth shall be blessed.

This promise given to Abram finds its ultimate fulfillment in Christ, whose earthly lineage is through Abraham (Matthew 1:1-16). Nevertheless, it also points to the fact that part of God's calling of Abraham, and later the setting-apart of the nation of Israel, was that they should be his representatives before the nations. This idea is shown repeatedly through the Old Testament and is inherent in their designation as a royal priesthood in Exodus 19:5-6.

Israel, as a chosen people, were to put on display for the surrounding nations to see, the joy, the glory, and the blessings of knowing and worshipping the one true God. As such, through their life, through their worship, and through their testimony, the people and the nations who did not know the one true God were supposed to look, and be curious, and be drawn to find out what made the people of Israel so distinct. As the surrounding nations looked upon this 'blessed' people, they were to be pointed to Yahweh. In modern parlance, the people of Israel were supposed to be on mission from God to the nations.

The result was to be just what is described in verse 2, that the nations might know the ways of the LORD and recognise his saving power. In short, through the blessed lives and the testimony of the faithful people of God others would learn who Yahweh is and what he is like. In doing so, they would recognise his greatness and power. Specifically, the people of Israel were to remember for themselves, and put on display to others, his greatness and saving power that led them from slavery in Egypt to the promised land. In a similar way, believers today are to put the greatness and saving power of God on display, for they are a walking testimony of how he still brings his people out of slavery to sin and death and into new life through Christ (1 Peter 2:9).

The third verse begins with a verb conveying the Hebrew jussive, indicating a desire or wish, (translated as "Let the peoples"). In this case the desire is that all people, everywhere, would praise God. This desire or call is also repeated in verse 5. As such, the biblical author in verses 1-3 has indicated that the purpose of God's blessing is so that the nations might know him, and then, knowing him, the right response for all people is to praise him.

The appropriateness that all should know and acknowledge the worthiness of God is demonstrated from Genesis to Revelation. He is great, majestic, and glorious beyond compare. There is no other like Yahweh. He alone is worthy and deserving of all honour and praise. While many in contemporary society, and frequently those who misrepresent or misunderstand the blessing of God, seek their own comfort, convenience, and reputation—that is, their own glory—the God of the Bible rightly does all things for the sake of *his own* glory. God blesses his people that through them others might know him, and together glorify him. God's blessing ought always to result in God's glory.

Yet this truth leads to an important warning, for, as Deuteronomy 6:14-15 reveals, God is a jealous God. When God is here spoken of as being jealous, and when in the same verse he forbids his people from the worship of anything else other than him, it is not because he is petty or insecure. It is that he is utterly matchless! He alone is the one true God. There is no one else and nothing else that compares to him. As such, Isaiah 42:8 declares,

> I am the LORD; that is my name;
> my glory I give to no other,
> nor my praise to carved idols.

God will not share his glory with any other because there is no other worthy of it. Therefore, when a person commits idolatry or engages in the worship of something other than God, or when people claim the fame or glory in a given situation for themselves, they grievously sin against God by trying to steal what is only rightfully his.

A pursuit of the blessings of God for the sole purpose of one's own comfort is by its very nature idolatry (looking to something other than God to meet the thirsts and desires of our hearts). This, when coupled with the false belief that one's own effort, righteousness, or even faith merits blessing, results in a prideful glory thief.

Yet, there is wonderful news. While God does all things for his own glory and pleasure, he has chosen to bring glory to himself in a way that brings blessing to his people. Surely, we need look no further than to Christ himself to see this glorious truth. Nevertheless, the patten is at least suggested in these opening verses of Psalm 67:

- He is glorified through his loving and generous acts of blessing toward his people.
- He is glorified when his people rightly recognise that he is the source of every good and perfect gift and respond to him in thanksgiving and worship.
- He is glorified when his people faithfully point others to the greatness of who he is, so that they can do as they are rightly designed and created to do—to worship him.

Conduits of blessing, not simply consumers

Before considering the remainder of the Psalm, it is appropriate to place the truth of verses 1-3 (and its covenantal connection) against the backdrop of the rest of the Old Testament narrative. The problem in ancient Israel was that the people who were supposed to enjoy the rich blessings of God and use them as conduits for the sake of the surrounding nations, lost sight of their holy calling. The result of this was that:

1. They began to see the blessings of God as a point of pride and boasting.
2. They began to believe that the blessings of God belonged to them purely for their own utilisation.
3. They began to assume that they could live for their own glory and still count on the blessings of God.
4. They lost sight of their calling to be a light to the nations.

One must surely wonder if such a tragic portrayal is not also precisely where much of today's church is.

1. We assume that God blesses us for our own sake.
2. We assume that we can do whatever we want with his blessings.
3. We use his blessings for our own glory not for his (have we remembered the warning of Deuteronomy 8:11-18?).
4. We look down upon those who do not know or follow him and criticise and condemn them for their life-style instead of living as physical, visible representatives, who put God's glory on display.

To such a people, Psalm 67 provides correction and perspective: God blesses his people so that the nations might know and praise him.

A right knowledge of God brings blessing to the nations

In verses 4 and 5, the Psalmist again calls upon all the nations to "be glad and sing for joy." It is noteworthy that "peoples," *'am*, and "nations," *le'ōm*, are used synonymously to give a sense of universality or entirety which is expressed further by the use of *kōl*, which depicts the idea of totality or the whole of something. As such, the idea conveyed is a reference to 'all people in every place.' The Psalmist's justification for calling on all people is that it is right and appropriate that the nations know and praise God, since he is the one who judges and guides them all. These two activities of God on behalf of all people, judging and guiding, are in themselves to be understood as blessings. We might point to these activities as demonstrations of his common grace (extended to the righteous and unrighteous alike). In essence the Psalmist declares that there is a joy that comes when people know of the sovereign rule and reign of God.

As Psalm 24:1 makes clear,

the earth is the LORD's and the fullness thereof,
the world and those who dwell therein.

All people and all nations belong to and are under the sovereign dominion of God. The exercise of his sovereignty is in Psalm 67 first seen in his judging of the peoples with equity, or uprightness: *mîšôr* denotes a blameless or straight/unperverted manner. As sovereign king, Yahweh has the right to judge, but unlike the unrighteous earthly rulers of a nation, the LORD is perfect in his judgments, both in holding the guilty to account, and in his attentiveness to the cause of the oppressed (see Psalm 9). Despite the injustice that a person might face in his present earthly circumstance, whether at the hand of another individual or under the rod of a callous ruling official, there is a joy that comes from knowing that the judge of the whole earth will do what is right (Genesis 18:25). No sin will go unpunished (either in the cross of Christ, who has borne the wrath that we deserved, or in God's righteous wrath against those who have rejected his holy Son), and no virtue will go unnoticed.

All nations and peoples ought rightly to sing for joy to the Lord, not only because he judges with equity, but also because he guides (*nāḥâ*) the nations upon earth. This divine guidance is not given in a mere general sense ('there's the map, now follow it!'), but is rather a "conducting of one along the right path."[6] This guidance frequently denotes a care and tenderness that is both loving and personal (Psalm 23:3). The same word is used in Genesis 24:48 when Abraham's servant gives thanks to the LORD for having guided his path to Rebecca, and in doing so, having made his quest for a wife for Isaac successful. It is found again in Exodus 13:21 where it describes the manner in which the LORD led Israel in the wilderness by means of the pillar of cloud by day and of fire by night. It might be suggested therefore, that far from being a distant directing of the affairs of the nations, it is speaking of the guiding presence of the LORD. The joyous response of the nations to the knowledge of God (verses 4-5) begins (at least in the Psalmist's perspective) as the blessed people of God live as conduits of his blessing to others. That is to say, when, through the testimony of the blessed people of God, people everywhere begin to learn of his upright judgments and his tender guiding, how can the nations not sing for joy!

---

[6] *Theological Wordbook of the Old Testament*, # 1341.

God is faithful in his blessing so that all nations may fear him.

Verse 5 repeats the refrain of verse 3, again desiring that all people would rightly praise God. The Psalm then closes with a final stanza in verses 6-7. Here we see something of a repetition or restatement of the theme of God's blessing with the yield of the earth (the harvest) held up as 'Exhibit A' in giving evidence of how the LORD has blessed his people. As previously noted, this has given rise to the suggestion that Psalm 67 may be a song of harvest. While this is a legitimate possibility, it is an ancillary point at best. Clearly, as has already been argued, God's blessing for the sake of his glory among the nations is given far greater emphasis.

Biblical Hebrew does not have a tense in the sense that we find in the English language, but rather its verb forms mark aspect. This means that what occurs in the English translations as past tense, "The earth *has yielded* its increase," and future tense, "God, our God *shall* bless us," ought not to be too strongly understood as conveying a sense of time. Rather, the yielding of the increase is marked as a Qal Perfect verb which typically expresses a completed action or state of being. As such, while not specifically related to time, this blessing of the earth's yield is something that the Psalmist has already witnessed and experienced. When attention is turned to the "God *shall* bless" phrase, repeated in verse 6 and 7, the Hebrew word *bārak* is employed again. Just as in the petition of verse 1, so also here, it occurs in the Piel Imperfect form. The Hebrew Piel stem denotes relationship, stressing that the action of the verb is put into effect by the subject of the clause, *'Elōhîm*. Accordingly, it is God who does the blessing without any other outside or compelling force. Furthermore, the Imperfect conjugation which typically expresses an incomplete action is also frequently used to point to something that is habitual or customary. A very loose paraphrase such as 'God, our God is not finished with his blessing yet, but because of his nature it keeps on coming,' might therefore be considered. Taken together, the idea seems to be that God has shown his faithful blessing in the past and we can look forward with confidence to his continued blessing ahead.

Surely, there is a sense in which this might be the testimony of every believer. God has blessed us, and we could recount many ways and examples. Moreover, because God is faithful to his promises and because it is in his nature to be generous, those who are now in Christ can look with confident expectation to further blessings ahead.

Yet here again, wise readers find themselves in danger of pressing a 'prosperity perspective' upon the text that if left unchecked might violate and distort the clear testimony of the balance of the biblical record. While it is undeniable that the land promises given to Old Testament Israel did contain a physical and material provision, as reflected in the yield of verse 6, a return to verse 1 is necessary in order to gain the correct interpretative key. Verses 6 and 7 are the confident assertion that the request of verse 1 will indeed be heard and answered. At the risk, therefore, of restating the heart of the request, the blessing is inseparably connected to God's being gracious and making his face to shine upon them. In short, the intimate enjoyment of favour with the LORD is the both the basis and the realm of divine blessing.

Surely this is what the Apostle Paul had in mind when he exulted in the blessings of which those who are in Christ participate in Ephesians 1:3ff. Believers now enjoy intimate favour and access to the unspeakable riches that are in Christ. What earthly treasure could even begin to compare to the blessing of having been chosen and adopted, redeemed and forgiven? It is from these blessings that New Testament believers are to be a blessing to the nations, that they too might come to know and praise the God of our salvation.

While Psalm 67 was a beautiful and appropriate prayer and song for the people of Israel, and indeed stands as such for the church today, we await the ultimate fulfilment of this Psalm with joyful anticipation. There is coming a day at the return of Christ when the glory of the LORD will cover the earth as the waters cover the sea (Habakkuk 2:14). Then all people will bow the knee in worship to our God.

One final time in verse 7 the Psalmist reminds his readers that the end goal of the blessing of God is the glory of God amongst the nations. Surely, there can be no better corrective to a false and self-focused prosperity mindset than to set our gaze fully on the pursuit of his glory. The framers of the Westminster Catechism were undoubtedly correct when they declared that the primary purpose of man is to glorify God and enjoy him forever. Perhaps the Psalmist would make the minor adjustment to state that the primary purpose of man is to glorify God and enjoy him forever, so that through their enjoyment others might come to glorify God and enjoy him forever.

Pastoral and missional implications of God's blessing and glory

Psalm 67 is clear that, though God's blessings are real and abundant, they are not solely for us or about us. The purpose of God's blessings is his glory among the nations. Yet, it is still right and appropriate that God's people consider his blessings (verse 4 illustrates this), and rejoice in him in response.

The chorus of the old hymn gives wise counsel when it says:

Count your blessings, name them one by one;
Count your blessings, see what God has done;
Count your blessings, name them one by one,
And it will surprise you what the Lord has done.[7]

In considering the truth of Psalm 67, and how those of us who are in Christ ought therefore to live in light of it, it is right to take an inventory of our blessings. The benefits of doing so are likely beyond enumeration, but four are offered here for consideration:

Taking an inventory of our blessings:
1. helps us to guard against robbing God of his glory and forgetting his mercy;
2. reminds us that every good and perfect gift comes from him;
3. leads to thanksgiving, worship, and joyful contentment;
4. challenges us to consider how we are using his blessings for the sake of our fellow believers, our unbelieving neighbours, and for the sake of his glory among the nations.

---

[7] Johnson Oatman, Jr. (1856-1926).

Reflect on his blessings

He has blessed us spiritually through Christ and in the knowledge of him. How might one who has been so blessed use this to glorify God and be a blessing?

He has blessed us materially: whether in homes, vehicles, possessions, or money. Does the way in which we steward what the Lord has entrusted to us reflect the goal of God's glory among all people?

He has blessed us relationally: God has graciously placed around us a sphere of influence that includes both believers and those who have yet to bow the knee to Christ. What does it look like to encourage them with what God has used to encourage us, or to comfort them with the comfort that we ourselves have received? God has given his people relational connections as a demonstration of his blessing and for the sake of his glory.

He has blessed us practically: whether in gifts, skills, abilities or education. What does it look like to give thanks to God for these and regularly employ them for the purpose of his glory?

In light of the purpose of this publication—to honour a servant of Christ whose life and ministry have been dedicated to the glory of God among the nations—I offer one final practical illustration of what it looks like to be a conduit of God's blessing.

In the Chicagoland area in which I live (the greater Chicago region in the U.S.A., for those not familiar with the local term), there are currently five world-class evangelical seminaries (at one of which I was honoured to be trained, and at another of which I have been privileged to guest teach on several occasions). Yet, despite the abundance of access to biblical and theological resources and education here, my work with *Carey* frequently takes me to regions of the world where men who hunger for God's word will travel for four days by foot, boat, motorbike, and bus to learn and be equipped from the Scriptures. They come for this training not only to grow themselves, but so they can return to their churches and villages to teach others. The need and the hunger amidst the global church is great. The blight of false teaching, like the so-called prosperity gospel, only goes to highlight the urgency of this need, and yet the workers are few. Whether you are reading this from the relative prosperity of the west, or from the comparative lack of resource in much of the developing world, let Psalm 67 both encourage and exhort you—our gracious God has blessed you for the sake of his glory among the nations. In honour of Dr. Bob Penhearow, but more importantly in joyful gratitude to Christ, would you take what has been entrusted to you and be a conduit of God's blessing for the sake of God's glory?

The Theology of the Genealogies of Christ in Matthew and Luke

Gang Wang

Introduction

As the first book of the New Testament, the Gospel of Matthew begins with the genealogy of Jesus Christ, the promised Messiah. Questions over the genealogy of Christ are focused on the discrepancies between the genealogies given in Matthew and Luke. Two different lists of names between King David and Joseph have perplexed serious biblical scholars over generations. Commentators propose various explanations, yet it is often said that there is no way to harmonise these two genealogies completely.[1] The purpose of this paper is not merely to provide another solution but rather to explore the depth of the theological significance of the genealogy of Christ in redemptive history.

Although the Apostle Paul warned young Timothy to shun theoretical debates over endless genealogies (1 Timothy 1:4), the importance of genealogy in Scripture is undeniable. From Genesis to Revelation, a fine line of God's chosen people emerges even beyond the narrow sense of genealogy. With numerous names, either well-known or unknown, genealogies not only outline the entire redemptive history in a concise way, but also reveal the eternal decree of God upon his people. The centre of all the biblical genealogies is Christ Jesus, from whom and through whom, the Second Adam, the everlasting life flows (Romans 5:21).

Following a Christ-centred principle, this paper examines concepts and biblical backgrounds of genealogy and the main questions around the two genealogies to locate the focus of the theological significance of the genealogy of Christ. As with Timothy, Paul also admonished Titus that foolish questioning over genealogies would only generate divisions and strife (Titus 3:9). However, the

---

[1] D. A. Carson, 'Matthew,' in F. E. Gaebelein (ed.), *The Expositor's Bible Commentary, Vol. 8* (Grand Rapids: Zondervan, 1984), 64.

mystery of godliness revealed in the incarnate Christ (1 Timothy 3:16) is praiseworthy and desirable for all those truly regenerated in him.

A preliminary analysis

In this section, a preliminary analysis will be made to outline and summarise the related issues and questions around the genealogies of Christ.

The concept of genealogy

A genealogy is simply called a family tree. The fundamental basis of genealogies is the concept of family, which is defined as "a group of people related either by consanguinity (by recognized birth) or affinity (by marriage or other relationship)."[2] So a genealogy shows the unity of a group of people tightly bonded to each other as one family by a biological or legal relationship. Outwardly, a genealogy appears to be multiple lists of names of individuals. In different cultures, it is often depicted in the form of a tree with one root, one trunk, various branches, twigs, and leaves. Genealogy has a natural flow or direction from older generations to younger ones. One of the most basic family relationships is the father-son relation. Although adoption or marriage could connect two individuals into a father-son relationship, the natural and essential foundation of the father-son relationship is the reality of biological birth, which ensures the same genes. The function of human genes is to keep genetic codes for a newborn baby to be like his or her parents in biological traits. This likeness of physiological characteristics testifies to the unity and common origin of the family.

Major questions and tensions

Different questions are raised about the two genealogies of Christ in Matthew and Luke; three of them are most often discussed. First and

---

[2] https://en.wikipedia.org/wiki/Family; cf. G. R. Osborne, 'Who was Jesus' Grandfather? What the two genealogies of Christ, found in Matthew and Luke, are really trying to say,' in *Christianity Today* 53, No. 12 (2009), 56.

foremost is the difference between the two genealogies. Secondly, attention is often drawn to the four unexpected women mentioned in the genealogy in Matthew: Tamar, Rahab, Ruth, and the wife of Uriah (Bathsheba). Thirdly, what is behind the unique structural layout of the genealogy in Matthew?

The tension between the different genealogies of Matthew and Luke seems to endanger the fundamental doctrine of the inerrancy of Scripture. Not only is Joseph's father different in the two genealogies, but almost the whole list of the names between King David and Joseph is different, except for Shealtiel and Zerubbabel. One of the most well-known solutions suggests that Matthew provides Joseph's genealogy while Luke's is Mary's genealogy. However, it is quite exceptional to give the mother's genealogy of a historical figure.

The tension around Jechoniah (Matthew 1:11) in the royal lineage in Matthew is also remarkable. A comparison of 1 Chronicles 3:16 with 2 Kings 24:6 reveals that Jechoniah is actually Jehoiachin, King Jehoiakim's son. In the Book of Jeremiah, the LORD pronounced a striking curse upon Jechoniah:

> Write this man down as childless,
> a man who shall not succeed in his days,
> for none of his offspring shall succeed
> in sitting on the throne of David
> and ruling again in Judah.[3]

One of the primary purposes of the genealogy of Christ is to testify that Jesus is the Messiah, the anointed king, and to show how Jesus shall sit on the throne of David as promised in the Old Testament (2 Samuel 7:12; Psalm 89:4). By showing the kinsman relationship of Jechoniah and Jesus, the genealogy in Matthew seems to contradict the fulfillment of the messianic prophecy in Jesus.

Among all the obstacles that keep Jesus from being fitted into the chosen family's lineage, the virgin birth might be the biggest stumbling block for many.[4] It would be simple, and readily accepted,

---

[3] Jer. 22:30.
[4] A. T. Lincoln, 'Luke and Jesus' Conception: a Case of Double Paternity?' in *Journal of Biblical Literature* 132, No. 3 (2013), 648.

if Jesus had a biological human father, but both Matthew and Luke blatantly affirm the virgin birth of Jesus. If that is the case, in what sense can Jesus be called "the son of David" (Matthew 1:1)? After all, Joseph was only the foster father of Jesus, and Luke puts it in this way: "being the son (as was supposed) of Joseph" (Luke 3:23). Even if the Lukan genealogy of Christ was of Mary, and Mary was actually of David's house and lineage, the gap between this human family and Christ, the Son of God, still needs to be overcome with a proper understanding of the genuine humanity of Christ.

A Christ-centred perspective

In order to comprehend the genealogies of Christ in Matthew and Luke and to answer the related questions, a Christ-centred perspective is essential.

A fundamental problem of human sin revealed

As people read Scripture and question the discrepancies and conflict between the two genealogies of Christ, all the questions tend to point to the inerrancy of Scripture. [5] Although insightful solutions and harmonisation are given as proper responses to the questions, the attitude toward the Scripture and the perspective to the texts need to be changed. The ultimate author of Scripture is the Holy Spirit, who is truthful, perfect, and sure (Psalm 19). Human authors and scribes are subject to errors, yet the Holy Spirit cannot err in divine revelation. It is crucial to remember that Scripture's purpose is to be "profitable for teaching, for reproof, for correction, and for training in righteousness" (2 Timothy 3:16). The Scripture is not some ancient document for critics to analyse, judge, or comment on, but the holy word for repentant sinners fearfully to accept. As multiple questions are raised from the surface of the texts in a theoretical manner from a human perspective, the focus should be turned to the fundamental problem of human sin revealed in the content of the texts of Matthew and Luke. Without seeing the fatal tragedy of the human race in the

---

[5] H. A. Sanders, 'The Genealogies of Jesus,' in *Journal of Biblical Literature* 32, No. 3 (1913), 184-193.

genealogy of Christ, it is futile to try to use human wisdom in finding answers in divine revelation.

As a family tree, a genealogy reflects three essential natures of a family: unity, continuity, and historicity. From a redemptive angle, both genealogies in Matthew and Luke reveal significant problems in this particular human family.

The unity of a family lies in the shared identity of each family member. Biologically, identical human genes unify all the family members in the genealogy to one ancestor. Who is Joseph's biological father? Whom did Zerubbabel beget? Scholars cannot deny the uncertainty in genealogies even with many valid proofs or evidence. In the second chapter of the book of Ezra, some Israelites were returning from the exile but could not find their names in the genealogies (Ezra 2:62; cf. Nehemiah 7:64). One of the most severe problems that both Ezra and Nehemiah faced was mixed marriage, which was regarded as the fundamental reason for the exile (Ezra 9; Nehemiah 13: 23-27). Throughout the history of Israel in the Old Testament, God repeatedly warned his chosen people to keep themselves from mixed marriage since that terribly corrupts the unity and purity of this family. Nevertheless, it was into this corrupted[6] family that Jesus was born.

The significance of a family's continuity is clearly demonstrated in the Bible, as a son, a male child, is often desired in biblical narratives. Tamar and Ruth were intentionally put in Matthew's genealogy to remind the readers how God graciously preserved and extended the lineage of Israel. Many times in Israelite history, internal and external crises fell upon the chosen family. When King Ahaziah died, his mother, Athaliah, arose to destroy the royal family (2 Kings 11:1). During the exile, Haman, the enemy of the Jews, plotted to destroy the chosen people throughout the whole kingdom of Ahasuerus in one day (Esther 3:6). As the prophet Isaiah said,

If the LORD of hosts
had not left us a few survivors,

---

[6] R. E. Brown, 'Matthew's Genealogy of Jesus Christ: a challenging Advent Homily,' in *Worship* 60, No. 6 (1986), 486.

we should have been like Sodom,
and become like Gomorrah (Isaiah 1:9).[7]

However glorious and great the nation of Israel was in the past, it was dramatically shrinking and diminishing at Jesus' time.

The historicity of a genealogy refers to the factual reality of the family on the platform of human history. Though there are many well-known names in the first part of the genealogies of Christ, the unknown names and missed generations after the glorious Davidic kingdom somehow predict a withdrawal from the platform of redemptive history, though even that would be only a temporary withdrawal. A genealogy itself proves the actual existence of a family lineage. When the unity of a family is ruined, and its continuity is broken, many such families eventually faded away in human history and only became remote legends for future generations.

The genealogy in Luke is traced all the way back to Adam. Thus, the fundamental problem of one human family is revealed to be a general problem of the entire human race. In Adam, the whole human family broke the commandment that God enacted. Before the fall, Adam had perfect humanity in bearing the image of God. After the fall, the image of God was broken because of sin. The damage became so universal that even human genes were no longer the same as before the fall. Consequently, death entered into the world through one man (Romans 5:12), and death continually endangers the continuity of every human family. Adam and Eve not only faced death, but also lost paradise, the home, the very platform of their family life. Ever since then, the whole world is under the curse, so that the human race, though initially one family, became scattered, discontinued, and lost from God, their creator and heavenly Father. After laying out the genealogy of Christ, Matthew recorded what the angel proclaimed to Joseph, "for he will save his people from their sins" (Matthew 1:21).

---

[7] Brown, 490.

The solution of Christ to the fallen family

The fundamental problem of the human family is ultimately from Adam. He was the first human being made by God in the image of God. The relationship between God and Adam was more than the relationship between God and other creatures. Because Adam reflected God's glory in the likeness of God, he might even call his creator Father. It was in such an intimate relationship that Adam fell. His sinful act was a blatant rebellion against God's word. Though that was just one commandment, Adam was actually guilty of offending the whole law (James 2:10). The nature of Adam's offence was a refusal to accept the family relationship based on God's image. Tragically, Adam and his race fell into the miserable status that the genealogies of Christ revealed. The very fact that Jesus, the Son of God, appears in the genealogy of the human family is good news for sinners. Christ entered into this fallen world and became a member of the human family so that that broken relationship with God the Father might be restored for lost sinners through the Son.[8] The restored relationship is based on faith in Christ Jesus (John 1:12). The redemptive work of Christ consists of three fundamental elements: incarnation, crucifixion, and resurrection.

Incarnation refers to that glorious mystery that the Word became flesh. It is to build a bridge over the insurmountable gap between the holy God and hopeless sinners.[9] To be the only mediator between God and man, Jesus needs to be, first of all, a real man. Because he is the great high priest for sinners, he needs to be a real human being so that he can bear human sins. According to the Creed of Chalcedon, Jesus is fully God and fully man. He is not an angel nor a phantom, but indeed a man with full humanity.

The humanity of Adam was granted by God when he was made, and that was essentially related to the image of God. Adam's humanity was undoubtedly affected and changed since the fall, because the image of God in Adam was broken, and the original

---

[8] Osborne, 56.
[9] R. Myles, 'Echoes of Displacement in Matthew's Genealogy of Jesus,' in *Colloquium* 45, No. 1 (2013), 41.

humanity was polluted because of the sinful nature that is transmitted to all Adam's descendants.

Nevertheless, Christ is sinless with pure, complete humanity from God, but not from the virgin Mary. What the virgin Mary provided is the flesh and blood that Christ took as his human body. Even Joseph, as a stepfather to Jesus, fostered the growth of Jesus by providing daily bread. It is also crucial that Jesus needs to be a real member of the human family by physically connecting to this particular couple, and through them to the whole human race. Jesus is not a visitor to the human family but a legitimate member, so that he may offer access to the tree of life to the entire human family. Furthermore, this Saviour must be not dead but living. If his life is limited, the bridge he builds for sinners would only last for a short time. Two thousand years ago, in that little town of Bethlehem, he was factually born of a virgin into this world. Three days after he died on the cross, Jesus factually rose from the grave.

> The Word became flesh and dwelt among us, and we have seen his glory, glory as of the only Son from the Father, full of grace and truth.[10]

Incarnation puts Christ between God and man, yet Christ still needed[11] to go to Calvary to atone for sins, that sinners might be justified by faith and brought to God as prodigal sons for reconciliation. Before his crucifixion, Christ provided the table for his disciples at the Passover. He gave the disciples the bread that symbolises his broken body on the cross. The purpose of Christ taking human flesh was that he might die together with other members of the human family. Those who believe in Christ are to die into Christ's death so that Christ might bring them together out of death as the ark brought Noah out of the flood in the past. Christ also took the cup, and told his disciples that this cup symbolises his blood that seals the new covenant with all who believe in the name of Jesus Christ. By shedding his precious blood on the cross, Christ atoned for believers' sins and so pacified the righteous wrath of God toward sinners. This is a critical prerequisite

---

[10] Jn. 1:14.
[11] W. A. Grudem, *Systematic Theology* (Grand Rapids: Zondervan, 1994), 569.

for sinners to be reconciled to the Father into that original family relationship.

As he was actually born into this world, Christ indeed died on the cross and was actually buried in the grave for three days. Though it is impossible to imagine the separation between the first and second persons of the holy Trinity, the death of Christ is substantial, at least in his humanity. The significance of his death implies an effectual release of sinners from the tyranny of Satan. This is demonstrated graphically when the chariots of Pharaoh were buried in the Red Sea. Any genuine members of God's family shall not yield to the power of the adversary. The passion of Christ gloriously triumphs over sin, Satan, and death. Through his crucifixion, Christ has cleansed and prepared the prodigals for the family reunion in heaven. He lived to identify himself with children of the first Adam, and he died for all God's elect to be in the last Adam for a restored family relationship with God the Father.

As the first Adam was put into a deep sleep to receive his wife, the last Adam died to give life to the bride of the Lamb, through whom the children of God are welcomed into God's family.

The resurrection of Christ is bodily; thus, a new and genuine life is given to God's children in Christ. The resurrected life in Christ is eternal, so the family of God shall stand forever. The problem of discontinuity in the human family is permanently resolved in Christ. The ascension of Christ is to the heavenly Father "from whom *the whole family* in heaven and on earth is named" (Ephesian 3:15).[12] The new creature, redeemed sinners, are brought to God the Father through the Son, not only to be justified and reconciled, but also to be adopted as dear children of God to inherit the richness of God's glory in heaven. In Christ, all the members of God's family obtain the glorious identity not only of citizens, but also of sons and daughters. The unity of God's family is unbrokenly built in Christ, the Rock of Ages.

All the previously discussed blessings and gifts will not be fully received until the promised Spirit of God falls upon the believers in Christ. Jesus specifically told his disciples, "if I do not go away, the

---

[12] The words in italics are borrowed from the NKJV.

Helper will not come to you. But if I go, I will send him to you" (John 16:7). Ten days after Jesus ascended into heaven, the Holy Spirit fell upon the disciples on the day of Pentecost.

As the power of the Holy Spirit was at work in giving life to the first Adam, the power of the Holy Spirit was also upon the virgin Mary in the conception of Christ,[13] the last Adam. It is in Christ that sinners are regenerated by the power of the Holy Spirit. As sinners put their faith in Christ and accept the new covenant through two essential ordinances, the image of God in Christ is moulded upon sinners' hearts by the Holy Spirit. When the Holy Spirit falls, the new heart begins to beat. The human family in the first Adam is destined to corruption, since the breath breathed into Adam's nostrils was only the breath of life, but the breath breathed into the redeemed is the very Spirit of Christ, Emmanuel, God with us. Christ is in God's children, and God's children are in Christ.

In his incarnation, Christ entered into the human family. In his death, Christ has released Adam's race from the corruptive nature of sin. In his resurrection, Christ regenerates sinners to the family of God. By God's eternal decree, Christ was born and adopted into a human family, so that all those who believe in his name shall be born again and adopted into God's family.

Answers to the questions in Christ's genealogies

The fundamental problem of sin revealed in the genealogies is the broken family relationship between God and man. Jesus Christ, the only mediator between God and man, as the eternal Son of God has become flesh, and became the Son of Man to restore the relationship of man to the Father in heaven. All the problems on the surface raised from the Gospel accounts need to be comprehended from this perspective of the doctrine of Christ's adoption. Though the concept or term, 'adoption,' may not be adequate fully to explain the questions in the genealogies, it is the key to understanding the theological significance of the genealogies of Christ in Matthew and Luke.

---

[13] J. M. Frame, *Systematic Theology: An Introduction to Christian Belief* (Phillipsburg: Presbyterian & Reformed, 2013), 883-893.

The most basic and profound family relationship is the relationship between a father and a son.[14] This relationship is based first of all on the genes that a son inherits from the father and also the fostering contribution of the parents to the growth of the son. On the one hand, it is the seed; on the other hand, it is flesh and blood. Both elements are essential in binding up two individuals together into this primary family relationship.

In the Old Testament, the law of levirate marriage is particularly specified in Deuteronomy 25:5-7. A dead man's brother was responsible for marrying the widow of his brother, and the firstborn son should succeed in the name of the dead brother. Thus, the son would have two fathers, one biological and another legal. The two brothers share genes firstly from the same father or same ancestor; secondly, they share the same woman as their wife. In this way, two father-son relationships are both legitimate.

This is quite different from adoption from outside of a family. In that case, there are no shared genes. Scholars notice that there is no adoption in Jewish law as that in the Roman legal tradition.[15] The question about the father of Joseph or Shealtiel might never get a definite answer. However, the divergence in the two genealogies clearly indicates the real possibility and legitimacy of the law of levirate marriage, applied in the family history of Israel.

Furthermore, the underlying principles of the law of levirate marriage are applicable to Jesus. As discussed in the previous section, Jesus shares the original humanity that Adam received when he was made, although the genes of Jesus came neither from Joseph nor from Mary. Nevertheless, Jesus received blood and flesh from Mary,[16] and also received daily bread from Joseph. Fulfilling the two fundamental elements of the basic father-son relationship, Jesus legitimately became a member of the human family. Without the legitimacy of

---

[14] U. Saarnivaara, 'The Genealogies of Jesus in Matthew and Luke,' in *The Lutheran Quarterly* 6, No. 4 (1954), 348-350.

[15] See L. N. Dembitz & K. Kohler, 'Adoption,' in *The Jewish Encyclopaedia, Vol. 1* (New York: Funk & Wagnalls, 1901), 206-208; J. H. Tigay, B.-Z. Schereschewsky, & Y. Gilat, 'Adoption,' in F. Skolnik & M. Berenbaum (eds.), *Encyclopaedia Judaica, Second Edition, Vol. 1* (Farmington Hills: Thomson Gale, 2007), 415-420.

[16] Brown, 488.

Jesus' adoption into the human family, sinners would not be able to unite with Christ in his physical death for bodily resurrection.

The fallen human family not only has a legitimate Saviour but is also desperately in need of such a Saviour. The puzzling questions over the gen ealogies of Christ should never become reasons for Christians to doubt biblical inerrancy but rather should lead sinners to the reality of the fallen condition of human beings. Two of the four women, Rahab and Bathsheba, are infamous for adultery, which is the worst cause of damage to a family's unity and individual identity. The other two women, Tamar and Ruth, played critical roles in the family crisis of broken lineage. Mentioning these special women in the genealogy of Christ is intended to remind the chosen family how fragile this family tree is because of their sins. Similarly, the curse upon Jechoniah pronounced through the prophet Jeremiah (Jeremiah 22:24-30) also demonstrates the hopeless problem of discontinuity in this family.

Those familiar with the Israelite history would lament with Nathanael in John 1:46, "can anything good come out of Nazareth?" All the questions on the surface turn sinners' attention to the fallen condition focus: a broken family relationship. Matthew's structured outline[17] of the genealogy emphasised the Davidic kingdom. Three groups of fourteen generations are to show and remind readers how this kingdom rose and fell. Matthew's aim is not to be accurate in numbers, nor to imply hidden meanings in symbolism, but to point to the only hope of the kingdom in Christ, the king of all kings. He is not only a member of the family of the Jews but also a family member of Adam. Salvation comes from the Jews (John 4:22) to all humankind. Christ was born through the virgin Mary. He is truly man and truly God. In him, the elect are adopted back into the family of God. In him, the reality, purity, and infinity of God's family stand.

Conclusion

There are rich spiritual lessons in the genealogies of Christ in Matthew and Luke. Other than Christ, Mary and Joseph are great examples of

---

[17] D. L Turner, 'Matthew,' in *The Baker Exegetical Commentary on the New Testament* (Grand Rapids: Baker, 2008), 61.

obedience. The virgin birth of Christ would be extremely hard for both of them to accept. However, Mary's response was, "Behold, I am the servant of the Lord; let it be to me according to your word" (Luke 1:38), and "when Joseph woke from sleep, he did as the angel of the Lord commanded him: he took his wife" (Matthew 1:24). Christians are to follow such examples of faith by humbly accepting the mighty work of God upon them. Where Adam and Eve failed, the redeemed children of God shall succeed by faith in Christ.

Contending for the sound doctrine of biblical inerrancy as well as the doctrine of the virgin birth of Christ, Christians may explore further and in-depth the doctrine of incarnation based on the genealogies of Christ. The relation of the two natures of Christ is essential to the proper understanding of the adoption of Christ into a human family. The doctrine of adoption is often ignored in most systematic theologies. How was Christ adopted into the human family through Mary and Joseph? How precisely should we define the concept of humanity? What does it mean for Christ to 'be made flesh,' 'become flesh,' or 'take flesh' while he is sinless? All these questions are utterly relevant as the genealogy of Christ is indeed a miniature of the redemptive history.

In Adam, the whole human family lost the life connection from God the Father. Being not ashamed to be identified with sinners (Hebrews 2:11), the Son of God died the sinner's death and became the firstborn from the dead (Colossians 1:18), and will eventually bring all God's children back to the Father in heaven.

> Oh, the depth of the riches and wisdom and knowledge of God!
> How unsearchable are his judgments and how inscrutable his ways![18]

Amen!

---

[18] Rom. 11:33.

The Prayer of the Great High Priest
(John 17:1-26)

Gareth Crossley

It has been said that the seventeenth chapter of the Gospel of John is, without doubt, the most remarkable portion of the most remarkable book in the world. In it the finest prayer in the world follows the best sermon in the world (chapters 13-16); from preaching, Jesus turns to prayer. In a sense this prayer is a pattern for all prayers. It shows that the glory of God should be the purpose, object, and goal of every prayer—not the good of the one who prays, not the conversion of others, not intercession for believers in suffering, in gospel outreach, nor even in spiritual crisis. Even though Jesus begins by mentioning himself, his overriding concern is the glory of his Father (verses 1-5). With less than twelve hours before crucifixion he prays, "Father, the hour has come; glorify your Son, that the Son may glorify you" (verse 1). The glory of God is uppermost. This is the priority for all prayer as is also evidenced in 'The Lord's Prayer:'

> Our Father in heaven,
> hallowed be your name.
> Your kingdom come,
> your will be done,
> on earth as it is in heaven.[1]

"Father, the hour has come" (verse 1)

"The hour has come:" the moment of crisis has arrived, the hour in which the Son of God would conclude his mission to the earth by yielding up his life on the cross. He is to be "the Lamb of God" taking "away the sin of the world" (John 1:29), the one to fulfil the prophecies, the types and symbols of the old order and bring in the new order. The hour of his triumph over the forces of evil and the prince of darkness is at hand.

---

[1] Matt. 6:9f.

Here are the words of the Lord Jesus facing his deepest crisis. He is about to complete his great undertaking and leave this world by means of a barbaric death on a cross. He is to be wrongly arrested, falsely accused, unlawfully judged, pitilessly mocked, crudely spat upon, viciously scourged; he is to be led away weak and bleeding, dragging a heavy wooden cross through the streets of Jerusalem to halt outside the city at the refuse tip and there be crucified as a common criminal among criminals, "numbered," indeed, "with the transgressors" (Isaiah 53:12). He is to endure the physical agony of crucifixion, to experience the horror of mental anguish as one "despised and rejected by men, a man of sorrows and acquainted with grief" (Isaiah 53:3). In anticipation the Son of God described his experience prophetically in Psalm 22:

> I am poured out like water,
> and all my bones are out of joint;
> my heart is like wax;
> it is melted within my breast;
> my strength is dried up like a potsherd,
> and my tongue sticks to my jaws....
> For dogs encompass me;
> a company of evildoers encircles me;
> they have pierced my hands and feet.[2]

This is the crisis of Christ, Son of the living God. Yet all this horror, with its bloody sweat and tears, is but a fraction of his true sufferings. The excruciating agony of the cross is not the physical dimension, the pain of the body; nor the emotional, the pain of the heart; nor the mental, the agony in his mind; it is the spiritual dimension. Others have died. Others have died with terror of body and mind, but none have died like this man *with such torment of soul*. It is the spiritual dimension in the sufferings of Jesus which mark him out as unique, and mark out his sufferings as unique. Not even a soul in the everlasting torments of hell will suffer as he suffered on that cross! It is this one, facing this end, who prays so poignantly in the upper room,

---

[2] Ps. 22:14-16.

"Father, the hour has come; glorify your Son that the Son may glorify you" (verse 1).

"Glorify your Son" (verse 1)

Jesus looks to the Father for the encouragement and support of his love, for he is to be the suffering Saviour who will be glorified in fulfilling every last detail of the Father's plan of salvation. The prayer that the Father may glorify the Son is not a selfish prayer. For the very next words demonstrate what motivates Jesus: "that your Son may glorify you" (verse 1). Some days before, when Greeks wanted to see Jesus, the Lord told Philip and Andrew,

> Now is my soul troubled. And what shall I say? 'Father, save me from this hour'? But for this purpose I have come to this hour. Father, glorify your name.[3]

He is to be arrested, led before the high priests Annas and Caiaphas, the governor Pilate, and King Herod. He is to be questioned, accused, and struck, made a laughing stock before the people as he is brought out clothed in a scarlet robe with a crown of twisted thorns on his head and a reed in his right hand (Matthew 27:28-29). How can he be glorified? When the Son of God is stripped and nailed to a wooden cross, how can he then be glorified *and* glorify the Father? Through prophecy his thoughts were revealed:

> I am a worm and not a man,
> scorned by mankind and despised by the people.
> All who see me mock me;
> they make mouths at me; they wag their heads;
> 'He trusts in the LORD; let him deliver him;
> let him rescue him, for he delights in him!'[4]

Jesus preserved his own dignity in the midst of the crude barbarism of the crucifixion. Willingly he goes to death. He lays down his life that

---

[3] Jn. 12:27f.
[4] Ps. 22:6-8.

he may take it again. No one takes it from him, but he lays it down of himself. He has power to lay it down, and he has power to take it again (John 10:17-18). This Son of the living God is the one "who for the joy that was set before him endured the cross, despising the shame" (Hebrews 12:2).

Yes, even in this, the Son of God will be glorified.

- Glorified in Gethsemane, as he courageously comes forward to meet the troops and officers with their swords and clubs.
- Glorified in his compassion, in healing the ear of Malchus.
- Glorified in his humility and self-control in the Jewish Court, Pilate's Praetorium, and Herod's Palace, as he, the co-creator, is ridiculed, taunted and tortured.
- Glorified as he is lifted up from the earth to draw all peoples to himself.
- Glorified as he successfully fulfils the task of redemption: "to finish the transgression, to put an end to sin, and to atone for iniquity, to bring in everlasting righteousness" (Daniel 9:24).
- Glorified in his conduct throughout the whole of his ordeal: his composure before his inquisitors, his quiet submission to crucifixion, his concern for his mother.
- Glorified in his grace, mercy, and compassion: praying for forgiveness upon his executioners, welcoming the repentant thief into his kingdom and presence.
- Glorified when he triumphantly cries, "It is finished!" (John 19:30)
- Glorified in his quiet confidence, as he places himself into the hands of God the Father in his final words.
- Glorified in an amazing resurrection from the dead.

His is a life of obedience, love, and trust, unruffled within, resolutely determined to do the will of God, the whole will of God, and nothing but the will of God. The Father does glorify the Son.

"That the Son may glorify you" (verse 1)

He wants, more than anything else in the world, to bring honour, praise, blessing, thanksgiving, and worship to the Father in heaven. He wants the angels to worship the Father on account of his submission and obedience. He wants the redeemed to worship, praise, and bless the Father in heaven on account of his submission and obedience.

The cross of Calvary demonstrates the perfections of the Lord God Almighty. It shows the impeccable holiness of God, the God who is light and in whom is no darkness at all (1 John 1:5), "the Father of lights with whom there is no variation or shadow due to change" (James 1:17), who cannot overlook sin. It shows the constant, inflexible righteousness of God, who must punish sins, transgressions, and iniquity; it shows the amazing grace of God in Christ, who made him who knew no sin to be sin for us, that we might become the righteousness of God in him (2 Corinthians 5:21); and it shows the magnificent love of Jesus for his Father and his people. There was no price on earth that Jesus would not pay for our salvation and the Father's glory.

The Son's eternal glory

On earth Jesus has glorified the Father by finishing the work the Father has given him to do (verse 4). He has spoken the words of God, communicated his teaching; he has completed the mission entrusted to him, lived the life appointed for him perfectly and completed it from beginning to end. Jesus now seeks to be glorified by the Father with the glory which he had with the Father before the world was created (verse 5).

Paul in his letter to the Philippians describes the excellence of the person and work of Christ in his life here on earth which culminated in death, "even death on a cross." He continues by indicating how *the Father glorified his Son* by highly exalting him and giving him the name that is above every name, so that at the name of Jesus every knee should bow, in heaven and on earth and under the earth, and every tongue confess that Jesus Christ is Lord.

Everything that Jesus did, and the reason for all his suffering, is summed up in the words, *"to the glory of God the Father."*[5]

The Son of God has existed eternally "in the form of God" (Philippians 2:6). He was there in the beginning of creation with God, God with God (John 1:1-2). There was no 'Jesus' before creation; indeed, he did not exist as such until his conception by the miraculous working of the Holy Spirit (Matthew 1:20). Humanity was prepared for the Son of God, who said to his Father, "a body have you prepared for me; ... Behold, I have come to do your will, O God" (Hebrews 10:5, 7). The Son of God "became flesh" (John 1:14).

Since therefore the children share in flesh and blood, he himself likewise partook of the same things.[6]

Before his incarnation the Son of God had a wonderful glory, "the glory as of the only begotten of the Father" (John 1:14[7]). The apostles, John, James, and Peter, were privileged to see that amazing phenomenon on the Mount of Transfiguration. Peter records that they

were eyewitnesses of his majesty. For when he received honour and glory from God the Father, and the voice was borne to him by the Majestic Glory, 'This is my beloved Son, with whom I am well pleased,' we ourselves heard this very voice borne from heaven, for we were with him on the holy mountain.[8]

That is when John saw the glory of Jesus the Son of God.

When Jesus prays for the same glory as he had before creation, he clearly indicates his pre-existent and eternal nature "in the bosom

---

[5] Philip. 2:8-11.
[6] Heb. 2:14.
[7] NKJV.
[8] 2 Pet. 1:16-18.

of the Father" (John 1:18[9]). Now he requests the same eternal glory for himself as he now is, and forever will be, 'the God-man.'

Knowing the only true God

The work of Jesus as the Messiah is to give eternal life to all those whom the Father gives him, and this is eternal life, that they may know the only true God, and Jesus Christ whom God has sent (verse 3; cf. John 3:16). The Father of Jesus is the only true God. "Turn to me," he says, "and be saved, all the ends of the earth! For I am God, and there is no other" (Isaiah 45:22).

> For great is the LORD, and greatly to be praised;
> he is to be feared above all gods.
> For all the gods of the peoples are worthless idols,
> but the LORD made the heavens.
> Splendour and majesty are before him;
> strength and beauty are in his sanctuary.[10]

Jesus said,

> No one knows the Son except the Father, and no one knows the Father except the Son and anyone to whom the Son chooses to reveal him.[11]

Jesus is the only way to God and the only way to knowing God (John 14:6).

Knowing God is to know also the true Messiah, Jesus Christ. It is to know that we are loved by him, saved by him, protected by him, led by him, and kept by him. It is the personal knowledge of being able to say, "The LORD is my shepherd" and therefore, "I shall not want" (Psalm 23:1). It is to have the highest opinion of him and with profound respect to honour, love, and obey, with the utmost gratitude for his grace and kindness. There is no comparison, for all other gods

---

[9] NKJV.
[10] Ps. 96:4-6.
[11] Matt. 11:27.

are dumb idols (Psalm 115:3-8). This is the God of all grace, the one who forgives all our sin, transgressions, and iniquity, this is the Christ who loved us and gave himself for us (Galatians 2:20). He is everything to us. Each believer can confidently say, "For to me to live is Christ, and to die is gain" (Philippians 1:21).

Prayer for his disciples

Jesus has expressed his concern to glorify the Father by finishing the work entrusted to him and so to gain eternal life for those whom God has given to him. He continues by praying further for those whom the Father has given to him (verses 6-9). They have kept God's word, which means that they have received what Jesus has said as the words of God. Years later the Christian converts in Thessalonica displayed the same reception of the word of God, and Paul prayed in gratitude,

> we also thank God constantly for this, that when you received the word of God, which you heard from us, you accepted it not as the word of men, but as what it really is, the word of God, which is at work in you believers.[12]

As they have kept God's word, so Jesus prays that God will keep them, that is, guard and protect them, and that they might enjoy the closest bond and union with God, like Jesus enjoys (verse 11; cf. 1 Peter 1:5). In praying for their protection Jesus does not ask for the disciples to be taken *out of the world* but rather to be guarded *in the world* against the evil one (verse 15), by God sanctifying them, separating them from the weakness of the flesh, from the allurement of the world, and from the influence of the devil. This sanctification, separation, and distinguishing of those who belong to Jesus is to be achieved through the sanctifying power of the truth, the word of God.

Real Christian discipleship is knowing God and knowing Jesus through a personal living relationship (verse 3), obeying God's word (verse 6), belonging to God and his Son (verses 9-10), and rejoicing with joy (verse 13), "joy that is inexpressible and filled with glory" (1 Peter 1:8).

---

[12] 1 Thess. 2:13

Prayer for his church

Jesus concludes his prayer by looking beyond the small body of men gathered around him, and, as in his mind's eye he looks down the years to come, he prays for his church (verses 20-26). This prayer is for all those who will be saved through the preaching and teaching of the apostles. The means that is used in order to bring about faith in Jesus Christ is, as always, the word. Jesus says it is through *their* word, not as if they had invented it, but because they heard it, accepted it, and preached it. This is the message of salvation, whether spoken or written. So the Saviour is praying for everyone who will come to faith right up to his return. Through the operation of the Holy Spirit in the mind and heart of those who hear this word thousands upon thousands are to be brought to salvation in Christ.

Jesus prays for the unity of his church worldwide

He has prayed for the apostles to share the oneness that is between the Father and Son (verse 11); now he asks that the oneness of *all believers* would be like that which exists eternally between the Father and the Son. Father, Son, and Holy Spirit are one in essence; believers, on the other hand are one in mind, effort, and purpose. God is love, and when we love one another we show the very essence of God. Only those who have been born from above, and are in the Father and in the Son, are also spiritually one, and offer a united witness to the world.

> There is one body and one Spirit—just as you were called to the one hope that belongs to your call—one Lord, one faith, one baptism, one God and Father of all, who is over all and through all and in all.[13]

The members of the church of Jesus Christ, having a unique relationship with their Lord and with each other, will be a testimony to the world. This testimony is twofold: that it is God who sent Jesus,

---

[13] Eph. 4:4-6.

and that he loves his people as he loves his Son (verse 23). It is staggering to learn that God loves us to this extent. What an amazing conclusion to this most wonderful prayer when Jesus says, "that the love with which you have loved me may be in them, and I in them" (verse 26). What a God, what a Saviour!

An Apostle of the Church: Does the office of apostle continue today?

Ray Tibbs

Since the earliest days of the church, many issues of Christian belief and practice have provoked a host of opinions amongst its adherents. Some matters have been very significant, and disputes have had a profound effect on the life and witness of the whole church. Some issues have less significance, with different viewpoints having a relatively localised effect. The subject of this paper is one of the latter. Students would ask me this question because they knew that some churches had apostles and they wondered if they should do the same. Many Christian churches of all types have exercised full, faithful, and fruitful ministries without addressing this issue. For those that have, the results have been diverse.

For that reason, this paper will not attempt any historical analysis of the topic. It will confine itself to a consideration of the biblical material and make a particular application. We will look only at the New Testament, as the Septuagint, while using the verb form many times, makes only a single use of the relevant noun in 1 Kings 14:6. In a paper of this brevity, it is impossible to consider all uses of the basic Greek term and its derivatives, so we will only look at key passages.

The meaning of the term 'apostle'

There is common agreement that the term translated as 'apostle' means 'one who has been sent.' The core of its meaning relates to *transition*. This is emphasised when it is compared with other terms which might appear to be synonyms:

- ambassador – the core relates to *representation*;
- messenger – the core relates to *communication*;
- servant – the core relates to *action*.

Each term is distinctive. All four terms could apply to the same person without contradiction. Each one can also stand alone without needing the others.

To understand apostleship, we must look at what it means to be sent. First, there is an assumption of connection. The sender must know the one whom he is sending. This would imply an authority by which the sender has the right to instruct the one who is sent. It would also imply consent on the part of the one sent, and his accountability to the sender.

There must be an assumption of purpose also. The sender must have a reason for sending the one who is sent and the one sent must know what the purpose is. As well as having the delegated authority to complete his task, the sent one has some freedom to choose how best to accomplish his assignment.

Then there is the assumption of preparation. The sender must ensure that the one sent has all the means at his disposal to achieve what he was sent to do. Thus, the one sent has the assurance that he is sufficiently equipped to accomplish the task.

This, in turn, assumes a known destination where the sender's purpose is to be achieved. Knowledge of the destination must be part of the equipping of the sent one. That may also require the prior preparation of the destination itself.

Finally, there is the assumption that the sender will assess the work of the sent one to ascertain whether or not the task is progressing satisfactorily and when it is deemed to have been accomplished successfully.

"The apostle and high priest of our profession"

The template for apostleship is our Saviour, the Lord Jesus Christ. This is how the writer to the Hebrews describes him in 3:1. The context of this reference is the demonstration of how Jesus is superior to Moses. The term 'apostle' is not sufficient in itself to convey all that the writer wants to say about Jesus. Angels were also 'sent ones' (1:14), but they were only ministering spirits, and most of the first chapter is devoted to showing the superiority of Christ to them. The term "apostle" is expanded by the addition of "high priest." His ministry in this regard was mentioned in 2:17-18, and is developed throughout the letter.

This high priest was sent. He did not rise up from amongst men as did others who had that title. Who sent him and where he came from is made clear in the opening verses of the letter. However 'sent' Moses may have been (Exodus 3:10-11), and whatever his designated role may have been amongst the people of God, he was never a high priest. That Jesus Christ is the high priest whom God has sent to us— fulfilling everything anticipated by the earthly shadows that went before him—is the very essence of Christianity: our "confession" (or 'profession'), as the writer expresses it. Jesus declared and embodied this truth about who he is, and it was miraculously confirmed throughout his ministry and by his resurrection. Upon this great truth rests our present faith and our future hope. It cannot be neglected (Hebrews 2:3).

Without applying the term 'apostle' to himself directly, Jesus repeatedly described himself as the one who had been sent.[1] An analysis of Jesus' statements shows that the points which he was emphasising were the identity of the one who had sent him, and the task which he had been given to do for him. This is summarised in John 3:17. During the course of his ministry, Jesus received explicit approval from his Father and confirmation of his identity through miracles. God owned him as his sent one, and after that work had been completed successfully, received him back into heaven as a lasting testimony to his satisfaction concerning what had been achieved in his name.

The apostleship of Jesus is unique. His identity as the Son of God has no equal. He had been sent directly by his Father. He had been with his Father in heaven before he was sent. He was sent to earth and the work he had agreed to do was clearly defined and could not have been done by angels or men. He was perfectly equipped by the Holy Spirit to complete the task he had been given. Preparations for his entry into the world had been made on earth through the history and religion of Israel and in its prophetic writings. In heaven, the Trinity had prepared a plan for the revelation of God to mankind which would

---

[1] Jn. 5:36-38; 6:29, 57; 7:29; 8:42; 10:36; 11:42; 17:3; etc.

secure the eternal salvation of the people of God, and initiate the concluding period of history, which would end with the judgment of mankind and the permanent establishment of the kingdom of God.

Nothing in the apostleship of the Son of God could be replicated and yet this term used to describe him—apostle—is given to other men. The fundamental meaning of the term remains unchanged, but its significance must be adjusted. It is evident that there must be levels of apostleship. No mere man called an apostle could be equated with Jesus Christ, the Son of God. Whatever the elements of his apostleship may be, no mere man has been sent by God in the same way as he sent his Son. The man may still be an apostle, but his significance is considerably reduced.

The twelve apostles

Jesus undertook the earliest part of his ministry alone. Gradually, disciples attached themselves to him, some by specific invitation, until a considerable number of followers had gathered around him. A turning point in his work was reached when he chose to invite some of them to engage in the work with him.[2] In each account these men are designated as "apostles." In Luke's account, this appointment is preceded by Jesus spending the night in prayer. In Matthew's account it is preceded by Jesus seeing so many people needing his help, and inviting the larger body of his disciples to "pray earnestly to the Lord of the harvest to send out labourers into his harvest" (Matthew 9:38).

When put together, these accounts provide a comprehensive description of apostleship. It was Jesus who was doing the sending. He had a clear reason for sending them. First, he made a selection out of a larger group. There is no explanation of why some were considered more suitable than others. The reasons for his choice were known only to him. He called named individuals, demonstrating some familiarity with them. He called them to himself for a time of preparation. He explained what he wanted them to do, giving them guidance and warnings. He also gave them authority over evil spirits

---

[2] Matt.10; Mk.3:13-21; 6:7-13; Lk. 6:12-16.

and the power to heal diseases. It was a limited commission with clear boundaries about time, place, and activity.

However, the accounts are not uniform in their presentation. Mark separates the calling from the sending, whereas Matthew unites them. Luke refers only to the calling and, uniquely, adds the sending of the seventy-two (Luke 10:1-20). Much of the preparation given in Luke is very similar to that given in Matthew. These variations can be reconciled as follows:

- Jesus selected 12 men, designated as 'apostles,' from the larger group of disciples.
- They were not sent out immediately, as their first calling was to be with him.
- They were sent out later as team leaders of the seventy-two (i.e., twelve groups of six who worked in pairs [hence seventy-two, not the more symbolic number of seventy]).
- The accounts of Matthew and Mark were written from an apostolic viewpoint. Matthew was one of the twelve and Peter may have been Mark's source. Luke, as usual, had a broader perspective.

When the seventy-two later returned to Jesus, they shared the outcome of their ministry. It was the apostles who had been given the power to exorcise and heal, but the whole group reported back what the whole group had witnessed. There is no suggestion that the other sixty had the same gifts and status as the apostles. They were apostolic assistants—sent, but in a subordinate, yet supportive, role to the apostles. A distinction is made between them. All may share the same task, but some help others to accomplish it. The apostles were those who had been called and equipped by Jesus as sent ones, working with the help of others, who had no such designation.

The apostles remained the constant companions of Jesus and were with him even though they were not sent anywhere else until after the resurrection of Jesus, when their original commission was renewed and expanded. Then, although the term 'apostle' is not always used, the same men (now eleven) are referred to.[3]

---

[3] Matt. 28:16-20; Mk. 16:14-18; Ac. 1:1-8.

Again, there is some variation in the accounts. It is likely that Jesus repeated his commission to the apostles, with some development on each occasion, until the full import of it could be grasped. It was so stupendous that they would not be able to absorb everything at once.

This time they were sent by the victorious, resurrected Jesus, with a new and greater commission. Their task was to go far and wide, bearing witness to Christ, preaching the gospel and making disciples everywhere. Their preparation would only be complete once the Holy Spirit had come upon them at Pentecost, for such work could only be done with the enabling of God. Their previous experience, of being with Jesus so much and being sent out by him before, meant that this task could not be given to others. They would need help to do it, as they had found before, but their singular, extended, and intimate relationship with Jesus marked them out from everyone else. He had chosen and prepared them for a mission of far greater significance than anything they had undertaken before.

The reference in Matthew 28:16-20 needs careful consideration. The apostles went to a mountain in Galilee as instructed (Matthew 28:10). By this time none of the apostles would have doubted the resurrection of Jesus because they had seen him so many times. The doubters (28:17) must refer to others. Is this the resurrection appearance referred to in 1 Corinthians 15:6? This is unlikely to refer to any gathering in Jerusalem. There were probably not as many as five hundred believers in Jerusalem at that time. Even if there were, where would they find a place to gather in private to meet the resurrected Jesus? The apostles could have gathered five hundred believers from the towns in Galilee where Jesus had been so well received. Some of that number may well have doubted what they saw and heard. If the remaining verses relate to this occasion, then the apostles were commissioned by Jesus in the hearing of about five hundred other believers. This would be a vital confirmation of the future ministry the apostles would exercise amongst other believers. Although the apostles would be based in Jerusalem and have their ministry authenticated there in other ways, these rural believers would not be behind their urban brothers and sisters in acknowledging the unique role of the apostles.

Even if this is not an accurate reconstruction of events, the unique status of these men could not be questioned. They had been personally selected by the Son of God to be his apostles. He had given them his exclusive attention for months. They had spent 'quality time' with him, in which he told them things which he never told anybody else. He gave them a task to do which others could not do because of the revelation he had entrusted to them. They alone were anointed by the Holy Spirit in Acts 2 and began their ministry immediately. Their ministry bore fruit straightaway. There could be no doubt that these men were chosen, sent, equipped, and blessed directly by the Lord Jesus himself.

But this raises other questions. What about Matthias and what about Paul? Matthias was not 'a sent one.' He had not received the same call and preparation from the lips of Jesus that the eleven had received. He may have become involved in the same task as the apostles, but we have noted the need for apostolic assistants. Peter's autocratic decision to look for a replacement for Judas was in keeping with earlier examples of his insistence that he knew what was best for the kingdom of God.[4] This well intentioned and biblically supported directive was inevitably ignorant of the plan of God still to be revealed.

It is not surprising that, at this point, Peter and the others were unclear about the definition and significance of their apostleship. They still had much to learn, and only the Spirit of God could teach them. They and the other believers would have considered the appointment of Matthias to be valid and treated him as one of them. Matthias had been with them since the early days and was probably one of the sixty who had been sent out with them. The fact remained, however, that he was not an apostle who had been personally sent by Jesus with the renewed commission. Despite this, he was considered to have equal status to the others. The Spirit would not have isolated him in by-passing him at the distribution of gifts. God is always taking into account our weaknesses and using our mistakes to his glory.

But in the unexpected providence of God, it seems that it was Paul who became the twelfth apostle. There are three accounts of

---

[4] E.g., Matt. 16:22.

Paul's conversion in Acts.[5] His conversion was synonymous with his apostolic commission (Acts 26:16-18). He was personally sent by the risen Jesus himself and this was confirmed by Ananias (Acts 9:15-16). In 1 Corinthians 15:8, Paul included his conversion experience in his list of the resurrection appearances of Jesus. Paul had never met Jesus before as far as we know. Jesus did more than identify himself as the object of Paul's venom. He showed himself to be alive, and familiar with Paul's activities. Only deity could overcome death and possess knowledge that defied space and time. It was not the light of reason that suddenly impacted upon Paul's life, but the risen Christ himself.

All the elements of apostleship previously identified as belonging exclusively to the original twelve can be seen in Paul's experience. First, there was selection. Jesus came specifically for Paul. Others in his party were affected by what happened, but not addressed directly. They saw the light and were fearful, but they could not hear any voice. Paul was singled out of that group as being personally known by Jesus. Jesus gave Paul a command, a commission, and a promise. Initially Paul was told to stand up, then he was called upon to testify, and finally he was promised protection and success. Jesus has authority over the purposes and revelation of God, as well as the physical and spiritual life of men. Paul discovered that all authority in heaven and earth had been given to Jesus. From that moment he was working for the person he had been working against.

Jesus appeared to Paul in order to appoint him as his servant and his witness (Acts 26:16). In a moment of time, Paul had experienced the glory, grace, authority, and omniscience of Jesus. He had been blinded to the world by the brilliance of the light of Christ. The life he knew had come to an abrupt end and the change was so overwhelming that even the desire for food and drink was eclipsed by the mixture of joy and anguish, peace and pain. His meat and drink would be to do the will of the one who sent him. He had seen the Son; he knew the truth; his sins were forgiven; God was reconciled; heaven was secured: all of grace.

---

[5] Ac. 9:1-19; 22:3-21; 26:9-23.

Paul probably learned more about Jesus in this encounter with him than the other apostles had learned in all the time that they were with Jesus. To some extent, his previous education and experience would have provided useful but basic instruction about the Christ, for Paul would have had a good grounding in Scripture. In his letters he quotes the Old Testament 141 times. His background was part of his preparation for apostleship, but there was more.

Paul suggests that he received direct revelation from Jesus, perhaps during his years in Arabia.[6] He seems to have been given particular teaching which, due to the special nature of his apostolic calling and writings, he incorporated into his ministry. The breadth, depth, and cohesion of Paul's understanding has a strong element of revelation in it. Whatever his background, gifts, and understanding may have been, the truth about Jesus is far too majestic and diverse to be merely a product of human reasoning.

Paul had to defend his apostleship repeatedly. His notorious past, the unorthodox circumstances of his commission, and his distinctive call to minister to Gentiles would all combine to raise suspicion for some believers. Although accepted by, and in fellowship with, the other apostles, he seems to have acted apart from them, never settling in Jerusalem. To have settled there would have made him a prime target for elimination by those whom he had previously served.

He considered himself to be one of the number of the apostles, and that number had significance. Jesus had established the symmetry between the twelve apostles and the twelve tribes of Israel in Matthew 19:28, while Judas was present. If he was to be replaced by one man and not two, then Paul is the most obvious candidate. The same numerical symmetry is implied in Revelation 4:4. The original sons of Jacob did not constitute precisely what became known as the twelve tribes of Israel, any more than the original twelve disciples of Jesus were precisely the same as those who came to be known as apostles. Although there is a numerical symmetry, this is a symbolic, rather than a literal, representation.

Paul shows how these apostles were the singular gift of Christ to his church.[7] He establishes that the victorious Jesus Christ dispensed

---

[6] 1 Cor. 7:10; 11:23; 15:3; Gal. 1:12; 2 Cor. 1-6.
[7] 1 Cor. 12:28; Eph. 2:20; 3:5f; 4:11.

gifts freely to his people for their good and the growth of his church. Jesus Christ knows what is best for his church and he has given three variations of the same gift to sustain it. Christ has given us servants of the word to help us grow into his likeness. The basis on which the church is built is the revealed word of God. It had been communicated to Old Testament prophets and to these apostles by God himself. They passed on his word faithfully. That word did not originate with them, but their words could be trusted.[8] Jesus Christ is the primary feature of this foundation. He provides the necessary stability and support. He also gives direction to the building, providing the origin for all the sight lines that are used. He was chosen and placed in that position by God, and remains precious to him (1 Peter 2:6).

God had revealed his word to the apostles and prophets. Directly inspired by the Holy Spirit, they were responsible for communicating divine truth verbally, and then, in some cases, in writing. They were eventually replaced, as their utterances were recorded and enshrined in the Bible. The apostles had been commissioned by Christ in person, and bore witness to his resurrection. They were given miraculous power, and their ministries were accompanied by great blessings.[9] The revelation committed to them remains the foundation of the whole church and every church.

That foundation is built upon by the next group of servants of the word. Evangelists take the basic good news of salvation in Jesus Christ and speak of it wherever they go. As people hear the truth from them and believe, churches are formed (e.g., 1 Corinthians 3:10-11). What they said is entirely consistent with, and derived from, the ministry of apostles and prophets. Without them, evangelists could not do their work.

Pastors and teachers continue the work begun by the other ministries, instructing and nurturing people on the basis of the same revealed truth. The life of the church develops as this third group of servants of the word care for and guide people according to the truth that is common to all, wherever they are. They build on the work of the evangelists, and both build on the revelation given to apostles and prophets. Some apostles did the work of evangelists too, and some

---

[8] Eph. 3:4f; 1 Cor. 3:10f.
[9] Lk. 6:13; Ac. 1:21f; 1 Cor. 9:1f; 2 Cor. 12:12.

evangelists may work as pastors and teachers, but these three groups are the indispensable components through which every local church is created. These apostles are foundational to every church today.

If the apostleship of Jesus was unique, then the apostleship of these men was also unique, but in a different way. This is another level of apostleship. They were personally sent by the Lord Jesus to us and to millions like us. Their ministry of revelation, now enshrined in the Scriptures, is the basis of all that we believe. It is still bearing fruit today across the world, and will do so for generations to come. Personally called by the risen Christ, given a worldwide commission to establish his church, and entrusted with an unparalleled revelation of the truth of God, their apostleship cannot be repeated.

Other apostles

However, the use of the term 'apostle' is not limited to the twelve. It is applied to others.

James. Galatians 1:19 seems to include James (the Lord's brother) in the number of apostles, and 1 Corinthians 15:7 appears to support that. In the latter refence, James is not linked to the apostles at all. Rather than reading "he appeared to James, then to [the rest of] all the apostles," it should read "he appeared to James, then to all the apostles." Grammatically, the Galatians reference does admit the suggested interpretation, but raises the question of how James was appointed. He became a significant leader in the Jerusalem church (Acts 15:13; Galatians 2:9). On the basis of what we have seen so far, either he was appointed by Jesus privately at the time of his resurrection appearance, similar to the experience of Paul, and that information was conveyed to the other apostles, or he was appointed by the other apostles, similarly to Matthias. Neither explanation seems satisfactory, given the absence of corroborating evidence for such a vital appointment. An alternative explanation, based on logic, is that Paul was simply referring to men of importance in the church, of whom James was one.

Barnabas. In Acts 14:4 and 14 this term is applied to both Barnabas and Paul. Acts 13:1-3 describes how these men were dispatched from the church in Antioch for missionary work. Although it was instigated by the Holy Spirit, the church fasted and prayed first, thereby making the commission their own. Barnabas and Paul were sent out by the church. They were apostles of the church, and all the elements of apostleship referred to earlier are found here. First, a selection was made. These individuals were known to the church and had already exercised an acceptable ministry within it. Preparation had already taken place. The task was given by the Spirit, approved by the church, performed by the men themselves, and evidently blessed by God. Their return to Antioch (Acts 14:26-28), demonstrated their sense of accountability to the church that commissioned them. Although the term 'apostle' was not used at that time, Barnabas had originally been sent to Antioch by the church in Jerusalem (Acts 11:22). The same criteria for apostleship had been fulfilled in that instance also. Barnabas was a valued member of the church in Jerusalem (Acts 4:36), and on that basis, he was given a special commission. Thus, he had been an apostle of the church in Jerusalem before he became an apostle of the church in Antioch. Both churches were the sending agency—identifying, preparing, and commissioning someone for a predetermined task. Barnabas was the 'sent one' in both instances.

Silas. In 1 Thessalonians 2:6 Paul refers back to his original visit to Thessalonica. He had not been alone, and refers to himself and Silas as apostles. After Paul and Barnabas had returned to Antioch, they split up. Barnabas took John Mark, and Paul chose Silas to accompany him. Acts 15:40 records that the church in Antioch commissioned them as they had commissioned Paul and Barnabas originally. Silas was an apostle in the same way as Barnabas.

Paul was therefore an apostle twice over. Predominantly, he was an apostle of Jesus Christ, and that shaped everything he did. But for a time, he was also an apostle of the church in Antioch. His roles were complementary, not contradictory. His apostleship from Jesus Christ did not preclude him from being an apostle of the church in Antioch. The latter role enabled him to fulfill the former role.

Andronicus and Junia. Romans 16:7 shows that this pair was known to Paul. Rather than them being "well known to the apostles," the best reading is 'outstanding among the apostles.'[10] This is probably not a reference to the original apostles, but could suggest that these two were amongst others who had been sent out by the church of Rome. If they were converted before Paul, they were probably experienced and mature. Alternatively, they may have been sent out to Rome by another church and were involved in the establishment of the church in Rome—hence his commendation. There is no other reference to them, so nothing is certain.

Epaphroditus. The same term for apostle is used in Philippians 2:25 but it is translated "messenger." The remaining verses of the chapter refer to the ministry which Epaphroditus exercised towards Paul. He had been sent by the church in Philippi to support Paul while he was in prison. Even though this was as much a practical as a spiritual ministry, the basic elements of apostleship were in place. The 'sent one' was identified, equipped, and commissioned for a task.

Apollos. In 1 Corinthians 4:6, Paul refers to himself and Apollos and in 4:9 to "us apostles." This refence does not necessarily apply to Apollos, but rather to Paul alone as one of the apostles of Jesus Christ. This is more likely, given the point that Paul is making in this passage. He is contrasting the status of the apostles and their consequent humiliation with his critics who exalted themselves and showed no humility.

Unnamed brothers. Once again, in 2 Corinthians 8:23, the term for apostles is translated as "messengers." Paul was sending Titus to Corinth along with others. They were commended as 'apostles of the churches' and a credit to Christ. Nothing else is known about them, so their apostleship cannot be examined, apart from noting that they were sent by the churches.

False apostles. In contrast to genuine apostles, some men were circulating and infiltrating churches, doing great damage, while claiming to be sent from elsewhere. This happened at Antioch, and Paul and Barnabas disputed with them. They claimed to represent the Jerusalem church, so Paul and Barnabas took the matter there. That church had not sent them, and addressed the issue by letter. This is all recorded in Acts 15. In Revelation 2:2, the church in Ephesus was

---

[10] As in the NASB.

commended by Jesus Christ for testing some interlopers and rejecting them as false apostles. Some people in the church at Corinth were undermining Paul's apostleship and setting themselves up instead. He warns the church against them (2 Corinthians 11:5, 13; 12:11). They had exalted themselves, claiming an authority which they did not possess. Jesus Christ had not sent them, and nor did any church, so they were to be dismissed.

In this section we have seen another level of apostleship. Paul identifies it in Galatians 1:1 as an apostleship which came from man. This is obviously a lower level of apostleship than those previously considered. In the heavenly realm, apostleship is applied exclusively to Jesus Christ. In the earthly realm, there are two variations of apostleship: those appointed directly by Jesus, and those subsequently appointed by his church. In Galatians 1:1, Paul was writing as an apostle of a different order. He knew what the apostleship of man was, because he had been appointed as an apostle from the church at Antioch. But that was temporary, lasting only for as long as it took to complete the given task. He was not despising it, but simply stating that his apostleship came from a higher source—the Lord Jesus Christ, who, in turn, was backed by God the Father.

All the examples in this section could fit into this last category— even James and Matthias, although they and the others may have understood it differently. Matthias was the choice of the church, a fact which God later appeared to confirm. The choice of Matthias did not come from Jesus, as did the choice of Paul and the eleven others. Apollos had gone to Corinth with the encouragement of the church in Ephesus (Acts 18:27), and Paul was still an apostle of the church in Antioch. If Paul is using the plural term to apply to himself and Apollos as 'apostles of men,' the force of his argument to the Corinthians is substantially reduced. Apollos seems to have been the kind of man who did not like to be sent anywhere, but worked on his own (1 Corinthians 16:12). Other men were glad to be sent (e.g., Timothy—1 Corinthians 4:17).

Did Timothy have 'the apostleship of man' if he was sent only by an individual and not a church? The noun form of the term is never used in such cases, suggesting an absence of formal recognition. But even if the criteria of apostleship were still met, he would have authority derived only from the one who sent him. He could act on Paul's behalf, but not with the authority of a church behind him. His given task would reflect that. The apostleship of man is just that— whatever form it takes. It can rise no higher.

Contemporary apostleship

The determining factor of any apostleship is the identity of the sender. That governs everything else. He chooses who to send, the task to be completed, and the preparation necessary for success. The sent one only possesses as much authority as the sender gives him, and it only relates to the assigned task. God sent his Son to be the Saviour of the world. Jesus knew that he spoke and acted with the power and authority of God, and some of his hearers recognised it. The Son sent his apostles into the world to proclaim the gospel of salvation and establish his church. Their ministry was authenticated by the "the signs of a true apostle" (2 Corinthians 12:12). Jesus gave them his power and authority to confirm the truth which they declared, which would be preserved for ever in the Bible. In obedience to Christ, the church sent out its own people to expand itself by the dissemination of the word of God, of which it was the custodian, but its apostles represent only human authority in having been sent by men.

The apostleship of man still exists today, and will continue for as long as the church lasts. It is not to be disparaged, but nor can it be ranked with the higher calling of the twelve. The church will continue to be a sending agency. It will select the personnel, define the task, and make sure that its personnel are sufficiently well prepared to accomplish the task successfully. The sent one goes on their behalf, and they remain committed to the one they send for as long as necessary.

We have seen that the term 'apostle' is inadequate in itself and needs expanding. Although he is a sent one, an ambassador represents the sender on any occasion when he is required to do so. He was sent as an ambassador, and this term is needed to explain the reason why he was sent. In the case of Jesus, his apostleship was defined by his high priesthood. Paul frequently described himself and his ministry in other ways apart from his apostleship (e.g., Titus 1:1), and Peter also qualifies his apostleship (2 Peter 1:1). John never applies the term 'apostle' to himself, but prefers other designations (e.g., 2 John 1). Some of those apostles sent by the church were also described in other ways (e.g., Romans 16:7). In itself, the term 'apostle' has relatively little significance when applied to the apostleship of man. Although apostles are being sent out today, we do not usually use that term to describe them. We may call them missionaries or church planters, for example, but they are still 'sent out ones.'

We have also found that not every task assigned to an apostle will be an openly spiritual one, even though it must be performed spiritually. This means that sometimes a church may send out a female apostle. As long as she is not given a leadership role which would involve ministering the word of God in circumstances which would give her authority over men, there are many other tasks which a church may send a woman to do. She would be no less of an apostle than men who are sent, but her task must be as biblically defined as theirs.

It must also be acknowledged that there are still false apostles today, who are not sent out by anyone, and are therefore accountable to no one. Claiming to be sent out directly by God is tantamount to claiming equality with Jesus Christ. Claiming to be sent out directly by Jesus Christ makes them equal to the twelve. The role of the apostle can be easily abused when it is regarded as a matter of status. The apostleship of Jesus was characterised by humble servanthood. His own apostles followed the example of the one who had sent them.

No apostle ever ruled as such. If they did, it was because their designated duty involved that work, rather than being intrinsic to their apostleship. They were to serve their sender first of all, and then they served those to whom they were sent in whatever manner was required of them. The twelve became distinguished from the elders of the church in Jerusalem (Acts 15:22), suggesting that their broader ministry did not give them an automatic right to rule the church indefinitely, even though in the early years, it was a necessity. In itself, apostleship only involves as much status as the sender invests in it.

A personal note

I write as an apostle. I thank God for my fellow apostle, Bob Penhearow. We attended the same church together in the 1970's, and were both sent out from it into pastoral ministry. Neither we nor the church ever used this term to refer to us, but it could properly be applied to us. It was the apostleship of man. I was the Barnabas to his Paul. Having confirmed my call to pastoral ministry, our church commissioned me to become the pastor of a small church in the English Fens. It sent me out and supported me financially and in prayer. I submitted regular written reports to the sending church. Its pastor and other members visited often. I was aware that I was representing the church that had sent me.

After I had started my pastorate, Bob was commissioned by the same church, for pastoral training in Canada. He had become another one of the church's apostles. While he was training, I invited him to join me for the summer vacation as a student intern at my church. Both of us were aware of being sent by, supported by, and still representing, the original church that had commissioned us both. In the providence of God, we were part of the same church for what was possibly the most blessed time in its history. During a period of less than 10 years, and partly due to the ministry of the pastor at that time, we were but two of at least 10 men who were sent out into various forms of Christian service by that church.

My new church embraced me as one of its own, and years later released me to take up a pastorate in London. I could not have moved on without securing their approval first. I was sent by this church to the new church. I took up my responsibilities in the second church, knowing that I had the loving support of the first church, as their apostle.

During this second pastorate, Bob was developing the concept of *Carey Outreach Ministries*, and asked me to join him in one of his early visits to Romania. I sought the permission of my church, and it willingly commended me for this trip and others that followed later, believing that it was an appropriate ministry for me to undertake. I had become their apostle now, taking with me their prayerful interest and practical support wherever I went. They could not go, but I could on their behalf.

Throughout Bob's involvement with *Carey*, his local church has always been a priority for him. He tried not to neglect it, and sought its active support for his wider ministry. To whichever country he went, he would be their apostle, sent by them to minister on their behalf.

Similarly, as each *Carey* lecturer serves churches in various parts of the world, he is freed up and equipped to do so by his home church. Each man is a sent one by his own church. It may be an apostleship of man, but hundreds of students will acknowledge their indebtedness to God for those distant churches who enabled these men to serve them in this way. The students may thank the men for their lectures, but they also thank their churches for identifying, equipping, and sending them to serve as lecturers.

As a para-church organisation, *Carey* has no right to supplant the authority of the local church. *Carey* does not send out anyone purely on its own behalf. It has been—and must remain—a ministry that facilitates the transition of apostles from some long-established churches to serve more recently founded churches, as happened in New Testament times. It recognises 'the apostleship of man' as being a valid, continuing ministry, and exercises its role as an apostolic assistant to help in the worldwide development of the church of Jesus Christ. This has been made possible by the faithful apostleship of the original apostles and the ultimate apostleship of Christ himself, so sacrificially completed. To fulfill the apostleship of men, we are not "sufficient in ourselves to claim anything as coming from us, but our sufficiency is from God" (2 Corinthians 3:5).

Theological Papers

The Beauty of God

Jonathan Bayes

One thing which I have come to appreciate very much about our brother, Bob Penhearow, is his evident delight in the beauty of God. Frequently, as he addresses God in prayer, I have heard him use the phrase, "our beautiful God." At one of our recent monthly *Carey* international prayer meetings via Zoom, as Bob was praying, I pricked up my ears at a phrase which he used, and then wrote it down: "what a beautiful and magnificent God you are!" I am convinced that this is not merely vain repetition, but rather an indication of genuine esteem for this aspect of God's being: the divine attribute of beauty has clearly captivated Bob. In recognition of this, it is my purpose in this paper to explore this element of the divine character.

A neglected topic

As far as I am aware, the attribute of divine beauty is never mentioned in any of the historic creeds, nor in any of the confessions of faith stemming from the Reformation period. To my knowledge, more recent confessions of faith globally are equally silent on this theme.

Neither has it figured very prominently in works of Reformed systematic theology. This, according to Herman Bavinck, is quite deliberate. He suggests that it is inadvisable to speak of the beauty of God. He argues that the Scriptures have a special word for God's beauty, namely 'glory,' and that while God's incommunicable glory does find a faint reflection in his creation, including in its beauty, nonetheless, to include beauty amongst the attributes of God risks blurring the distinction between figurative, analogical language and inappropriate literal language.[1]

Joel Beeke and Paul Smalley, however, make a more positive, albeit passing, reference to this doctrine. They describe God as

---

[1] H. Bavinck, *Reformed Dogmatics, Vol. 2: God and Creation* [English translation by John Vriend] (Grand Rapids: Baker, 2004), 254.

"supremely beautiful and desirable," and connect his beauty with both his glory and his holiness.[2]

Bob Letham includes a section on the beauty of God in his chapter on God's attributes. Although he includes a citation from Karl Barth, his own elaboration on this theme is tantalisingly brief. Letham denies that there is a concept of beauty to which God conforms, but affirms that our greatest joy should be to be animated by God's beauty in the face of Jesus Christ.[3]

A pleasant exception to this rather cursory treatment of God's beauty is found in Wayne Grudem's *Systematic Theology*. He equates God's beauty with his perfection. Whereas 'perfection' is a negative concept—God lacks nothing desirable, 'beauty' is its positive counterpart—God has everything desirable. Grudem sees the practical implication of this as being that all our legitimate desires can find their fulfilment only in God, and continues by stressing that we are to reflect God's beauty in our lives by living in a way that is in accordance with his character, and by delighting in God's excellence as we see it manifested in the fellowship of the church.[4]

While applauding Grudem's unusual attempt to give the beauty of God a worthy place in the list of divine attributes, I have to say that I do find his treatment a little frustrating. To reduce beauty to things desirable, and to major on its practical ramifications, seems to me to miss out on the implications of the term itself, and risks reducing God to that which satisfies our desires. While he certainly does fulfil that function, I would hope that the beauty of God can be discussed in a more than merely functional way. There is something intrinsically beautiful about God himself and in himself. Beauty is more than merely the fulfilment of my desires. Something beautiful makes an impression on me, irrespective of any functional usefulness which it may have. I worry that Grudem's account risks reversing the priority and initiative, putting the fulfilment of our desires in the place where

---

[2] J. R. Beeke & P. M. Smalley, *Reformed Systematic Theology, Vol. 1: Revelation and God* (Wheaton: Crossway, 2019), 514, 581.
[3] R. Letham, *Systematic Theology* (Wheaton: Crossway, 2019), 163f.
[4] W. Grudem, *Systematic Theology* (Grand Rapids: Zondervan, 1994), 219f.

God in his essential being ought to stand, albeit that I am sure that this was not Grudem's intention.

Beauty has, to use modern parlance, 'the Wow! factor.' It is that aspect of the theme which I hope to explore as I proceed, while noting that we are dealing here, as in all things which concern the immense, mysterious triune creator-redeemer God, with matters that far transcend the limits of our finite understanding.

Having alluded to Bob Letham's reference to Karl Barth, it would be prudent to glance at Barth's own exposition of this theme. I fear that my comment with reference to Grudem is equally applicable to Barth. Having introduced the concept of divine beauty, he immediately goes on: "If we can and must say that God is beautiful, to say this is to say how he enlightens and convinces and persuades us." Later in the same paragraph Barth continues by saying that God "acts as the one who gives pleasure, creates desire and rewards with enjoyment."[5] Once again these comments seem to define God's beauty in terms of its benefits for us, rather than seeing it as something intrinsically wonderful in God himself, irrespective of its external impact.

'In the eye of the beholder'?

Having said this, we recognise that there is some truth in the saying, 'beauty is in the eye of the beholder.' When we speak of beauty in everyday things, we often associate it with our five senses. A spectacular view across the snow-covered hills is a beautiful scene, which appeals to the sense of sight. The song of a thrush sounds beautiful to the ear. A delectable lily has a beautiful scent. A piece of silk has a beautiful texture to the touch. A piece of lemon drizzle cake tastes beautiful.

The Scriptures certainly recognise these sensuous aspects of the concept of beauty, most especially the beauty that appeals to the eye. The first instance of the word in the English Standard Version is found in Genesis 12:11, which informs us that to Abram, Sarai, his wife, was "a woman beautiful in appearance," attractive to his sight, an

---

[5] K. Barth, *Church Dogmatics, Vol. 2, Part 1* [English translation by T. H. L. Parker & J. L. M. Haire] (London: T. & T. Clark, 1957), 650.

assessment with which the Egyptians concurred (verse 14). There are many subsequent references to the physical attractiveness of beautiful women, some positive, others not. Other instances of beauty of appearance include animals, flowers, landscapes, ornaments (crowns and jewellery), and buildings, especially the temple within its setting in Zion.

We are told in Joshua 7:21 that at Ai Achan "saw among the spoil a beautiful cloak." Perhaps, in this instance, the beauty appealed both to his sight and to his sense of touch. Maybe there is also, in part at least, an allusion to the beauty of sweet taste in the reference to "a green olive tree, beautiful with good fruit" in Jeremiah 11:16. The sound of "a beautiful voice" is also mentioned in Ezekiel 33:32. Maybe there is also a hint at the beauty of scent in the words of Hosea 14:6: "his beauty shall be like the olive and his fragrance like Lebanon."

Of course, not everyone enjoys a snow scene. A tone-deaf person may well find no beauty in bird song. For some people the lily's smell may be too overpowering to be described as beautiful. It may be that certain individuals find the feel of silk irritating. And what appeals to my taste can make my friend feel sick! So there certainly is something subjective about beauty in created things.

The recognition of divine beauty may be compared to the response of our senses to created beauty, but it goes far deeper. It is not an external perception. We are talking now about spiritual discernment, about the eye of faith, about the vision of the heart, about Spirit-given perception. Moreover, we are speaking of the response which is right as a matter of absolute obligation, and one which flows from a living relationship with the living God.

In Isaiah 53:2 we read this comment regarding the LORD's suffering Servant:

he had no form or majesty that we should look at him,
and no beauty that we should desire him.

E. J. Young's observation seems pertinent: "the appearance of the servant was such that man, judging from a wrong perspective, would completely misjudge him."[6] Beauty may be in the eye of the beholder, but the beholder may have deficient eyesight and insight.

When we consider the beauty of God, we are pursuing something about God himself, which is essentially beautiful, whether or not that beauty is perceived by sinful human onlookers. We are, inevitably, affirming something which is objectively true about him, not something which is open to subjective assessment. If we fail to find the living God beautiful, that is a symptom of our fallenness, of our sinful inability to appreciate him as we ought to.

Our duty is to embrace and worship God because he is the very epitome of beauty, the very definition of what is beautiful, not merely because as such he satisfies all our desires (though he certainly does), but simply because we thereby acknowledge reality, and we seek to give him the glory for his beauty, not merely to benefit ourselves.

Biblical emphases

I think that it is valid to say that when we consider the attributes of God, it is the Old Testament which is our main source. Generally speaking, the New Testament takes it for granted that God's character is such as he has already revealed himself to be prior to the coming of Christ. The New Testament's main role as regards the doctrine of God is, in the light of the incarnation of God the Son and the outpouring of God the Holy Spirit, to begin to clarify the fact that the one God exists in three persons. Certainly, as regards the truth of God's beauty, it is to the Old Testament that we must turn.

Psalm 27:4

Probably the best starting point for the exposition of this theme is Psalm 27:4. Here David expresses the chief desire of his heart:

> One thing have I asked of the LORD,
> that will I seek after:
> that I may dwell in the house of the LORD

---

[6] E. J. Young, *The Book of Isaiah, Vol. 3: Chapters 40-66* (Grand Rapids: Eerdmans, 1972), 342.

all the days of my life,
to gaze upon the beauty of the LORD
and to enquire in his temple.

It is generally acknowledged that the specific background occasion to
this Psalm is unidentifiable. However, the summary by Delitzsch
seems indisputable: "Cut off from the sanctuary, the poet is himself
threatened on all sides by the dangers of war."[7] References to
adversaries, foes, and enemies appear in verses 2, 6, 11, and 12, and
to an opposing army and war in verse 3. It seems that David was
writing at one of the times when he was preoccupied with the duty of
fighting the LORD's battle, and was therefore unable to attend worship
at the tabernacle (a preferable rendering in verse 4, given the date of
the Psalm prior to the building of Solomon's temple).

Against that background of deprivation from the corporate
worship of the LORD's people, David's longing is to dwell
permanently in the LORD's house. No doubt he is speaking
metaphorically. It is not his intention to camp out in the physical
tabernacle. Rather, his desire is for "intimate communion"[8] with God.
The underlying motivation is to be able to gaze indefinitely,
constantly, endlessly, upon the LORD's beauty.

The Psalm begins with the statement, "The LORD is my light."
There is a close connection between light and beauty. As Victor Hugo
wrote, "To love beauty is to see the light."[9] F. W. Grant's comment
on the opening phrase of this Psalm is therefore pertinent: he
recognises that in the light God himself is manifested, and notes that
in it "beauty, warmth, the vigour of life itself, are all found."[10]

The Hebrew word translated 'beauty' in verse 4 is *nō'am*. It
reappears in Psalm 90:17, which refers to "the *beauty* of the LORD our

---

[7] F. Delitzsch, *Biblical Commentary on the Psalms* (Edinburgh: T. & T. Clark, 1892),
355.

[8] J. A. Alexander, *The Psalms Translated and Explained* (Edinburgh: Elliot & Thin,
1864), 122.

[9] V. Hugo, *Les Miserables, Vol. 5* (New York: Crowell, 1887), 121 [English
translation of "Aimer la beauté, c'est voire la lumière"].

[10] F. W. Grant, *The Numerical Bible, Vol. 3: The Psalms* (New York: Loizeaux,
1897), 124.

God."[11] Its root meaning has to do with pleasantness.[12] This hints at the impact that something beautiful may make on those who observe it, though Samuel Meier, acknowledges that it may also refer to "the intrinsic attractiveness of an object or action." Strangely, however, he makes no reference to its use as a quality of God.[13]

It is instructive to note the explanations of God's beauty given by commentators. There are those who reduce the term to signify "all that makes God an object of affection and desire to the believer."[14] Such an explanation merits the same objection as I have made with reference to Wayne Grudem.

However, amongst those commentators who do offer a more objective definition of beauty as a divine attribute, we find a striking consistency. Henry Law speaks attractively of "the lovely charm of his transcendent grace,"[15] and the beauty of God's grace is the theme also in a number of other commentaries.[16]

That said, I am yet more taken with the approach which sees God's beauty as the harmony of all his perfections. Two quotations may illustrate this understanding of God's beauty. The first comes from Matthew Henry. He says that David

> knew something of the beauty of the Lord, the infinite and transcendent amiableness of the divine being and perfections;

---

[11] Though the ESV here renders it 'favour,' with 'beauty' mentioned as an alternative in the footnote; D. Kidner, *Psalms 73-150* (Leicester: IVP, 1975), 331, quite appropriately writes: "*'favour'* is too colourless a word."

[12] W. Gesenius, *Hebrew and Chaldee Lexicon to the Old Testament Scriptures.* [English translation by S. P. Tregelles] (London: Bagster, 1868), 317f.

[13] S. A. Meier, '5838 *nā'am*,' in W. A. VanGemeren (ed.), *New International Dictionary of Old Testament Theology and Exegesis* (Grand Rapids: Zondervan, 1997), Vol. 3, 121f.

[14] Alexander, 121.

[15] H. Law, *Daily Prayer and Praise: The Book of Psalms Arranged for Private and Family Use, Vol. 1: Psalms 1-75* (Edinburgh: Banner of Truth, 2000), p. 136.

[16] E.g., Delitzsch, 357; A. F. Kirkpatrick, *The Book of Psalms* (Cambridge: CUP, 1906), 141; A. Maclaren, *Expositions of Holy Scripture: Psalms* (Carluke: Online Bible Edition, 1995-2016), on Ps. 90:17; W. A. VanGemeren, 'Psalms,' in F. E. Gaebelein (ed.) *The Expositor's Bible Commentary, Vol. 5* (Grand Rapids: Zondervan, 1991), 245.

his holiness is his beauty; his goodness is his beauty. The harmony of all his attributes is the beauty of his nature.[17]

The second, somewhat longer, quotation comes from Andrew Gray, as abridged by Spurgeon:

> Another thing, which we may call an element of beauty in God, is the combination of his various attributes in one harmonious whole. The colours of the rainbow are beautiful, when taken one by one: but there is a beauty in the rainbow, which arises not from any single tint; there is a beauty in it which would not exist if the several hues were assumed in succession—a beauty which is a result of their assemblage and collocation, and consists in their blended radiance. In like manner so the several perfections, which coexist and unite in the nature of God, produce a glorious beauty. Holiness is beautiful; mercy is beautiful; truth is beautiful. But, over and above, there is a beauty which belongs to such combinations and harmonies.[18]

I believe that these two writers have grasped the point admirably: the beauty of God is the harmonious assembly, the blended combination, the perfect balance, the simultaneous brilliance, of all God's attributes. The truth of the simplicity of God forbids us to separate his attributes from one another. As Peter Sanlon puts it,

> God's simplicity means that there are no divisions or parts to him. God's attributes and his existence are identical.... Simplicity means that God is identical with his attributes and, consequently, each attribute is identical with each other attribute.[19]

That, we might say, is exquisitely beautiful!

---

[17] M. Henry, *Commentary on the Whole Bible* (Carluke: Online Bible Edition, 1995-2016), on Ps. 27:1-6.

[18] From A. Gray, *Gospel Contrasts and Parallels* [1862]; quoted by C. H. Spurgeon, *The Treasury of David* (London: Marshall, 1869), Vol. 2, 10.

[19] P. Sanlon, *Simply God* (Nottingham: IVP, 2014), 60f.

The beauty of holiness

Relevant to this aspect of our discussion is the biblical emphasis on 'the beauty of holiness.' Sadly, that phrase, which appears four times in the Authorised Version and the New King James Version, has disappeared from the English Standard Version, which replaces it with less exotic language, speaking instead of "the splendour of holiness," and, on one occasion of "holy attire."

Three times God's people are exhorted to worship him in the beauty of holiness.[20] In these contexts the phrase is open to some ambiguity. Is what is in view the beauty of God's holiness, or the beauty of the holiness in which alone his people can approach him in worship?

Warren Wiersbe is one example of those who take the latter view. His exposition of the exhortation begins like this: "God desires holiness for his people." Wiersbe then expands on this comment with the challenge to separation and distinctiveness. He tells how the triune God is seeking "to lead us into a life of holiness."[21]

With all due respect, though, I think that Wiersbe is mistaken in his interpretation of this phrase. It seems to me that John Collins is right to find 2 Chronicles 20:21 decisive for understanding its meaning.[22] Here Jehoshaphat

> appointed those who were to sing to the LORD and praise *the beauty of holiness*, as they went before the army, and say,
> 'Give thanks to the LORD,
> for his steadfast love endures forever.'[23]

If the beauty of holiness was something which Jehoshaphat's advancing army could praise, then it must be the beauty of the holiness of the LORD himself.

---

[20] 1 Chr. 16:29; Pss. 29:2; 96:9.
[21] W. Wiersbe, *Prayer, Praise and Promises: A Daily Walk Through the Psalms* (Grand Rapids: Baker, 1992, 2011), 245.
[22] C. J. Collins, '2075 *hdr*,' in VanGemeren (ed.), Vol. 1, 1015.
[23] The words in italics I have inserted from the AV/NKJV into the ESV translation

In this phrase the word rendered 'beauty' is a different one from that used in Psalm 27:4. It is $h^a\underline{d}\bar{a}r\bar{a}h$. Gesenius translates it as 'ornament,' or 'adorning.' [24] God's holiness is his ornamental adorning with beauty. The implication is that this is what we can see of God. Nonetheless,

> the major emphasis is on the Lord and his appearance, not on the worshipper except as the realization of God's actual presence evokes awe.[25]

However, this word does assert that the inner depths of God's being are hidden from our view, which is, of course, absolutely true. There is in the essence of God an ineffable profundity which to us is totally impenetrable. Nevertheless, the beauty of his holiness is a genuine display of his unfathomable reality. We are certainly not talking about ornamentation which is a mere cover-up.

There is a close connection between God's simplicity and his holiness. To say that God is holy is to affirm two things simultaneously. The first is his moral excellence. But the second, and more important, thing is his absolute distinctness in every conceivable respect from all other realities, every one of which is but a part of his creation; in this sense, as Louis Berkhof points out, God's holiness "is sometimes spoken of as his supreme and central perfection."[26] A. A. Hodge explains it like this:

> The holiness of God is not to be conceived of as one attribute among others; it is rather a general term representing the conception of his consummate perfection and total glory.[27]

God's holiness may be used as a summary term for the simplicity of his nature, in which the sum total of all his attributes blend together beautifully into a harmonious whole.

---

[24] Gesenius, 126.

[25] *Theological Wordbook of the Old Testament*, # 477.

[26] L. Berkhof, *Systematic Theology* (Edinburgh: Banner of Truth, 1958), 73.

[27] A. A. Hodge, *Outlines of Theology* [1879] (Edinburgh: Banner of Truth, 1972 reprint), 163.

Some commentators have indeed noticed this in their remarks on those texts which refer to the beauty of holiness. Spurgeon cites two examples in his comments on Psalm 96:9. We may start with a brief extract from the late eighteenth-century writer, Legh Richmond:

> Whatever we can understand as meant by beauty or holiness, we see in the attributes of God, whether we consider them in all their harmony, or contemplate any one of them in particular.

Spurgeon also quotes, at greater length, Joseph le Coute, writing in 1874 on the subject *Religion and Science*:

> Shall I call holiness an attribute? Is it not rather the glorious combination of all his attributes into one perfect whole? As all his attributes proceed from the absolute, so all again converge and meet in holiness. As from the insufferable white light of the absolute they all seem to diverge and separate into prismatic hues, so they all seem again to converge and meet and combine in the dazzling white radiance of his holiness. This, therefore, is rather the intense whiteness, purity, clearness, the infinite lustre and splendour of his perfect nature—like a gem without flaw, without stain, and without colour. All of his attributes are glorious, but in this we have a combination of all into a still more glorious whole. It is for this reason that it is so frequently in Scripture associated with the divine beauty. The poetic nature of the psalmist is exalted to ecstasy in contemplation of the "beauty of holiness," the "beauty of the LORD." Beauty is a combination of elements according to the laws of harmony; the more beautiful the parts or elements, and the more perfect the harmonious combination, the higher the beauty. How high and glorious, therefore, must be the beauty of this attribute which is the perfect combination of all his infinite perfections![28]

---

[28] Spurgeon, Vol. 4, 189.

In the house of the LORD

At this point I want to return for a moment to Psalm 27:4. It is surely significant that David's desire to gaze upon the LORD's beauty is to be fulfilled in the house of the LORD, in his tabernacle. C. S. Lewis has brought out the significance of this most helpfully. He emphasises the unity of the whole of life which characterised the Jewish outlook. There was no dualistic divide either between everyday activity and worship, nor between the rituals of worship and the presence of God. The tabernacle was the place of sacrifice, and it was in the sacrificial rites that they met with God and beheld his beauty.[29]

There is significance for us in these observations. Two things should, I think, be highlighted.

The first is that we are reminded that we, together with all our fellow believers, now form the spiritual temple. Paul reminds the Corinthian Christians (and his words are equally applicable to us today) "that you are God's temple and that God's Spirit dwells in you" (1 Corinthians 3:16). The redeemed people of God have become the locus of the divine beauty. Whenever we gather for worship, the beauty of God is reflected in the fellowship of the saints.

Secondly, the significance for God's beauty of the sacrificial centre of worship is as pertinent today as it was in Old Testament times. Just as the worship of the tabernacle was focused around the offerings, so Christian worship is centred on that to which all the Old Testament offerings were but signposts—the ultimate sacrifice of Christ on the cross. Paradoxical as it may seem, that ugly event is actually the summit of the divine beauty. It is at Calvary pre-eminently that we see the harmonious consistency of the totality of the divine nature, for it is there that

steadfast love and faithfulness meet;
righteousness and peace kiss each other.[30]

---

[29] C. S. Lewis, 'The Fair Beauty of the Lord,' in *Reflections on the Psalms* (London: Collins, 1958), 51-61.
[30] Ps. 85:10.

Hebrews 9:12 tells us that "by means of his own blood" Jesus "entered once for all into the holy places..., thus securing an eternal redemption." If God's holiness is his beauty, then the heavenly holy places are the locale of that divine beauty, beautified by his resplendent presence. As the definitive revelation of the divine beauty, our Saviour is eligible to take his place in those beautiful surroundings—in the very presence of our beautiful God. In this connection another of Spurgeon's quotations is worth citing, this time from Edward Hyde on Psalm 45:2:

> In one Christ we may contemplate and must confess all the beauty and loveliness both of heaven and earth; the beauty of heaven is God, the beauty of earth is man; the beauty of heaven and earth together is this God man.[31]

The beauty of Christ

This leads us into a further observation. We cannot talk about the beauty of God without turning our attention to the beauty of Christ. As children we used to sing,

> Let the beauty of Jesus be seen in me—
> All his wondrous compassion and purity.[32]

The beauty of Jesus is a theme which occurs prophetically in several Old Testament contexts. We shall glance at two texts from the book of Isaiah.

First, Isaiah 4:2 informs us of a coming day when "the branch of the LORD shall be beautiful and glorious." That 'the branch' is a prophetic title for Christ is clear enough from several other texts, including Jeremiah 23:5-6:

> Behold, the days are coming, declares the LORD, when I will raise up for David a righteous Branch, and he shall reign as king and deal wisely, and shall execute justice and

---

[31] Spurgeon, Vol. 2, 325.
[32] A. W. T. Orson (1886-1967).

righteousness in the land. In his days Judah will be saved, and Israel will dwell securely. And this is the name by which he will be called: 'The LORD is our righteousness.'

John Gill describes Christ, particularly in his humanity, as "'beautiful,' being laden with the fruits of divine grace."[33] All the diverse elements in the totality of God's grace—including the "wondrous compassion and purity" of the chorus—cohere harmoniously in Christ, making him the apex of the divine beauty. Alec Motyer notes that, of the texts using 'the branch' as a title for the Messiah, Isaiah 4:2 uniquely calls him 'the branch of the LORD:' "the Messiah springs from a dual ancestry as he belongs in the 'family tree' of both David and the Lord."[34] And so, as Andrew Davis observes, the beauty in view here, through the human life of Jesus, is "a radiant display of the attributes of God."[35]

Our second text is Isaiah 33:17, which entices us with the promise, "your eyes will behold the king in his beauty," again prophetic of the coming reign of Christ. Andrew Davis whets our appetite with this comment: "The greatest beauty our eyes will ever see is the radiant Christ, seated on his throne in the new Jerusalem; and that vision will complete our salvation."[36]

In these two verses we have two further Hebrew terms for beauty. Isaiah 33:17 uses $y^o phî$, which is a regular Hebrew word for beauty. More significant is the term $s^e bî$, used in Isaiah 4:2. It refers to such beauty as is "the best in regards to splendor and honor,"[37] and has connotations of desirability.[38] Our prayer must be that consideration of the beauty of God, especially as it is revealed in the Lord Jesus, will stimulate in our hearts a yet deeper desire for our beautiful Saviour. In line with my earlier comments, I do not mean that the beauty of the triune God may be defined in terms of the satisfying of our desires, but rather that we should desire him for no other reason

---

[33] J. Gill, *Exposition of the Old Testament* (Carluke: Online Bible Edition, 1995-2016), on Isa. 4:2.

[34] J. A. Motyer, *The Prophecy of Isaiah* (Leicester: IVP, 1993), 65.

[35] A. M. Davis, *Exalting Jesus in Isaiah* (Nashville: Holman, 2017), 28.

[36] Davis, 187.

[37] *Theological Wordbook of the Old Testament*, # 1869.

[38] C. J. Collins, '7382 $s^e bî$,' in VanGemeren (ed.), Vol. 3, 738.

than he is intrinsically worthy that his beauty should be deemed, in itself, the very quintessence of absolute desirability.

One further comment on Psalm 27:4 is in order. In verse 9 David refers to God as *ᴱlōhîm*, using a general title. However, it is surely significant that his desire is "to gaze upon the beauty of the LORD." Here he uses God's personal name, Jehovah.[39] When the LORD proclaimed this name in Exodus 34:6-7, expounding its meaning, his starting-point was his mercy: this was the chief quality to which he drew attention. He then expanded on the meaning of mercy, defining himself as "gracious, slow to anger, and abounding in steadfast love and faithfulness, keeping steadfast love for thousands, forgiving iniquity and transgression and sin." And David's longing, by reference to the name Jehovah, is to gaze on this cluster of attributes. These are the divine characteristics which make it possible for David, even when he does use the title *ᴱlōhîm* in verse 9 to call the LORD the "God of my salvation."

To a sinner like David—and us—the harmonious beauty of God which is most adorable is the symmetry of this set of qualities which are bound together by mercy, and it is these qualities, supremely, which are made manifest in the life, death, and resurrection of our Lord Jesus Christ. This is where we reach the apex of God's beauty. We must not fall into the trap of saying that this is merely because mercy is what we most need—though it certainly is. But God's uppermost aim in displaying his mercy to a sinful world is that he might be glorified for his mercy (Romans 15:9). We glorify him as we adore the scintillating, all-surpassing beauty of his mercy.

This connects also with the Bible's repeated stress on the beauty of God's holiness. In 2 Chronicles 20:21, the reference to praising the beauty of holiness is immediately followed by an indication of the content of that praise: "Give thanks to the LORD, for his *mercy* endures forever."[40] As mentioned earlier, one aspect of God's holiness is his absolute distinctiveness from every other reality, and the property

---

[39] Although the current scholarly consensus is the rendering Yahweh, I prefer to retain the traditional form, Jehovah, since it remains more familiar to the wider Christian public.
[40] The word 'mercy' is borrowed from the AV/NKJV; ESV reads 'steadfast love.'

which sets him apart most emphatically is his mercy. To him, indeed, be glory and praise for the beautiful holiness of his mercy in Christ.

Historical survey

One thing which is interesting to note is that the reticence about God's beauty which we observed in the confessions and theological works of the Reformed tradition has not been universal throughout Christian history. I want at this point to refer briefly to a few representative examples of theologians from different periods of church history who have dealt with this truth.

Jonathan Edwards

I shall start with one who does stand in the Reformed tradition, but is an exception to its general trend—Jonathan Edwards. I shall focus on his *Treatise Concerning Religious Affections*.[41]

The beauty of God's nature, Edwards says, is true, supreme, and infinite, and "is infinitely diverse from all other beauty,"[42] though, of course, all other beauty is a pale reflection of the defining beauty which is God.

He is rightly insistent that the genuine believer (as opposed to the hypocrite) admires, loves, and delights in God because of the inherent glory of his beauty, not for any benefit which he may derive from him. This resonates with the criticism which I made earlier of Grudem's approach. God's beauty is admirable in itself, not merely as the satisfaction of our desires. In fact, there would be an infinitely glorious beauty in God's grace "whether it were exercised towards us or no."[43]

In analysing God's glorious beauty, Edwards sees it as consisting pre-eminently in his holiness, which is "the beauty and sweetness of the divine nature."[44] He says that the beauty of holiness "is the beauty

---

[41] J. Edwards, 'A Treatise Concerning Religious Affections' [1746], in *The Works of Jonathan Edwards, Vol. 1* (Edinburgh: Banner of Truth, 1974 reprint), 234-343.
[42] Edwards, 290.
[43] Edwards, 277.
[44] Edwards, 265.

of the Godhead, the divinity of divinity."[45] God's moral perfection is the heart of his beauty, and for the true saint God's holiness is "a most beautiful thing."[46]

In addition to holiness Strachan and Sweeney identify six more attributes in particular which, they claim demonstrated for Edwards God's beauty: eternal self-existence, greatness, loveliness, power, wisdom, and goodness.[47] Actually, though, Edwards notes "the beauty of all God's moral attributes," and then observes that "his moral attributes cannot be without his natural attributes," for all God's attributes imply one another, and the beauty of God's holiness "renders all his other attributes glorious and lovely."[48] Hence the saints on earth "admire and extol all God's attributes, either as deriving loveliness from his holiness, or as being a part of it." So whichever of God's attributes is in view, "his holiness is the beauty that engages them."[49]

Edwards stresses the point that God's beauty shines most brightly, and is most affectingly exhibited, "in the face of an incarnate, infinitely loving, meek, compassionate, dying Redeemer."[50] Moreover, in line with the earlier comments, "the first foundation" of delight in Christ is "his own beauty."[51] Edwards speaks of "the spiritual beauty of his human nature," which "is summed up in his holiness," and expressed in such qualities as his meekness, patience, and compassion, and this beauty is "the image and reflection" of "the beauty of his divine nature."[52]

This has gospel relevance in that "the exceeding beauty and dignity" of Christ's person is proclaimed in the gospel as it exhibits "his word, works, acts, and life."[53] As a result, there is a genuine

---

[45] Edwards, 284.
[46] Edwards, 261.
[47] O. Strachan & D. Sweeney, *Jonathan Edwards on Beauty* (Chicago: Moody, 2010), 26-38.
[48] Edwards, 279.
[49] Edwards, 280.
[50] Edwards, 244.
[51] Edwards, 277.
[52] Edwards, 279.
[53] Edwards, 291.

"evangelical humiliation," a true change of heart, resulting from the "discovery of God's holy beauty."[54]

The Cappadocian Fathers

We now travel backwards in time to the fourth century to take a glance at the writings of the Cappadocian fathers, Basil the Great, Gregory of Nyssa, and Gregory of Nazianzen. References to the beauty of God are plenteous in the writings of the fathers, and this trio will serve as representative.

In a homily on the text "Rejoice always" (1 Thessalonians 5:16), Basil comments that the condition of the angels is one of unmitigated gladness as they "enjoy the ineffable beauty and glory of our Creator." The command to rejoice always is urging us on to that life which we too shall enjoy in glory once our present sufferings are in the past, and it will be a life of "calm and quiet." The implication is that we too, like the angels, will be taken up with the adoration of the beauty of God.[55] Gregory of Nyssa emphasises the example set by the angels for us to follow even now: "their work and their excellence is to contemplate the Father of all purity, and to beautify the lines of their own character from the source of all beauty." In imitation of this, our souls should look to the beauty above in an "intellectual contemplation of immaterial beauty."[56]

All three of these writers refer frequently to God as the 'archetype' of beauty. God is the measure by which all beauty is defined, the standard against which everything that claims to be beautiful is assessed. Thus, Gregory of Nyssa can write, "the Deity is in very substance beautiful."[57] Gregory of Nazianzen speaks far less frequently of God's beauty than do his two associates, though even he can speak of God as "that which is really beautiful," in contrast with

---

[54] Edwards, 294.

[55] Basil, *Twenty-four Homilies, Homily 4*. [cited by P. Schaff, 'Sketch of the Life and Works of St. Bail,' in *The Nicene and Post-Nicene Fathers, Second Series, Vol. 8* (Albany: Ages, 1996-97), 89f.]

[56] Gregory of Nyssa, *On Virginity*, 4-5.

[57] Gregory of Nyssa, *On the Soul and Resurrection* (Nicene and Post-Nicene Fathers, Second Series, Vol. 5, 870).

the things of flesh,[58] and as "the most beautiful" of the objects of thought as distinct from sight.[59]

But how is God's beauty to be defined? In his work on the six days of creation, Basil refers to the beauty of God the creator in the middle of a list of adulatory expressions:

> It is he, beneficent nature, goodness without measure, a worthy object of love for all beings endowed with reason, the beauty the most to be desired, the origin of all that exists, the source of life, intellectual light, impenetrable wisdom.[60]

Basil here accumulates terms to magnify the glory of God. Probably he sees much overlap, so that God's beauty includes his beneficence, his goodness, his worthiness, his creative power, his life, light, and wisdom. Everything, in other words, about God is beautiful, so much so that he is truly the most desirable, lovable being—again, not because of the benefits that this brings us, but because that represents his own intrinsic glory.

Gregory of Nyssa also multiplies expressions to bring out the characteristics of the beauty of God. "The divine beauty is not adorned with any shape or endowment of form, by any beauty of colour, but is contemplated as excellence in unspeakable bliss."[61] This is "that beauty which has no source but itself," the essential, absolute, primal, unrivalled beauty, the beauty which is "above all increase and addition, incapable of change and alteration."[62] God's beauty is boundless, incomparable, invisible, formless, simple, immaterial, but its essence is goodness expressed as love: "God's life will have its activity in love; which life is thus in itself beautiful."[63]

As we survey the beauty of creation, we are directed upwards to realise the beauty of the creator. Gregory of Nyssa pictures the beauties in the created world as a ladder by which we may climb to

---

[58] Gregory of Nazianzen, *Oration 21*, 2.
[59] Gregory of Nazianzen, *Oration 28*, 30.
[60] Basil, *Hexaemeron*, 1.2.
[61] Gregory of Nyssa, *On the Making of Man*, 5.
[62] Gregory of Nyssa, *On Virginity*, 11.
[63] Gregory of Nyssa, *On the Soul and Resurrection*, 873.

the higher beauty, as a hand to lead us to the greatest beauty of all, and as a message which instructs us to turn our thoughts to the beauty of God.[64] Basil writes, eloquently:

> If the sun, subject to corruption, is so beautiful, so grand, so rapid in its movement, so invariable in its course; if its grandeur is in such perfect harmony with and due proportion to the universe: if, by the beauty of its nature, it shines like a brilliant eye in the middle of creation; if finally, one cannot tire of contemplating it, what will be the beauty of the Sun of Righteousness?[65]

Not that God is on a par with whatever we may deem beautiful in his creation: he is "above all beauty," and as we are captivated by the beauty of the visible world, we are to "raise ourselves to him,"[66] recognising in him the epitome of a beauty which is transcendent and ineffable.

By reference to the threefold 'holy' in the song of the seraphim in Isaiah 6:3, Gregory of Nyssa emphasises "the beauty in each person of the Trinity," in contemplation of which the seraphim were "awestruck."[67] He makes but a passing application of this truth to the Holy Spirit, who is "always beautiful."[68]

Basil's references to the Holy Spirit have far more to do with our dependence on the grace of the Spirit if we are to be able to "gaze intently on the beauty of the glory of God."[69] He comments: "the mind which is impregnated with the Godhead of the Spirit is at once capable of viewing great objects; it beholds the divine beauty, though only so far as grace imparts and its nature receives."[70]

Basil notes that part of the Spirit's work in the life of the believer is the purification of the eye of the soul to which "the image of the invisible" is then revealed. All three Cappadocians refer from time to

---

[64] Gregory of Nyssa, *On Virginity*, 11.
[65] Basil, *Hexaemeron*, 6.1.
[66] Basil, *Hexaemeron*, 1.11.
[67] Gregory of Nyssa, *Against Eunomius*, 1.23.
[68] Gregory of Nyssa, *On the Holy Spirit*, 626.
[69] Basil, *Letters*, 150.1
[70] Basil, *Letters*, 233.1.

time to humanity, created in the image of God, as the reflection of the divine beauty. However, in this context Basil appears to be referring to Jesus Christ,[71] and alluding to the words of Colossians 1:15. As the image restored, the Saviour came to rescue us from the ugliness into which we have been plunged by sin and to raise us again to that divine beauty. Basil then adds: "in the spectacle of that image you shall behold the unspeakable beauty of the archetype."[72] The image of God revealed in the incarnate Christ is, for Basil, a reflection of the divine beauty of the triune God, which is itself beyond description.

Gregory of Nyssa, too, speaks of the Son as the image of the archetypal beauty of the Father, and uses as an analogy the relationship of a ray to the sun: the ray is like the sun in every way— "in beauty, in power, in lustre, in size, in brilliance, in all things at once."[73]

Gregory of Nazianzen also refers to Christ as "the image of the archetypal beauty,"[74] and suggests that "nothing can be more lovely or more beautiful" than Christ's body, "adorned by the passion, and made splendid by the Godhead"[75] in resurrection and exaltation.

Basil urges us, in order to see the supreme beauty, to "fix our eyes on the beauty of the image of the invisible God"[76]—that is to say, to focus our contemplation without distraction on our Lord Jesus Christ. As we do so, we are enabled, in the Son as the image of the Father, to perceive the beauty of the image. From there we are led on to perceive the archetype, and so to glimpse the image of the Father by "gazing at the unbegotten beauty in the begotten."[77] Basil is clear that the beauty of the distinct persons of the triune Godhead is one and the same.

Basil brings out the practical implication of the contemplation of God in his beauty: it keeps our mind aloof from worldly things, and

---

[71] So B. E. Fitzgerald, *Basil the Great on the Holy Spirit* (Souderton: St. Philip's Anchorite Church, 2003), 9 (https://www.st-philip.net/files/Fitzgerald%20Patristic%20series/Basil-Great_On_the_Holy_Spirit. pdf).
[72] Basil, *On the Holy Spirit*, 9.23.
[73] Gregory of Nyssa, *Against Eunomius*, 1.36.
[74] Gregory of Nazianzen, *Oration 38*, 13.
[75] Gregory of Nazianzen, *Oration 45*, 25.
[76] Basil, *On the Holy Spirit*, 18.47.
[77] Basil, *Letters*, 38.8.

ensures that all our energies are devoted to "the acquisition of the good things which are eternal."[78] Such language might seem to hint, yet again, at the satisfaction of our desires as the primary motive, rather than at our being captivated by God in his beauty as himself the object of our desire. However, Basil's point is that our desires are themselves shaped by the beauty of God, that being weaned off lesser things is the route to our sanctification after the image of the divine beauty.

Gregory of Nyssa offers a stimulating vision of the life of the soul in the world to come, a life in which "none of its habits are left to it except that of love, which clings by natural affinity to the beautiful," and true beauty never gives rise to "insolent satiety," nor will there ever be any sense that the limit of appreciation of the beautiful has been attained.[79] Preaching at the funeral of a sister, Gregory of Nazianzen admires the foretaste which she had of Christ's heavenly beauty through her cultivation of the vision of his love, so that death only "transferred her to exceeding joys."[80]

Sam Storms

We now fast forward to the twenty-first century. Sam Storms is a contemporary theologian who has given considerable thought to the truth of the beauty of God, particularly in his book, whose title is borrowed from the words of Psalm 27:4, *One Thing*.[81]

Storms associates the word 'beauty' with a series of other terms in connection with God, including glory, splendour, majesty, grandeur, and radiance. He also uses a vast variety of descriptive words to convey the wonder of God's uncreated, independent, and unending beauty: it is ineffable, incomparable, transcendent, sublime, indescribable, unfathomable, incomprehensible, absolute, unqualified, luminous, and immeasurable.

---

[78] Basil, *Letters*, 2.2.
[79] Gregory of Nyssa, *On the Soul and Resurrection*, 872f.
[80] Gregory of Nazianzen, *Oration 8*, 19.
[81] S. Storms, *One Thing: Developing a Passion for the Beauty of God* (Fearn: Christian Focus, 2004).

When Storms analyses God's beauty into its component parts he refers specifically to God's holiness, goodness, power, grace, kindness, and love. But perhaps his best definition of God's beauty is found in the phrase, "the sweet symmetry of his attributes," on which he enlarges in terms of the unfathomable depths of God's greatness, the baffling wisdom of his deeds, and the limitless extent of his goodness.[82]

Storms relates God's beauty to the truth of his trinitarian nature. He writes:

> God delights infinitely in his own beauty. When God the Father beholds himself in the Son he is immeasurably happy. He gazes at the Son and sees a perfect reflection of his own holiness. The Father rejoices in the beauty of the Son and Spirit, and the Son revels in the beauty of the Spirit and Father, and the Spirit delights in that of the Father and Son.

God "enjoys himself! He celebrates with infinite and eternal intensity the beauty of who he is as Father, Son, and Holy Spirit."[83]

Storms amplifies this trinitarian aspect of God's beauty most emphatically in connection with the Son. We behold "the beauty of our radiant and resplendent God as he has made himself known in his incarnate Son, Jesus Christ."[84] Storms refers more than once to the beauty of Christ, and speaks of "the beauty of Christ's love."[85] And the staggering reality is that Scripture portrays "the majesty and beauty of the eternal Son of God in the weakness of human flesh."[86]

To us the vision of God's beauty is mediated through various mirrors. In addition to the beauty of Christ himself, it is displayed in Scripture, creation, providence, redemption and the church. The written word of God eloquently reveals our God of beauty. In the works of his hands, in the heavens, on the earth, in things of immense magnitude or things of infinitesimal minuteness, the amazing beauty

---

[82] Storms, 53.
[83] Storms, 22f.
[84] Storms, 161.
[85] Storms, 40.
[86] Storms, 58.

of the creator is made known. "The physical world is a window to the beauty of God."[87]

This inexpressible beauty of God compels a response on our part. We are captivated, awestruck by it. Storms is clear that the entire purpose of our existence is that we should relish and rejoice in the beauty of God. He describes the divine beauty as "all-satisfying,"[88] but without falling into the trap for which I earlier criticised Wayne Grudem of subordinating God's beauty to the satisfaction of our desires. Storms speaks of "disinterested delight." He compares our delight in God's beauty to the joy which may result from staring at a beautiful painting, which does not "have an 'in order that' appended to it, as if it existed to help me achieve some higher or more ultimate goal." A beautiful work of art is "just there, to be admired, marveled at, and enjoyed."[89] In the same way, the delight which we find in the beauty of God is not just a step on the way to finding some yet higher fulfilment; it is the way in which we glorify him—and his glory is the pre-eminent concern.

In fact, Storms points out, the encounter with divine beauty "is profoundly transforming." The "beauty takes hold of us, and challenges the allegiance of our hearts." It calls us to "reshape our lives."[90] When we see the beauty and splendour of all that God is for us in Jesus, "we cannot help *wanting* to serve him. There is a splendor, a beauty about God and his ways that *lures* human beings to him."[91] The result is that the joy and delight in beholding the beauty of God in Jesus Christ serves to liberate our hearts from sin's slavery. It is to the glory of his name that our joy in his beauty should increase.

As his final comment, Storms reminds us that human effort alone will never apprehend the spiritual beauty of Jesus. The sovereign initiative of divine grace is vital. We see, savour, and enjoy the beauty of God only because there has been infused within us "by the regenerating work of the Holy Spirit a new taste, a new sense of the

---

[87] Storms, 108.
[88] Storms, 46.
[89] Storms, 49.
[90] Storms, 55.
[91] Storms, 129, quoted from G. R. McDermott, *Seeing God: Twelve Reliable Signs of True Spirituality* (Downers Grove: IVP, 1995), 114 [italics original].

sweetness and beauty and grandeur of God in Christ." I therefore echo the words with which Storms concludes his book: "Thank you, Lord."[92]

Awe

I close by referring to the words of the following song by Mark Altrogge:

> You are beautiful beyond description,
> Too marvellous for words,
> Too wonderful for comprehension,
> Like nothing ever seen or heard.
> Who can grasp your infinite wisdom?
> Who can fathom the depth of your love?
> You are beautiful beyond description,
> Majesty, enthroned above.
> And I stand, I stand in awe of you.
> I stand, I stand in awe of you.
> Holy God, to whom all praise is due,
> I stand in awe of you.[93]

These words depict a splendid diagram of the indescribable beauty of God. God is an ineffable marvel. He is an incomprehensible wonder. He is incomparably unique. He is the God whose wisdom is infinitely transcendent, the one whose love is impenetrably profound. He is the God of sovereign, majestic exaltation, the one whose holiness is universally praiseworthy. All these attributes—and every other characteristic of his glorious being, for these are merely representative of his harmonious totality—make up the beauty of God.

Confronted by the reality of such a God, our only legitimate response is, indeed, awe. And I, for one, am grateful to Bob Penhearow for his constant prayerful articulation of that joyful, grateful, loving, adoring awe at the beauty of God.

---

[92] Storms, 188.
[93] M. Altrogge (b.1950) © 1986, Sovereign Grace Praise. Quoted by permission.

The Five *Solas*

Steven West

Dr. Bob Penhearow has been unfailingly kind to me. He has taken a great deal of time out of his very, *very* busy schedule to encourage me in my academic teaching and writing, as well as in my pastoral ministry. I have appreciated his love for the triune God, for the truth of God's word, and for the local church in its manifestations all around the world. Bob is marked by a heart for seeing pastors and leaders trained in the great truths of the faith that will feed their hearts as well as their minds, and enable them to teach and feed their people in turn. Thankfully, Bob doesn't confuse the deep truths of Scripture with theology that is needlessly abstract or esoteric. He has been concerned that preachers and teachers be well-trained in the fundamentals of biblical and systematic theology, so that both they and their congregations can know and live out the truth.

Carey's doctrinal distinctives represent a Reformed, evangelical, baptistic orientation. Although there is charity for all and latitude on many secondary and tertiary issues, the theology of the mission is unashamedly and avowedly rooted in Scripture, and is in harmony with the great credal and confessional statements of church history. The justly famous theological slogans of the Reformation—the five *solas*—are precious to Bob and, just as they summarised the heart of the theology of the Reformation, they encapsulate a great deal of the mission's theology as well. A teaching and preaching ministry that is built on these foundational truths can nourish and strengthen the people of God in any culture, in any language, at any time.

The last point of *Carey*'s Doctrinal Statement reads as follows:

15. The *Solas* of the Reformation

We believe in the 5 *SOLAS* of the Reformation: The Scriptures, being the only source of divine revelation (*Sola Scriptura*), teach us that salvation is by Grace Alone (*Sola Gratia*), through Faith Alone (*Sola Fide*), in Christ Alone (*Solus Christus*), to the Glory of God Alone (*Soli Deo Gloria*). *2 Tim.*

3:14-17; Ep. 2:8-9; Ro. 10:1-4; He. 9:11-15, 23-28; 1 Co. 10:31.[1]

In this point *Carey* identifies the heart of Reformation theology, and also provides a quick view into the logical links between the doctrines. It is the Scriptures that teach that salvation is *by* grace *through* faith *in* Christ *to* the glory of God. Philosophically, these doctrines are not merely consistent with each other, they are coherent (i.e., they are mutually reinforcing and are to be considered not merely as individual truths, but as an organic whole). Although entire books have been written on each *sola*, this chapter will endeavour succinctly to expound each doctrine for its individual meaning, identify its underlying logical structure, and examine its relationship with the other four *sola* statements.

Sola Scriptura

At a pedantic level, the *Carey* statement on the *solas* contains an inaccuracy. If the context is ignored, the claim that the Scriptures are "the *only* source of divine revelation" is false. Literally everything that exists bears testimony to the existence of God, and thus everything that exists is revelatory in some capacity. The commonplace distinction between general and special revelation is well-accepted in theology, as it ought to be. Creation is revelation. The incarnate Christ is revelation. God's providential acts are revelation. Clearly *Carey* is not denying this reality. The statement, then, that the Scriptures are the *only* source of divine revelation is made with a particular, contextual focus. The claim is really that the Scriptures are the *only* place where we find God's special, inspired, verbal revelation. The canon of Scripture is—in a completely unique and exclusive way—God's holy word.

The introduction to *Carey*'s statement of beliefs establishes this understanding at the very beginning, as does the first doctrine articulated in the statement. The preamble states:

---

[1] www.careyoutreach.org/about-us/what-we-believe

Carey International Pastoral Training (CIPT) accepts the Holy Scriptures as the only supreme and complete authority in all matters of doctrine and practice.

Immediately following the introduction, the doctrinal statement opens with the declaration that:

> We believe the Bible—the sixty-six books of the Old and New Testaments, to be the complete Word of God: as originally written, they were verbally inspired by the Spirit of God, and therefore entirely free from error. The Bible is the final authority in all matters of faith and practice. *2 Pt. 1:20-21; 2 Tim. 3:16; Ro. 15:4; I Th. 1:13; I Tim. 3:13.*[2]

At the time of the Reformation, we know that the concept of *sola Scriptura* fell foul of the teaching of the Roman Catholic Church. The pope and the traditional teachings of the Church were accorded a place of authority over the beliefs and practices of the people. In some places and at some times, the Bible was literally taken out of people's hands. Translating the Bible into a language that common people could read was a capital offense in some jurisdictions. Martin Luther wasn't innovating when he based his views on Scripture and held to God's word as the ultimate authority, but he was recovering a high view of Scripture which had for a long time been set aside by the Roman Catholic Church.

When Luther had to answer for his teaching he famously remarked:

> Unless I am convinced by Scripture and plain reason—I do not accept the authority of the popes and councils, for they have contradicted each other—my conscience is captive to the Word of God. I cannot and I will not recant anything, for to go against conscience is neither right nor safe.[3]

---

[2] www.careyoutreach.org/about-us/what-we-believe
[3] From Luther's speech at the Imperial Diet of Worms, 18th April, 1521.

Carey lecturers teach believers in many different cultures around the world, and Luther's statement here can be helpful for everyone. It also provides some special insight which helps those who are mired in cultures that are postmodern and relativistic, as we'll see.

In terms of relativism, notice that Luther recognises the contradictory nature of appealing to multiple, competing human authorities. Although Luther did not live in a postmodern cultural milieu—he didn't even live during the time of modernism—he was aware that finite human beings can only speak with relative degrees of authority and truth. To bring the discussion more towards the present, after the subjective-turn in epistemology, combined with the corresponding loss of confidence in religion, people could only be their own authorities. Yet finite, fallible creatures are not sufficient to stand as ultimate authorities. People disagree: who adjudicates? Even grounding authority at the level of the cultural community or society is never sufficient. How does a collection of fallible finite beings somehow become authoritative? How do we adjudicate between cultures? How could the Allied Nations judge the Axis Powers? If there is no court of appeal beyond human beings or human communities, then there is no court of appeal! If a given society is its own ultimate standard, then moral reform within that society is also impossible, since what the society dictates is by definition right in an authoritative way. In this welter of confusion, we need a genuine, ultimate authority.

Very interestingly, Luther connected Scripture with *plain reason*. A vital principle undergirds his point: Scripture is *understandable*. It doesn't do any good to have an ultimate standard of authority which is incomprehensible. Thankfully, the Scriptures can be understood. Theologians sometimes refer to the attributes of Scripture, and they usually identify four. First, Scripture is necessary. It is necessary in order for us to understand certain truths about God and his great plan of redemption. Second, Scripture is sufficient. At every stage of redemptive history, what God had specially revealed to his people was sufficient for his purposes and sufficient for their needs. Now that Christ's earthly work is finished and he has ascended to the right hand of the Father, and the canon has been completed, the canon is sufficient and cannot be added to before the Lord's return.

Third, Scripture has the attribute of authority. Fourth, it is clear. The doctrine of clarity (sometimes called *perspicuity*) does not mean that absolutely every verse is as easy to interpret as every other verse, but it does mean that the basic message of Scripture is clear enough to be understood by anyone. Even children can understand the Bible at some levels!

This last characteristic of Scripture—the attribute of clarity—is essential for a Christian response to relativism and postmodernism. In Genesis 1, God speaks and a world is created. His word is capable of achieving something as remarkable as creation *ex nihilo*. God is omniscient, and so he knows the limitations and usefulness of language. He knows what it can and what it cannot accomplish. Postmodernism began as a linguistic theory, casting doubt on the ability of language to communicate. There is obviously a great degree of technical nuance that can go into a discussion on such matters, but for now we'll bypass virtually all of that to say this: God talks, and God knows how to communicate. In Genesis 1 God speaks to Adam and Eve, and he expects them to understand his words. God created human beings with linguistic faculties; we are communicators, because God is a communicator. Our minds are designed for the production and interpretation of speech. When words are written down they retain their meaning. God has spoken, and he has spoken clearly and understandably. When we approach the Scriptures, we can have confidence that they are a message from God—who knows how to communicate—to us, who are built to receive his communication and revelation.

The logic behind *sola Scriptura*, then, is that when God speaks, his words must be authoritative in an absolute and ultimate sense. The nature of the word of God is grounded in the nature of God himself. God is omniscient, so he cannot be mistaken. He is truth, so he cannot lie. Purposeful deception or communicating something false that you mistakenly take to be true exhaust the categories for misleading speech. Nothing that God says can be wrong. It is normally from this theological axiom that the doctrine of the inerrancy and infallibility of Scripture is deduced. If every word of Scripture is God-breathed and God is incapable of error, then every word of Scripture will be accurate and true, when interpreted in its context according to proper rules of hermeneutics. Since *only* the Scriptures are the breathed-out word of God, then only the Scriptures are marked by absolute authority. The Bible is our authority only because God is our authority.

At this point the relation that *sola Scriptura* sustains to the other *solas* is readily apparent. Whatever is revealed in the Bible is true. When it comes to the main elements of God's redemptive plan centred on Christ Jesus, the teaching of Scripture is not only true, it is crystal clear. These are the great things that God wants us to know. So what does the Bible teach us about salvation? It teaches us that salvation is by grace alone (*sola gratia*).

Sola Gratia

That there could be no salvation apart from the grace of God was not a point of debate in the Reformation. Protestants and Roman Catholics alike acknowledged that it was the grace of God that planned and accomplished salvation through Jesus Christ. God did not owe anyone salvation, so salvation was an act of grace. The debate came when the issues surrounding grace, faith, the human response, and works were analysed together. For the Reformers, it was *only* the grace of God that allowed us to be saved. It was Christ's merit, and none of ours, which brought about salvation, and it was God's sovereign will, rather than our fallen natures, that allowed us to respond to the gospel.

In Ephesians 2:5 Paul writes:

> even when we were dead in our trespasses, [God] made us alive together with Christ—by grace you have been saved.

Then just a few verses later he writes:

> For by grace you have been saved through faith. And this is not your own doing; it is the gift of God, not a result of works, so that no one may boast.[4]

---

[4] Eph. 2:8f.

The repetition of "by grace you have been saved" signals that this is the key idea in the passage. Paul also underscores the fact that our salvation is the gift of God. It is his work on our behalf that allows us to be saved; he gives us in Jesus Christ what we do not deserve. Since we do not deserve salvation, this by definition means that salvation is by grace.

The Reformers connected the doctrine of *sola gratia* with the doctrines of original sin, human depravity, God's overarching general sovereignty, and his specific sovereign choice in predestination and election. If people inherited the sin nature from Adam, and if they were dead in trespasses and sin, then not only would they not respond positively to the gospel, they would actively resist it and suppress the truth in unrighteousness. Regeneration would have to precede conversion. If such were the case, then the very fact that someone was made spiritually alive in Christ could only be because of God's pre-decision to predetermine that they would be saved. This decision to elect a people for salvation occurred in the secret counsels of God in eternity past, and was not based on any foreseen merit or on any particular response that people would make to the gospel. The sole and exclusive reason why anyone was saved by Christ was 100% grace. It was grace from beginning to end; it was grace alone all the way through.

Sola Fide

Salvation by grace alone is logically connected to faith alone (*sola fide*). We have already seen how the two are brought together in Ephesians 2:8:

> For by grace you have been saved through faith. And this is not your own doing; it is the gift of God.

We are saved *by* grace and *through* faith. The grammar of this passage indicates that the entire package of salvation by grace through faith is the gift of God. It is not only grace that is the gift of God (grace is a gift by definition), it is the faith that is the gift of God as well. God needs to give faith to people so that they can receive his gift of salvation by grace. *Sola fide* flows out of *sola gratia*.

In *sola fide*, faith is not something which contributes to our salvation in a meritorious way. Faith is instrumental; it is the instrument through which we receive the benefits of salvation. Faith cannot be considered a good work of ours that contributes to our merit before God, since Paul explicitly says that we are saved by grace through faith, and that this is "not a result of works, so that no one may boast." If faith were a work, then that would give us some claim—no matter how small—to some aspect of our own salvation. Salvation would be a composite of Christ's work plus our choice, or Christ's work plus our contribution of faith. Against this view, the Reformers insisted that faith was not a human work nor a human initiative—God regenerated his elect so that they put their faith in Christ in conversion. Faith was exercised by human beings, but it was only made possible by God's grace.

It is important to recognise that our works *never* contribute merit towards our salvation. Faith is not a work that brings us into the kingdom, and at no time during our Christian lives are our works achieving for us any kind of salvific merit. Works are the evidence of salvation; they are the fruit, not the root. This is why the New Testament can often speak of us being judged by our words and deeds: what we do and say is evidence of the state of our hearts. A regenerated heart brings forth good works as a consequence of its orientation to God, and by the active power and presence of the Holy Spirit. Where there are no good works there is no salvation, but it is not the works themselves which save. The ground of salvation is not our own personal merit, or a treasury of supererogatory merit that was stockpiled by particular saints in church history. Human works do not contribute to salvation, and faith is not an exception to this theological principle.

The Reformation was about far more than the doctrine of justification by faith, yet nonetheless this was a key issue separating Protestants from Rome. Justification by faith alone was drawn from passages like Romans 1:17, which states:

For in it [the gospel] the righteousness of God is revealed from faith for faith, as it is written, 'The righteous shall live by faith.'

In Romans 3:28, Paul wrote: "For we hold that one is justified by faith apart from works of the law." Famously, Luther added the word 'alone' after the word 'faith' in his German translation. In doing so, he was attempting to bring out Paul's meaning. It is not by works, but only by faith, that we are justified. This justification is a legal, forensic declaration by God that gives us the standing of being judicially innocent in his sight. We are innocent of transgression, and we are clothed in the righteousness of Christ. This comes through faith—faith alone.

Solus Christus

If faith is an instrument by which we receive merit, where does that merit come from? Salvation is by grace, but *how* can God be gracious to sinners and provide them with salvation? The answer is that God graciously provides salvation by uniting us by faith with his Son, the Lord Jesus Christ. It is through Christ alone that people can be saved.

The centrality of Christ in evangelical Christianity is taken for granted, to the point where it can be central in name only but not in practice. One of the things that has characterised Bob's preaching and teaching is a love of biblical theology, where he clearly expounds how lines of theology develop throughout the canon until they reach their fulfillment in Jesus. For *Carey*, the centrality of Christ isn't merely given lip service, it is taught explicitly and implicitly in every course. Ethics, counselling, and pastoral theology, as well as biblical studies and systematic theology, are focused on Christ. This is as it ought to be. Christ is the centre of Scripture, and should be the centre of all that we do.

Solus Christus has many entailments and implications, but at its basic level it is a modal claim. It is not simply asserting that salvation *is* only in Christ, it is asserting that salvation *could not* come through anyone else. Christ is the only Saviour, but he is also the only one who *could be* our Saviour. This modal reality is grounded in two truths: (1) Christ's two natures; (2) Christ's work. For *solus Christus* to be valid, it is important for us to recognise that only a person with both a divine and a human nature could be qualified to do the work that Christ did.

Although it took the early church some time to work out a credal formulation on the person and natures of Christ, a proper Christological understanding existed long before its codification. Recognising the deity and humanity of Christ was something that the earliest followers of Christ did. In the New Testament, the apostolic witness is clear that Christ was both God and man. Through debates and challenges—and in response to various sub-Christian formulations and understandings—a definitive credal statement of Christological orthodoxy was made in Chalcedon in 451. The creed declares:

> We, then, following the holy fathers, all with one consent, teach men to confess one and the same Son, our Lord Jesus Christ, the same perfect in Godhead and also perfect in manhood; truly God and truly man, of a reasonable soul and body; consubstantial with us according to the manhood; in all things like unto us, without sin; begotten before all ages of the Father according to the Godhead, and in these latter days, for us and for our salvation, born of the virgin Mary, the mother of God, according to the manhood; one and the same Christ, Son, Lord, only-begotten, to be acknowledged in two natures, unconfusedly, unchangeably, indivisibly, inseparably; the distinction of natures being by no means taken away by the union, but rather the property of each nature being preserved, and concurring in one person and one subsistence, not parted or divided into two persons, but one and the same Son, and only-begotten, God the Word, the Lord Jesus Christ, as the prophets from the beginning have declared concerning him, and the Lord Jesus Christ himself taught us, and the creed of the holy fathers has handed down to us.

Those familiar with the theological debates can see how the language of this credal statement is intentionally designed to respond to unorthodox opinions and arguments about Christ. Even without that background knowledge, however, the creed makes it clear that Christ was the eternal Son of the Father. He was the second person of the Trinity, with all of the attributes of deity. He was *fully* God. Yet to his full, essential deity, he added a full, genuine humanity. These natures were not mixed into a hybrid or third thing. Each nature retained its full set of attributes and characteristics. *Kenotic* Christology, which sees the Son abandoning some of the attributes of his divine nature, was a novel, liberal-theological interpretation of Philippians 2:7, that was never taught in the history of the church until the 1800's. Christ humbled himself, but he did not stop being fully divine.

Christ was also truly and fully human. This is a doctrine that cannot be compromised upon. He had every human faculty that is part of the essence of human nature. Christ had a human mind and human will. One key difference from us, however, was that he did not inherit a sin nature from Adam. The second person of the Trinity operated both as God and as a man. One person, two natures. This raises the question of *why* Christ had to be fully God and fully man. In other words, why was the incarnation necessary?

An important text for answering this question is Hebrews 2:14-15:

> Since therefore the children share in flesh and blood, he himself likewise partook of the same things, that through death he might destroy the one who has the power of death, that is, the devil, and deliver all those who through fear of death were subject to lifelong slavery.

In order to destroy the power of death, Jesus had to die and then be raised to life again. In order to die and defeat death, Christ needed to be a human being. In order to pay for human sin, Christ needed to be a man to substitute himself in the place of fallen sinners. He needed to be *fully* human because every faculty we have is stained and affected by sin. There is a theological expression, 'what is not assumed is not redeemed.' This means that if Christ did not assume a part of our nature, then that part of our nature is not redeemed in the atonement. In order for us to be fully redeemed, Christ needed to be our complete substitute in every way.

Only Christ could provide an acceptable, substitutionary atonement, and he is the only one who actually accomplished atoning for the sins of God's people. Christ lived a perfect human life, and had no sin of his own. Yet he was willing to suffer in our place and pay the penalty for our sin, redeeming us and reconciling us to God. The atoning work of Christ is the *only* atonement in heaven and on earth. There is no other name by which we can be saved. It is the two natures of Christ that made possible his atoning sacrifice. In death he paid for our sin, and in his life he earned a full human righteousness through his perfect obedience. Our sins are imputed to him, and his righteousness is imputed to us. We are united with him in his death, and united with him in his resurrection and ascension. We are in him and he is in us. Salvation is accomplished only in Christ. Eternal life is found only in Christ. There is only one Lord and Saviour for the world. We can only be righteous in Christ alone. Only Christ can bring us to the Father. Everything that we need is found '*solus Christus.*'

Soli Deo Gloria

In the same way that in times past many Christians of a certain persuasion fixed the initials 'DV' (*deo volente*, 'God willing') to their statements of future plans, so today many Christians influenced by Reformed theology add *SDG* or write out *soli Deo gloria* at the end of an expression of work or service to the Lord. It's the sort of sentiment that is often added to a book Preface by the author or editor. This is all well and good, provided it doesn't devolve into a pious platitude, or something that we add unthinkingly, out of habit, or because that's simply the vernacular of our particular ecclesiological circle. When properly considered and applied to our own life and works, this slogan is a deep and rich summary statement: it means that everything we do should be done to the glory of God.

Like ending a prayer by saying, 'in Jesus' name,' the words can be used even when the heart is not engaged. To make a candid confession, in the first journal article I ever published—entitled *Is Sola Scriptura Self-Referentially Incoherent?* (I answered 'no' to that question)—I decided to sign off with that slogan. Although I do believe that I wanted God to be glorified, as a young man writing his first article for peer-review, I also hoped that it would make me sound a little bit smart; I wanted to know my church history, and using *Latin* is surely even more impressive than using Greek or Hebrew! Using the slogan is no guarantee that you *mean* it: I wanted God to be glorified, but I also wanted my share of recognition, at least as a side-benefit. How much of our ministry work is for our own sake, building our own kingdom? At best, I imagine that our motives are mixed. We do desire for there to be *Deo gloria*, but our hearts resist what our mouths confess: we cheat a little on the *soli*. For me, my use of that phrase actually didn't make me look very clever—it made me look either ill-informed or careless. Knowing about the five *solas*, I wrote *Sola Deo Gloria*. The editor graciously corrected my error, in the galley-proofs changing my *Sola* into the grammatically-proper *Soli*.

Most of us can agree on this life-principle that everything we do ought to be done for the glory of God. Likely the most famous question and answer in the history of Protestant catechisms is found in the very first words of the Westminster Shorter Catechism. Many of you likely have the following words memorised:

What is the chief end of man?
The chief end of man is to glorify God and enjoy him forever.[5]

In other words, the entire point of our existence is to bring glory to God. One of the proof texts for this catechetical statement is taken from Paul: "So, whether you eat or drink, or whatever you do, do all to the glory of God" (1 Corinthians 10:31). All of our lives are to be lived *soli Deo gloria*. I imagine that it would be difficult to find a follower of Jesus Christ who would dispute this truth in theory.

One very insightful recent study of *soli Deo gloria* is found in a book authored by David VanDrunen. VanDrunen argues that *soli Deo gloria* is the glue that holds the *solas* together. He also argues for a point that I found completely convincing and compelling. VanDrunen writes:

...a common emphasis in contemporary discussion of *soli Deo gloria*—that we are to glorify God in all of our contemporary pursuits—gets at one important aspect of the Reformation theology of the glory of God but risks distorting its larger message. *Soli Deo gloria* was never primarily about us and our conduct before God. According to Reformed orthodox

---

[5] Westminster Shorter Catechism (1647), Q. 1.

theology, God is inherently glorious and he glorifies himself in all of his works. That is the heart of the matter. [6]

In one sense, we can say that the reason why we should add *soli Deo gloria* at the end of our works is that *God himself* does everything for the purpose of his own glory. When we act to glorify God, we are acting from the same motives as God himself. God will not share his glory with another—glory is for him alone. Yet, incredibly, God invites us to participate in—not steal—his glory. United with Christ, who brings many sons to glory, we share in the glory of Christ. Ultimately, God is glorified through Christ. *Solus Christus* is for *soli Deo gloria*. Objectively, everything in the universe brings glory to God alone. Subjectively, our motives for everything we do should be for the glory of God alone.

Soli Deo gloria includes worship, but it is not reducible to times when we are singing, praying, or ascribing verbal praise to God. The angels in heaven surround the throne, giving their praise and worship to God and to the Lamb, proclaiming their glory, but glory to God alone is more, not less, than verbal declarations. It is sweet to worship God through Jesus Christ, but everything we do in our lives ought to bring God glory. How can it be otherwise? As the Scriptures teach, we are saved by grace alone, through faith alone, in Christ alone, to the glory of God alone.

Concluding thought

The five s*olas* provide an excellent foundation for many different doctrines. They are logically related to one another, flowing into each other and strengthening each other. Behind all of them is an unshakeable view that God is the ultimate reality, and that everything comes from him and redounds to his glory. If we are to know God, he must speak. If we are to be saved, the plan and accomplishment of salvation can only come from his grace. We cannot add our works to what God has done on our behalf, so salvation must be by faith alone. Since only God can save, but a human being needs to live and die to

---

[6] D. VanDrunen, *God's Glory Alone: The Majestic Heart of Christian Faith and Life* (Grand Rapids: Zondervan, 2015), 43.

redeem, and give life to, sinners, the second person of the Trinity had to become a man to be our representative. Salvation can only be found in Christ alone. As a result, all glory goes to God alone.

Bob Penhearow and *Carey* have stood for, taught, and lived-out these foundational truths. Because of Bob's vision and work, these truths are being taught all over the world, and they are being taught to teachers who will pass them on to thousands of other believers. This is a rich legacy and a rich ministry, and Bob would be the first to say—and to mean—that it is all *soli Deo gloria.*

Historical and Biographical Papers

Lights in the Darkness:
Pastors Chang and Chu of Shanxi[1]

Raymond Martin

Shanxi Province in northern China is an area where there have been great famines in the past resulting in numerous deaths. The spiritual famine in this part of China was also great until the gospel first reached Shanxi in 1876. It was during a time of famine relief that the Lord began to open hearts to the good news. David Hill, an English Methodist missionary, was used by God to reach a Confucian scholar and opium addict who became one of the greatest Christians in the church of China, Pastor Hsi. This paper is about two lesser known, but remarkable, servants of Christ in the southern part of Shanxi, west of the Fen River, Pastors Chang and Chu. The grace of God powerfully transformed these two men and made them, in this impoverished province, mighty instruments for God, who reached hundreds of others for Christ.

Chang—the Buddhist priest

The story begins in a Buddhist temple in a little village named Mulberry Crag about twelve miles from the city of Taning, which means, 'The City of Great Peace.' Chang Chi Pen, the only son of his parents, had been brought to this temple as the fulfilment of a vow which they had made to the temple priest. In a way reminiscent of the story of Hannah, though certainly not directed to her Lord, they had waited long for a son to be born, and promised to devote him to Buddha if 'the gods' had mercy on them and gave them a son. Chang Chi Pen was born and the parents kept their promise, but the one true and living God had other plans for their only son. When Chang was only eight years old, he began his training to become a Buddhist priest.

---

[1] The English spelling of Chinese names and places in this paper is the same as used in the writings of the missionary authors, which is the Wade-Giles system or a modification of it. Pinyin spellings are slightly different: for example, Taning is Daning and Siaoyi is Xiaoyi in Pinyin.

He promised to keep the ten vows of a virtuous and ascetic life, and received personal instruction from the village priest. He learned the Buddhist classics, studied music, and, after years of training, made the solemn vow to follow Buddha and his teachings, in a formal ceremony in which he was branded on his shaven head. It seemed that he was set for the rest of his life as a Buddhist priest, but he was troubled at times by doubts about the teachings of the Buddhist faith. Surrounded by numerous images of gods in the temple every day, his heart was restless.

One evening, while having a discussion with the temple priest, his old teacher suddenly said to him:

> These three religions of ours, Confucianism, Buddhism, and Taoism, do not contain all the truth. Another religion will come from the west as Buddhism did, and that will be the truth. Should this come in your lifetime be sure to welcome and investigate it.[2]

These words had a profound impact on Chang who later had a dream in which he heard a voice saying, "The true light will come from the west to enable men to walk in the right way." When the village priest died, Chang was appointed as head priest not only of the village, but of Taning County. His Buddhist practice was not that of a mystic in meditation, but one in which he devoted himself to helping the sick and diseased of his county. The afflicted would come to him for healing and ask him to call upon the gods for help.

Followers of Buddha believe that he is 'The Enlightened One' and that the way of salvation is by becoming 'enlightened' through self-effort. But one day, the true light suddenly began to break into the darkness of Chang's soul.

In 1878, during an inspection tour of another temple in Taning, Chang came across a book with a strange title as he was examining some of the Buddhist literature in the temple. The title of the book, *Ma ko Fuyin*, seemed to Chang to read, "The Happy Sound of the

---

[2] M. Broomhall, *In Quest of God: The Life Story of Pastors Chang and Chu, Buddhist Priest and Chinese Scholar* (London: CIM, 1921), 9.

Horse." It was actually a copy of the Gospel of Mark! In Mandarin, the character *ma* means a 'horse' and the verb *ko* means 'to permit.' As Chang read it literally it seemed to be about 'a horse permitting a happy sound.' But what caught Chang's eye were the characters on the cover of the book which read, "Western Chronology." Remembering the words of his teacher, the old temple priest, and his own dream that truth and light would come from the west, his curiosity was aroused to read and study this book which he had found in the temple. It had apparently been left there by a priest who obtained it from a missionary who had passed through Taning some time previously, selling gospel literature.[3]

Back in Mulberry Crag, Chang read his newly found treasure with great interest, but could not understand the names and places he was reading. The one thing that did impress him was how often the characters for happiness were repeated. As a Buddhist priest, his goal in life had been to escape from suffering and finally to reach immortality in Nirvana, the end of the cycle of rebirth. But now he was reading a book which spoke of the happiness that he had found so elusive. How could he attain to this happiness? What was the teaching of this unusual book from the west? Chang needed someone to help him understand this fascinating little book. His thoughts turned to his young friend, Chu Wan Yi, a Confucian scholar, whom he invited to come and read with him.

Chu—the Confucian scholar

Although only about twenty years old, Chu was highly regarded as a brilliant young man and classical scholar. He had not only studied the Confucian classics for his Bachelor of Arts degree, but had also read the Buddhist and Taoist writings in his search for wisdom and light for the practice of virtue.[4] As Chang and Chu were reading the Gospel

---

[3] The exact time and identity of the missionary who had brought the Gospel of Mark to Taning is uncertain.
[4] The Confucian Classics consist of the Five Canonical Classics: Canon of History, Canon of Poetry or Odes, Canon of Changes, Record of Rites, and the Annals of Spring and Autumn. Also, the Four Books: The Book of Great Learning, The Doctrine of the Mean, The Analects of Confucius, and The Works of Mencius. See

of Mark, the people of Shanxi were experiencing terrible suffering and starvation through a time of famine and epidemics. Chang's parents had passed away and although he had continually called to the lifeless gods in his temple for help and relief from the sorrows and suffering, no answer had come, just as no answer had come from Baal when his deluded worshippers had cried out to him (1 Kings 18:26-29). With heavy but hopeful hearts, these two friends pressed on in their study of Mark. Marshall Broomhall describes the scene for us:

> We may therefore picture these two men, the one in his Buddhist robes and the other in his scholar's gown, distressed and perplexed in mind beyond measure by the unspeakable calamities and sorrows of famine—seated night after night amid the weird and awesome surroundings of the temple, where the gods had turned deaf ears to all their cries, poring, in the dim light of a primitive Chinese lamp, over the pages of the mysterious little book that had come from the West. Hungry and thirsty, their souls fainted within them, and yet they were nearer than they knew to him who is the bread and water of life. The more they read the deeper their interest and wonder grew. Life as they knew it was hard and relentless, but here was love such as they had never conceived.[5]

So devoted to the study of the Gospel were Chang and Chu that they burned incense to the book, and also to Jesus and the twelve apostles, along with the gods of the temple. The light of the word slowly began to break into their spiritual darkness, and they gathered other seekers from the village to read and study with them. This continued for a year, but then Chang came into possession of the Gospel of Matthew after learning of a foreigner travelling through Taning selling books. We can imagine the two seekers and their friends working their way through the names in the genealogy of Jesus in the first chapter of Matthew, but with a sense of awe due to the reverence Chinese have for their ancestors.

Lit-Sen Chang, *Asia's Religions: Christianity's Momentous Encounter with Paganism* (Vancouver: China Horizon and Horizon Ministries Canada, 1999), 40-43.
[5] Broomhall, 30.

Chang was especially moved by the Lord's warm invitation to weary and burdened sinners in Matthew 11:28, "Come to me, all who labour and are heavy laden, and I will give you rest." The last word in the invitation in Mandarin is 'peace,' which is just what Chang and Chu were seeking amidst their tribulations. Another passage which made a deep impression upon them was Matthew 7:13-14:

> Enter by the narrow gate. For the gate is wide and the way is easy that leads to destruction, and those who enter by it are many. For the gate is narrow and the way is hard that leads to life, and those who find it are few.

In the providence of God, some of Chu's students obtained the entire New Testament and brought it to the village for the seekers to study. More light from the word broke in upon them as they learned about God as a loving heavenly Father, how we can come to him in prayer, and that there is a kingdom of heaven that came with Jesus Christ. They also learned from further reading into the epistles of Paul that idolatry is sinful, and something that they must turn away from to worship and serve the true and living God and his Son Jesus Christ. The teachings of the word of God were making a powerful impact on their souls as they meditated daily on the truths of Scripture. They could not be the same after the entrance of the word had brought light into their hearts and given them the knowledge of the Lord. They had not yet met a foreign teacher and had learned everything they knew from their reading and study of the New Testament Scriptures.

Chang was so affected that he knew he could not continue to be the head Buddhist priest of his county. It was time to make his decision and follow the word of God. He was about forty years old at the time when he left the Buddhist priesthood and began working as a farmer. He also married a widow with two sons, who sadly never shared the joys of his faith. This was but one trial that Chang would endure as he and Chu were called to suffer many things for Christ.

Spiritual growth through trials and sufferings

About four years after Chang and Chu began studying the Scriptures faithfully, Chu made a journey through the mountains of South Shanxi to the city of Pingyangfu where he met Samuel Drake of the China Inland Mission. The Confucian scholar had many questions about the Bible for the missionary, and Drake warmly responded to his humble inquiries. Chu later spent more time at the mission where he met several other Chinese Christians for the first time, including Pastor Hsi who helped him to understand the Scriptures better and gave him deeper insights into the word, including the important subject of prayer. Chu was not the same after this, as he too knew that the time of change had come and that he must leave his Confucian past to follow Christ. Drake later wrote about his impression of Chu in a letter to his family:

> His manner immediately on acquaintance produced a pleasing and assuring effect. There was evident frankness and humility of mind, while there was no suspicion of obsequiousness. His simple naturalness made me feel that I could trust him with perfect security.[6]

Chu's humble character was evident to other believers, but he and Chang were called to develop the fruit of patience when they were told that they must wait for a year to be baptised. The reason for this rule at the Mission Station was to encourage newly professing believers to continue on in faithfulness of purpose to the Lord to demonstrate the genuineness of their faith. Chu was greatly disappointed by this rule but Chang knew that he had a personal issue to deal with before he could be accepted for baptism. He had been an opium smoker for some time, and this habit was deeply offensive, even to many unbelievers. Through prayer and faith, he was enabled to overcome this vicious habit and find deliverance by the grace of God. Chu suffered the loss of his only child and also his brother who, just before he died, joyfully cried out, "Thank God, thank God, Jesus is able to save." This experience of death without fear strengthened Chu's faith. Shortly after this he suffered persecution for the first time when he was beaten on his hand and threatened that his degree would be taken away for being a follower of 'The Western Sage,' as Jesus

---

[6] Broomhall, 40.

was referred to by some in China. Chu responded to this threat by saying,

> I counted my degree as nothing in comparison with the excellency of Christ Jesus my Lord, for Jesus has greater glory in store for me than any earthly degree.[7]

About a year later, Chang and Chu made another trek through the mountains to the Mission. Chang suffered swollen feet on this journey and Chu tried to persuade him to turn back, but he refused to do so and patiently bore the pain. The day of joy finally came, and he was baptised and welcomed into the church, along with Chu. They had proven to be faithful disciples of Jesus, but more trials of their faith lay ahead for them. Chang was publicly beaten with a total of three hundred blows by the lictors for refusing to pay a portion of his taxes for the support of idols, then cast into a cold and filthy cell for forty days. Although he was always gracious and gentle to others, this painful experience was never forgotten:

> The effects of this cruel treatment received at this time Chang carried to the end of his days. In after years, when he became the pastor of the church in the very city where he had suffered, he always evinced the most sympathetic and tenderhearted spirit towards any Christian who was persecuted or who might be called upon to suffer as he had. His one weakness, in fact, as a pastor, was possibly his keen anxiety to shield the converts from all persecution and hardship.[8]

Chu also suffered greatly for Christ after refusing to bow and worship the great Chinese philosopher Confucius at one of the annual festivals in his honour. As the assembled crowd cried out, "Confucius, Confucius, how great is Confucius," and prostrated themselves three times to an idol in his honour, Chu, like the three Hebrews in the Book of Daniel, remained standing. For this act of obedience to his Lord, Chu was beaten one hundred times. These sufferings for Christ only

---

[7] Broomhall, 46.
[8] Broomhall, 63.

served to strengthen the faith of Chang and Chu, and encouraged them to speak of their Saviour with greater boldness. Like the apostles in the Book of Acts, they went forth "rejoicing that they were counted worthy to suffer dishonour for the name" (Acts 5:41). They were determined not only to build up the little church in Mulberry Crag, but zealously to reach out to other parts of Shanxi with the gospel of grace.

A passion for evangelism

Chang and Chu had eagerly shared their faith in Christ from the very beginning of their Christian lives. Not only had they gathered others to study the Gospel of Mark with them when they were still groping for the truth, they had also told others in the village about Jesus when the light of the gospel had shined into their hearts. Among the first to hear the word of life from their lips was a poor farmer named Yang, who had been addicted to opium smoking and gambling. This man's wife was afflicted with an illness and no one was able to help her. However, a certain doctor told the farmer to go to Chang and Chu for help. When he came to the church and told them of his trouble, Chang exhorted him to repent of his sins, turn from his idols, and believe in the Lord Jesus Christ. Yang obeyed the word and destroyed the idols in his home. A short time later, his wife and brother were both restored to good health and they all began to gather with the house church in the village. Yang and his wife became faithful workers for the Lord in evangelism and teaching others. Chu's mother was another of the first converts in the village. In no way ashamed of her son for having left his Confucian beliefs, she warmly embraced Jesus as her Lord and excelled in the ministry of hospitality. A missionary described her as

> one of the nicest and truest gentlewomen in China, with a face literally lit up with the light of heaven. It is a heavenly satisfaction to see what the grace of God can do in the hearts of those who have only known Him for a short time.[9]

Not content with merely reaching out to others in their small village, Chang and Chu had a vision to take the gospel to other parts of Shanxi

---

[9] Broomhall, 55.

Province where people had never heard of Christ. They made a five-day journey across the mountains over roads that were often just rough footpaths and beds of streams to the area of Siaoyi, one hundred miles north of Mulberry Crag. Here they met an old friend named Hu who belonged to a sect called the 'Pill of Immortality Religion.'[10] When they told Hu about the love of Jesus, and how their faith in him had brought them peace and joy that they had long been seeking, Hu and his wife both became believers and burned their idols. He then took Chang and Chu from house to house so that they could proclaim the good news of salvation in Jesus Christ to others in Siaoyi. As a result of this outreach,

> eight families destroyed their idols and turned to the Lord. Three of those who put away idols at that time afterwards became deacons of the church which sprang up in that district.[11]

The church in Siaoyi was shaken by trials of faith, and hindered by a lack of regular teaching. Only two of the believers could read. Chu committed to visiting them more regularly to strengthen their faith, and this church became one of the strongest in Southern Shanxi. A year after the initial visit to this area, fifteen families had "turned to God from idols to serve the living and true God" (1 Thessalonians 1:9). The zeal of Chang and Chu was bearing fruit in Mulberry Crag and beyond.

New doors for ministry began to open for them as reports of their work reached others who had come to China to serve as missionaries,

---

[10] Some Taoist religious practitioners believed in immortality through the ingestion of elixirs. Wing-Tsit Chan, *The Way of Lao Tzu* (Englewood Cliffs: Prentice Hall, 1963), 26, observes, "The practice of divination, astrology, faith healing, witchcraft, and the like had existed from very early days. By the fourth century BC, there was in addition, the belief in immortals who were supposed to live in islands off the China coast. The belief was so widespread and so firm that feudal lords sent missions there to seek elixir from them."

[11] The practice of new converts burning their idols was common in missionary work in China. See H. Davies, *Among Hills and Valleys in Western China* (London: Partridge, 1901), 121f, and M. Broomhall, *The Chinese Empire: A General and Missionary Survey* (London: Morgan & Scott, 1907), 215. The report of the work in Shanxi Province and Siaoyi was written by Albert Lutley of the China Inland Mission.

including some of the famous Cambridge Seven.[12] W. W. Cassels, who later became the first bishop in western China of the Church of England, and Montagu Beauchamp settled in the city of Taning to lead the work of the China Inland Mission in that area. A nother missionary, F. W. Baller, took up residence in Sichow. Chang and Chu had hoped for the day when experienced Christian missionaries would come to live among them to encourage them in Christ and work with them in the ministry. Cassels wrote about Chu after spending time with him:

> The more we see of Chu, the more we praise God for him. He is a man with a great deal more animation than most Chinese that we have had anything to do with. Rather reserved, perhaps, at first, but when he begins to speak about the spread of the gospel, his face lights up and he talks away so fast and so enthusiastically that it is quite impossible for us to follow him.[13]

Baller wrote of the spiritual refreshing he enjoyed one night after he had travelled fifty miles to visit Chu in Mulberry Crag:

> On entering the cave house of Elder Chu…I saw that which refreshed me at once. On the table lay copies of the Old and New Testaments. Both were open and had evidently been studied. On the left-hand side of the cave John 3:16 was written on a good-sized piece of paper and on each side was a suitable inscription in favour of the word of God. At the end of the cave several passages from the Gospel of John were neatly written on enlarged sheets of paper which were flanked by similar inscriptions. To feel that I was under the roof of a Christian in such an out-of-the-way place took away a great deal of my weariness.[14]

---

[12] The Cambridge Seven included: W. W. Cassels, C. T. Studd, Montagu Beauchamp, Stanley Smith, D. E. Hoste, and C. H. and A. T. Polhill-Turner. See M. Broomhall, *W. W. Cassels, First Bishop in Western China* (London: CIM, 1926), 40-44.
[13] Broomhall, *Cassels*, 68f.
[14] Broomhall, *Quest*, 87. Cave houses are still common in Shanxi. The writer knows two Christian teachers who taught in a house church seminary located in a cave in Shanxi a few years ago.

It was through fellowship in Christ that 'iron sharpened iron' and strengthened all of these believers for the work of Christ. In time, more workers, including women missionaries, would join the work to reach women and children. Chang would be set apart as pastor in the Taning area, and Chu would be appointed as a missionary pastor of the Western Hills area of South Shanxi, where he continued to preach the gospel and visit the new churches that had been planted. The light that had first burst into the village temple with two men reading the Gospel of Mark was shining into many hearts. But there were also difficult spiritual valleys through which they must pass as servants of Jesus.

From despair into peace and joy

Chu's spiritual character was outstanding, but he experienced a period of deep distress after suffering a serious illness during some winter travelling. He had chills and a high fever, and became delirious as he had night visions which terrified his soul. Scripture passages gave him both hope and fear as he applied the verses to himself. He was overwhelmed with a sense of his personal failures and sins. Chu sank into a dark night of the soul:

> Looking upon the cattle in the fields, he felt he was not equal to a beast. The beast did its duty; it did not sin, it had no soul and therefore was not in danger of hell fire. As he looked upon nature he felt he was not equal even to a tree. The tree grew steadily in size and beauty; it was long-lived and served a useful purpose, while he was a mere cumberer of the ground. For some weeks even prayer had been almost impossible. The fact that he had begrudged the losing of his degree, that he had thought his worldly honour in any sense comparable to the great grace of preaching the gospel, was a proof that he was utterly unworthy. He must have been deceived either by the devil or by himself as to the condition of his own heart. What

should he do? He dared not desist from preaching and yet he
felt so unworthy.[15]

Chu continued to struggle in his soul, and cried out to the Lord either
to take away his burden of sin, or to release him from the ministry. He
longed for the assurance of sins forgiven, and feared the fires of hell
from which he had warned sinners to flee to Christ. His dreams
continued to torment him, but the Lord intervened for his servant. He
was invited by W. W. Cassels to travel with him to Pingyangfu to
meet Hudson Taylor.

Chu had heard so much about Taylor, and greatly admired him
because of his love for China. Taylor's devotion to Christ, his
missionary vision and passion, and his life of faith and prayer had
been a source of inspiration for the Chinese servant. He longed to meet
him, but continued to wrestle with feelings of his unworthiness. He
even felt unworthy to ride a mule to meet Taylor, as riding was
regarded in China as a position of superiority, but all that he could
think was that he was a lowly and unworthy sinner. He decided that
when he met Hudson Taylor, he would ask him to be relieved of his
ministry and be permitted simply to be a humble believer and member
of the church. However, when he arrived in Pingyangfu, he received
the news that he had been nominated to be the pastor of the work of
the Western Hills. Rather than causing him to rejoice, the news only
sank him deeper into depression.

The next day, Chu and Hudson Taylor met together for
fellowship and to discuss the work of the Shanxi ministry. Chu
confessed his weaknesses and feelings of inadequacy to the esteemed
missionary leader, but Taylor reminded him of Paul's words in 2
Corinthians 12:9 that 'Christ's power is perfected in our weakness.'
Taylor's knowledge of the Bible, and personal experience, had taught
him that the men that God uses greatly are weak people who recognise
that God is with them. Chu also shared his spiritual burdens with
Pastor His, who was present at the meeting, and he and Hudson Taylor
persuaded the converted Confucian scholar to accept the call to be the
pastor of the Western Hills and Siaoyi.

---

[15] Broomhall, *Quest*, 100.

We can imagine the joy in the hearts of both Pastor Chu and Hudson Taylor, Chu in meeting the 'Venerable Pastor' and missionary, and Taylor in seeing wonderful fruit of his China Inland Mission in Southern Shanxi. Chu wanted Taylor to pray for him that his sins might be forgiven, but Taylor prayed instead that he would have grace for his ministry, be filled with the Holy Spirit, and labour in faithfulness to the Lord that he might receive the Master's reward, 'Well done.'

The Lord used this meeting with the missionaries and other Chinese leaders to lift Chu's spirit and give him a measure of peace. Later on, he would experience great joy and power in his ministry for Christ. The personal assurance that he was accepted with God through the Lord Jesus Christ, and that God was able to build him up and give him a future inheritance with his sanctified people gave him 'joy unspeakable' that remained a lovely mark of the Holy Spirit's work in his soul:

> This experience was no passing emotion, for from that time joy was his outstanding characteristic, and he became one of the most attractive and successful preachers of the gospel that God has given to his church in China. The sedate, unimpassioned manner of the Confucian scholar gave way in Chu to an enthusiasm and a demonstrativeness which was most unusual in a Chinese.[16]

Kingdom progress and great persecution

The work of Christ in Southern Shanxi continued to expand as Chang and Chu, working together with China Inland Mission teams, reached out everywhere with the gospel. Chang journeyed to the city of Kichow south of Taning, where he preached the good news of salvation and distributed Bibles and gospel literature. The Lord blessed his efforts, and a new church was established in that area. In Hotsin, another town further south, Chu and Albert Lutley teamed together and preached at the yearly fair to large crowds, and sold thousands of books and tracts. A new convert named Tan, who had

---

[16] Broomhall, *Quest*, 112f.

been addicted to opium smoking, met them to share how he had become a new creation in Jesus. Tan was the first convert in Hotsin, and later became a deacon in the church. He was a man of tremendous zeal, who led his whole family to Christ and was used to destroy completely idolatry in his village. Through his efforts, the village temple was thrown down, and a new church was built with the old materials. Hotsin became a hotbed of evangelism, and even sent the gospel to the neighbouring province of Shaanxi where the Nestorians had first brought Christianity to China in the seventh century.[17]

The church in Taning sent out teams of evangelists two by two to visit nearby towns and villages. Chang worked with two deacons, Li and Wang, to visit scattered believers and pray for the sick and demon possessed.[18]

Chang also followed the example of Pastor Hsi, and established opium refuges to help those in bondage to this drug. Evangelism was always at the forefront of every effort. The gospel was preached with spiritual power to illiterate farmers and Confucian students with equal compassion for their souls. The work in Siaoyi was wonderfully blessed through the tireless and sacrificial work of Emily Whitchurch, who assisted Pastor Chu and others in the systematic evangelism of the entire district, including every village within five miles. Whitchurch also went to market towns, where she and a Chinese woman evangelist shared the gospel with hundreds of other women. People everywhere, both believers and unbelievers, were encouraged to memorise chapters and verses of the Gospels.

From the light that had first burned in the darkness of a Buddhist temple in a tiny mountain village, the flame had spread to five cities and numerous villages in South Shanxi. The number of new believers added to the church in about twenty years was over four hundred and fifty, with many hundreds more enquirers and people with interest in learning more about the faith. The kingdom of grace had come to the

---

[17] The Nestorians were also known as 'The Church of the East.' They arrived in Xian, Shaanxi, in 635 with their form of Christianity which included some Taoist concepts. See M. Palmer, *The Jesus Sutras: Rediscovering the lost religion of Taoist Christianity* (London: Piatkus, 2001).

[18] Demon-possession was a common occurrence in China. See J. L. Nevius, *Demon Possession and Allied Themes* (Chicago: Revell, 1894).

Western Hills of Shanxi. But, as the apostles had warned the new converts of South Galatia on their first missionary journey that "through many tribulations we must enter the kingdom of God" (Acts 14:22), so the young believers of Shanxi were soon to pass through great persecution for their faith at the hands of the Boxers.

The Boxer Rebellion was a violently anti-foreign movement encouraged by Empress Dowager and other authorities in the government. In the view of many Chinese, foreign countries had done enormous harm to China and selfishly taken advantage of her people for their own evil purposes. The enormous problem of opium addiction was a plague upon the nation. One writer at the time observed:

> You may go through China and find tens of thousands of towns and villages with no trace of the Bible or of Christian influence, but you will scarcely find a hamlet where the opium-pipe does not reign. We have given China something beside the gospel, something that is doing more harm in a week than the united efforts of all our Christian missionaries in a year. Opium demoralizes the people, and makes more slaves than the slave-trade.

One missionary was preaching to a crowd in the open air about hell when someone called out, "Yes, we know about hell; since England sent us opium China has been a hell."[19]

The feeling of resentment towards foreigners was widespread, but the Empress added fuel to the fire. The Boxers were influenced by Taoist superstitions and demonically-inspired leaders. As Broomhall observes:

> The district west of the Fen River, in common with the whole of the province and many other parts of China, began to be gradually disturbed by bands of men who professed to be spirit mediums. These men quickly gathered around them large numbers of lads, whom they instructed in pseudo-religious practices and incantations, by means of which they appeared

---

[19] Davies, *Hills and Valleys*, 131.

to become possessed by a spirit, and were thereupon declared invulnerable against sword or bullet. In this state they would fall to the ground in a kind of frenzy, after which they became filled with a senseless hatred of all things foreign or Christian.[20]

The believers in Shanxi were deeply concerned, not merely for themselves, but for their beloved missionary friends with whom they had laboured side by side in the gospel. They quickly urged them to hide in caves and the hills. It was impossible however, to escape from the frenzy and fury of the murderous Boxers. The China Inland Mission suffered the loss of nearly sixty adult workers and twenty-one children who were cruelly put to death, including the godly Emily Whitchurch, who had been such a valued co-worker of Chu. More Christians were martyred in Shanxi Province than in any other part of China so that Shanxi became known as the 'Martyr Province.' Many Chinese believers were killed in this violent uprising. Chu was able to escape by keeping on the move and living in a cave by a stream. He led a man who helped him to hide to faith in Christ even as he was going through this terrible time of tribulation. Chang also escaped and hid for several weeks until his son was captured and threatened with death unless he revealed his father's hiding place to the Boxers. In the merciful providence of God, Chang's reputation as a man of love and compassion for the afflicted enabled him to be set free instead of being killed, after some who knew him well pleaded for his life.

Chang later wrote a letter to the relatives of some of the women missionaries who had been martyred for Christ, in which he said:

Our three beloved lady missionaries were of one heart and full of zeal. Our native brethren and sisters in the surrounding district were delighted to receive the gospel from them, and as a result this church gradually increased.[21]

---

[20] Broomhall, *Quest*, 146.

[21] M. Broomhall, *Last Letters and Further Records of Martyred Missionaries of the China Inland Mission* (London: Morgan and Scott, 1901), 46.

He added words of sympathy and comfort with verses from the Scriptures for the grieving parents who had willingly given their loved ones for the gospel in China. His pastoral heart bled with love for those who had died for Christ.

The awful stress and trials of those days of persecution took a toll on Chang and Chu. They died within a year of each other. The work which the Lord had begun in the Buddhist temple with two seekers did not die though. Days of revival, and also more testing, would follow but 'the gates of hell' did not overcome the church in South Shanxi. Many years later, a fitting tribute to the two pastors and an update on the work of Christ was written by one who knew the story so well:

> Between forty and fifty years have elapsed since the time when Chang the priest and Chu the scholar sat together in the precincts of the Buddhist temple at Mulberry Crag, poring over the pages of the little Gospel which had come into their possession. At that time there was no Christian church and there was no follower of the Lord Jesus Christ in the whole region west of the Fen River, but during the years covered by our story approximately fifteen hundred persons had learned to know the blessedness of sins forgiven and the helpfulness of Christian fellowship. Of these not a few sealed their testimony with their blood, or by lives gladly laid down in devoted service. Today nearly one thousand communicants still remain, and to these may be added some fifteen hundred more who are under definite Christian instruction.[22]

The light that came from the west in the gospel of Christ into the hearts of a Buddhist priest and a Confucian scholar shined into many others in the hills of Southern Shanxi, to "give the light of the knowledge of the glory of God in the face of Jesus Christ" (2 Corinthians 4:6).

---

[22] Broomhall, *Quest*, 188.

History and Faith in the Thinking
of John Gresham Machen[1]

Michael Haykin

In the early stages of what has come to be known as the Fundamentalist-Modernist controversy, John Gresham Machen (1881-1937), then Professor of New Testament Literature and Exegesis at Princeton Theological Seminary, set this struggle in the overall framework of church history. The struggle, he noted,

> is one of three great crises in the history of the Christian church. One came in the second century when Christianity was almost engulfed by paganism in the church in the form of Gnosticism. There was another in the middle ages when legalism was almost dominant in the church, similar to the modern legalism which appears in the Liberal church. Christianity today is fighting a great battle, but I, for my part, am looking for ultimate victory. God will not desert His church.[2]

This third "great battle," of which Machen here speaks, had erupted within the ranks of his ecclesial community, Northern Presbyterianism, in 1922, when Harry Emerson Fosdick (1878-1969), a liberal Baptist minister, trumpeted forth the question from the pulpit of the First Presbyterian Church in New York, 'Shall the

---

[1] It is a privilege to have this essay included in this Festschrift for Dr. Robert Penhearow, whose zest for the expansion of the impact and glory of the Gospel, especially through theological education, I have deeply appreciated.

[2] J. G. Machen, 'Christianity vs. Modern Liberalism,' in *The Moody Bible Institute Monthly* 23 (April 1923), 352. I am indebted for this reference to the late Rev. J. G. Shepherd of Burlington, Ontario. For an overview of this controversy, see G. M. Marsden and B. J. Longfield, 'Fundamentalist-Modernist Controversy,' in D. G. Reid, R. D. Linder, B. L. Shelley & H. S. Stout (eds.), *Dictionary of Christianity in America* (Downers Grove: IVP, 1990), 466-468.

Fundamentalists Win?'[3] Machen's answer to this question, as he looked at the church's victory in the previous "great crises" of her history, was an unequivocal 'yes.'[4] Here Machen's confidence in a sovereign God is abundantly evident. But his deep interest in history is also apparent. In fact, W. Stanford Reid has argued that Machen was above all a historian.[5] For proof, Reid appeals to Machen's 1915 address *History and Faith*, which Machen gave at his installation as Princeton's Associate Professor of New Testament in May of that year. Machen's opening sentences asserted:

> The student of the New Testament should be primarily an historian. The centre and core of all the Bible is history.[6]

Now, whether or not Reid is correct in describing Machen as first and foremost a historian, there is little doubt that Machen was aware that absolutely central to his disagreement with liberalism was the question of the nature of history as it related to Christianity.[7] The

---

[3] On Fosdick, see C. W. Whiteman, 'Fosdick, Harry Emerson,' in Reid *et al.*, 446f. For his role in this conflict, see B. J. Longfield, *The Presbyterian Controversy: Fundamentalists, Modernists, and Moderates* (New York, Oxford: OUP, 1991).

[4] The story of his part in this struggle has been told a number of times. See especially N. B. Stonehouse, *J. Gresham Machen: A Biographical Memoir* (Grand Rapids: Eerdmans., 1954); W. Stanford Reid, 'J. Gresham Machen,' in D. F. Wells (ed.), *The Princeton Theology* (Grand Rapids: Baker, 1989), 93-111; D. C. Davis, 'Machen and Liberalism,' in C. G. Dennison & R. C. Gamble (eds.), *Pressing Toward the Mark: Essays Commemorating Fifty Years of the Orthodox Presbyterian Church* (Philadelphia: The Committee for the Historian of the Orthodox Presbyterian Church, 1986), 247-258; Longfield; J. Piper, 'J. Gresham Machen's Response to Modernism' (Unpublished paper, Bethlehem Conference of Pastors, January 26, 1993). Machen's role in this controversy has been discussed in a superb study by D. G. Hart, *Defending the Faith: J. Gresham Machen and the Crisis of Conservative Protestantism in Modern America* (Grand Rapids: Baker, 1995).

[5] W. S. Reid, 98.

[6] J. G. Machen, 'History and Faith,' in *The Princeton Theological Review* 13 (July 1915), 337 [found also in N. B. Stonehouse (ed.), *What Is Christianity? and other addresses* (Grand Rapids: Eerdmans, 1951)].

[7] Longfield, 48. In an essay on Machen's view of history G. M. Marsden, 'Understanding Gresham Machen,' in *The Princeton Seminary Bulletin* NS 11, No.1 (February 1990), 48, has written that the "problem of history has arguably been *the* twentieth-century problem." For an adaptation of this essay, see G. M. Marsden,

liberals, according to Machen, were "impatient of history." From their vantage-point, he went on to observe,

> history...is a dead thing.... The true essence of the Bible is to be found in eternal ideas; history is merely the form in which those ideas are expressed. It makes no difference whether the history is real or fictitious; in either case, the ideas are the same. It makes no difference whether Abraham was an historical personage or a myth; in either case his life is an inspiring example of faith.... It makes no difference whether Jesus really lived and died and rose again as He is declared to have done in the Gospels; in any case the Gospel picture, be it ideal or be it history, is an encouragement to filial piety.

Machen was confident, though, that to give up history is to give up the gospel. For, Machen pointed out, the term 'gospel' means 'good news,' that is,

> tidings, information about something that has happened. In other words, it means history. A gospel independent of history is simply a contradiction in terms.[8]

Before we examine Machen's approach to the relationship of history and the Christian gospel in more detail, it will be helpful to outline his early career before becoming a defender of the faith.

Machen's early years

Machen was born in 1881 in Baltimore, Maryland, then at the crossroads of Northern and Southern life.[9] His father, Arthur Machen (1826-1915), a lawyer, was a Southerner in his sympathies, even though he grew up in Washington, D.C. In the middle of the Civil War, for instance, he began to attend regularly Franklin Street

---

Understanding Fundamentalism and Evangelicalism (Grand Rapids: Eerdmans, 1991), 182-201.

[8] Machen, 'History and Faith,' 337f.

[9] For information on Machen's parents and early years, see Stonehouse, *Machen*, 17-57; Marsden, 'Understanding Gresham Machen,' 55f; Longfield, 28-41.

Presbyterian Church in Baltimore, a church which joined the Southern Presbyterian Church just after the war and whose pastor, J. J. Bullock, was a firm supporter of the South.

His mother, Mary Gresham Machen (1849-1931) was, in the words of George Marsden, "indelibly a daughter of the lost cause" of the Confederacy.[10] During the war she had lived in Macon, Georgia, while her brother fought under the Confederate flag. Later, after her marriage to Arthur Machen, she would join the Baltimore chapter of the United Daughters of the Confederacy. Despite the defeat of the South and the many hardships that this brought, she still managed to grow up a privileged member of ante-bellum Southern aristocracy.

Mary passed on to young Gresham the values of this aristocratic elite—in politics, for instance, he would be a radical libertarian and a firm advocate of racial segregation[11]—as well as her robust Calvinist spirituality. As a young boy he was taught the Westminster Shorter Catechism, which, by his teen years gave him a good command of the riches of Scripture and Reformed doctrine.[12]

In 1898 Machen went to Johns Hopkins University in Baltimore, graduating three years later with a B.A. in classics. At the urging of his pastor, Harris E. Kirk, he went on to Princeton Seminary in 1902, though at the time he had no intention of entering vocational ministry. Princeton was renowned as "a Gibraltar of orthodoxy," her faculty justly proud of the school's "unswerving fidelity to the theology of the Reformation."[13] Since the founding of the seminary in 1812, a noteworthy line of theologians—among them Archibald Alexander (1772-1851), Charles Hodge (1797-1878), Archibald Alexander Hodge (1823-86), and Benjamin B. Warfield (1851-1921)—had

> upheld Reformed confessionalism…, defended high views of biblical inspiration and authority…, organized their thinking with the aid of the Scottish philosophy of common sense,

---

[10] Marsden, 'Understanding Gresham Machen,' 55.
[11] Marsden, 'Understanding Gresham Machen,' 56f.
[12] Longfield, 32.
[13] Stonehouse, *Machen*, 61f. On Princeton's resistance to change, see D. G. Hart, 'The Princeton Mind in the Modern World and the Common Sense of J. Gresham Machen,' in *The Westminster Theological Journal* 46 (1984), 3f.

and...had a surprisingly large place for the role of the Holy Spirit in religious experience.[14]

Three years of study at the seminary gave Machen skill as a biblical exegete, particularly with regard to the New Testament, but no clear direction as to his future. In his final year of study, he won a fellowship in New Testament which encouraged him to think of spending a year abroad honing his abilities as a scholar. He decided to spend the academic year of 1905-06 in Germany studying with such well-known New Testament scholars as Adolph Jülicher (1857-1938), Johannes Weiss (1863-1914), Wilhelm Bousset (1865-1920), and Johann Wilhelm Herrmann (1846-1922). On a previous visit to Germany in the summer of 1904 he had concluded that the two institutions which Germany most needed were the Sabbath and American football![15] This time, though, he would learn that there was something even more basic that was wanting: evangelical scholarship.

Sitting at the feet of these German scholars Machen was exposed to the full force of liberalism. Although Machen had had religious doubts before he ever set foot in Europe, his experience in Germany shook his faith to the core. Fifteen years earlier another American visitor to the halls of German academia, a Michigan student by the name of D. C. Davidson, compared the experience of theological study in Germany to a furnace in which his Christian convictions were tried to the very depths. "I have encountered many a fiery temptation," Davidson later wrote, "but I have never had a temptation cross my pathway so subtle and dangerous as that of German destructive criticism."[16] Machen's experience was similar in many respects, but whereas Davidson was rescued by the preaching of C. H. Spurgeon (1834-92) only a few months after the trial of his faith, it would be a good while before Machen knew his feet to be planted again on the solid rock of orthodoxy.

---

[14] M. A. Noll, 'The Spirit of Old Princeton and the Spirit of the OPC,' in Dennison & Gamble (eds.), 238. For a good history of Princeton Theological Seminary, see D. B. Calhoun, *Princeton Seminary* (Edinburgh: Banner of Truth, 1994, 1996), 2 vols.
[15] Stonehouse, *Machen*, 84.
[16] D. C. Davidson, 'In the Furnace of Unbelieving Theology,' in *The Banner of Truth* 293 (February 1988), 16-19.

Of all the scholars whom Machen heard lecture during this time in Germany none impressed him so much as Wilhelm Herrmann. Hardly known today, Herrmann was at that time probably the leading liberal theologian in Europe. Among his students were a number who would be well-known figures on the scene of twentieth-century theology, including Rudolf Bultmann (1884-1976) and Karl Barth (1886-1968). As a lecturer Herrmann was captivating. Machen noted in a letter to his father that he "speaks right to the heart," refusing "to allow the student to look at religion from a distance as a thing to be *studied* merely." In another letter to his father Machen observed that in "New England those who do not believe in the bodily resurrection of Jesus are, generally speaking, religiously dead," but this was not the case with Herrmann. Though he denied the bodily resurrection he "believes that Jesus is the one thing in all the world that inspires *absolute* confidence, and an *absolute* joyful subjection." Machen was certainly not ignorant of definite flaws in Herrmann's theology, yet he confessed to his father that his chief feeling with respect to him was "one of the deepest reverence."[17]

Herrmann was convinced that historico-critical research into the life of Christ can never provide an unassailable footing for Christian faith. "No historical judgment...ever attains anything more than probability." It is, he averred, "a fatal error to attempt to establish the basis of faith by means of historical [*historisch*] investigation."[18] The assurance that faith needs can only come directly from the person of Christ himself. As a person reads the New Testament, the love and moral seriousness that characterised the inner life of Christ shines through its pages, impacting the reader, and transforming his or her life. True faith is rooted in this encounter with the inner life of Christ as it is portrayed in the New Testament. This encounter "sets us free from the mere record [of the Scriptures], because it presses in upon us

---

[17] Stonehouse, *Machen*, 106f.
[18] W. Herrmann, *Communion of the Christian With God* [English translation by J. S. Staynton] (New York: Putnam's, 1906), 72, 76. The following account of Herrmann's theology and view of history is indebted to D. L. Deegan, 'Wilhelm Herrmann: A Reassessment,' in *Scottish Journal of Theology* 19 (1966), 188-203; G. W. Bromiley, *Historical Theology: An Introduction* (Grand Rapids: Eerdmans, 1978), 397-404; C. Welch, *Protestant Thought in the Nineteenth Century, Vol. 2: 1870-1914* (New Haven: Yale UP, 1985), 44-54, 152-157; and Longfield, 41f.

as a power that is present through its work upon us."[19] It is thus that the inner life of Christ constitutes for Herrmann the "saving fact" of the New Testament. Since this is the case, the truth or falsity of the historical details of Christ's external life is of little significance.

Herrmann admits that the events of Christ's life and ministry, by means of which the faith of the early disciples was saved from shipwreck, have immeasurable importance for the church in every era. If they had not taken place, then there would be no written record about Christ. But later readers have no direct access to these events, since the accounts in the gospels are shrouded in myth. Yet such historical errors and myths in no way impede the New Testament's witness to the personal character of Jesus. For Herrmann, the "power of Jesus' inner life breaks through all the veils of tradition and provides the believer with a firmer ground of faith than the determination to accept the resurrection of Jesus by submission to the apostolic witness." [20] Herrmann's thought in this regard is well expressed by the following words of the liberal church historian Adolf von Harnack (1851-1930), which were intended for popular consumption:

> We must not try to evade the gospel by entrenching ourselves behind the miraculous stories related by the evangelists. In spite of these stories, nay, in part even in them, we are presented with a reality which has claims upon our participation. Study it, and do not let yourselves be deterred because this or that miraculous story strikes you as strange or leaves you cold.... The question of miracles is of relative indifference in comparison with everything else which is to be found in the Gospels.[21]

Machen's traumatic, first-hand encounter with German liberalism came to a close in the summer of 1907 when he accepted a one-year

---

[19] Herrmann, 74.
[20] Deegan, 200.
[21] A. von Harnack, *What is Christianity?* 2nd ed. [English translation by T. B. Saunders] (New York: Putnam's; London: Williams & Norgate, 1901), 32. On Machen's contact with von Harnack, see Hart, *Defending the Faith*, 41f.

appointment at Princeton as an instructor in New Testament. The invitation to return to Princeton may well have been a concerted effort on the part of the faculty to rescue Machen from the clutches of liberalism.[22] Machen seriously contemplated returning to Germany at the conclusion of that academic year, but happily his career became steadily entwined with the halls of Princeton. He stayed on, teaching New Testament, seeking to resolve the doubts that plagued him, slowly yielding to scriptural truth and the winsome influence of his colleagues, of whom the chief was Benjamin Warfield. Thus, by the time that he was formally installed as Assistant Professor of New Testament in 1915 and gave his inaugural address on *History and Faith*, he had come to adhere firmly to the Princeton tradition.

History and Faith (1915)

This inaugural address makes it abundantly clear that the clouds had lifted and Machen had resolved the doubts that had bedevilled him ever since his time in Germany. *History and Faith* is thus a public reply to Herrmann and the liberal perspective on history and the reliability of Scripture.[23]

Machen begins with the basic assertion, already noted, that a "gospel independent of history is simply a contradiction in terms."[24] Biblical faith and history are inextricably yoked together. For instance, in the scriptural account of the life, ministry, death, and resurrection of Christ various historical assertions are made. He is said to be born of a virgin; to have lived "a life of perfect purity, of awful righteousness, and of gracious, sovereign power;" to have died a death that is never viewed as a "mere holy martyrdom"—a common assertion in early twentieth-century liberal circles—but seen as "a sacrifice for the sins of the world;" to have been resurrected bodily, which was "a mighty act of God" and a fact of history, not "a vision, an hallucination," as some liberals asserted; to being still alive and ever-ready to help those who turn to him; to be "in mysterious union with the eternal God." This composite picture drawn from the Pauline

---

[22] Marsden, 'Understanding Gresham Machen,' 50.
[23] Stonehouse, *Machen*, 206; Longfield, 48.
[24] Machen, 'History and Faith,' 338.

corpus and the four Gospels is, Machen asserts, the portrayal of nothing less than "a supernatural person."[25]

Liberal scholars, however, seeking to retool Christianity to fit the naturalistic viewpoint of the surrounding culture, wanted nothing to do with a supernatural Jesus. They felt that ancient ideas of God and his supernatural intervention in the world had little to say to men and women living in modern, twentieth-century urban cultures. They thus attempted to separate the natural from the supernatural in the New Testament accounts about Christ, and so "disentangle the human Jesus" from the divinity thrust upon him by the early church. But, as Machen points out, the supernatural Jesus is the only Jesus that we know. The scriptural record simply does not give us the liberty of separating the divine and the human in the life of Christ. The "divine and human are too closely interwoven; reject the divine," and ultimately, Machen asserted, "you must reject the human too."[26]

Then look, Machen suggested, at the beginning of the Christian movement. What is to account for it? During his life and earthly ministry Christ had won "comparatively few" disciples. Left to their own resources these disciples can hardly be credited with beginning what we know as Christianity. They were "far inferior" to Christ "in spiritual discernment and in courage" and had not the "slightest trace of originality." They had been "abjectly dependent upon the Master" during his earthly life, and had, moreover, never "succeeded in understanding him." And "what little understanding, what little courage" they did have was dissolved after his death. "How could such men," Machen asked, "institute the mightiest religious movement in the history of the world?"[27] Simply looking at the historical record, Machen concluded, it is obvious that something extraordinary must have happened between the death of Christ and the bold preaching of the first disciples. Well, Scripture explains the transformation by means of the resurrection of Christ. History is relentlessly plain. The foundation of the church is either inexplicable, or else it is to be explained by the resurrection of Jesus Christ from the dead. But if the resurrection be accepted, then the lofty claims of

---

[25] Machen, 'History and Faith,' 339-342, 347.
[26] Machen, 'History and Faith,' 342f, 347f.
[27] Machen, 'History and Faith,' 345f.

Jesus are substantiated: Jesus then was no mere man, but God and man, God come in the flesh.

As we have seen with the theology of Wilhelm Herrmann, the liberal remoulding of Christianity emphasised Christian experience at the expense of historical truth. Although Machen had a tendency to respond to this distortion of biblical Christianity by focusing on the historical and logical truth of the Christian faith, he was not oblivious to the necessity of experience. Thus, as he drew his address to a close, he stated:

> The resurrection of Jesus is a fact of history; it is good news; it is an event that has put a new face upon life. But how can the acceptance of an historical fact satisfy the longing of our souls? Must we stake our salvation upon the intricacies of historical research? Is the trained historian the modern priest without whose gracious intervention no one can see God? Surely some more immediate certitude is required.
>
> The objection would be valid if history stood alone. But history does not stand alone; it is confirmed by experience.
>
> An historical conviction of the resurrection of Jesus is not the end of faith but only the beginning; if faith stops there, it will probably never stand the fires of criticism. We are told that Jesus rose from the dead; the message is supported by a singular weight of evidence. But it is not just a message remote from us; it concerns not merely the past. If Jesus rose from the dead, as he is declared to have done in the Gospels, then he is still alive, and if he is still alive, then he may still be found. He is present with us today to help us if we will but turn to him.... Christian experience cannot do without history, but it adds to history that directness, that immediateness, that intimacy of conviction which delivers us from fear.[28]

The historicity of the resurrection is substantiated as men and women are led to put their trust in the message that Christ is risen from the dead, and find that that trust is not misplaced. Machen was thus very conscious of the fact that there is a subjective side to the Christian life.

---

[28] Machen, 'History and Faith,' 349f.

As he stated in a 1927 address to the General Assembly of the Free Church of Scotland:

> We cannot tell all that it [i.e., Christianity] is by...merely historical method...we cannot tell all that it is by looking at it merely from the outside. In order that we should tell all that it is, we must ourselves be Christians; we must know Christianity in our own inner lives.[29]

Moreover, it should be noted that Machen did not believe that demonstration of the historicity of the resurrection and other facts about Christ necessarily issued in faith. Contrary to the opinion of some contemporary critics, notably William Owen Carver (1868-1954), a professing evangelical who, for most of his career, taught missions at Southern Baptist Theological Seminary, Louisville, Kentucky,[30] Machen was not forgetful that the work of the Spirit is absolutely fundamental for faith. In a later work, *What Is Faith?* (1925), Machen thus asserted that it is only where the Spirit has removed "the blinding effects of sin" that a person will come to "believe in the resurrection of Christ and thus accept the claims of Christianity."[31] And in his *Christianity and Liberalism* (1923), to which we now turn, he affirmed:

> The more one observes the condition of the Church, the more one feels obliged to confess that the conviction of sin is a great mystery, which can be produced only by the Spirit of God. Proclamation of the law, in word and in deed, can prepare for the experience, but the experience itself comes from God. When a man has that experience, when a man comes under conviction of sin, his whole attitude toward life is transformed; he wonders at his former blindness, and the message of the gospel, which formerly seemed to be an idle tale, becomes now

---

[29] J. G. Machen, 'What Is Christianity?' in N. B. Stonehouse (ed.) *What Is Christianity?*, 18. See also Hart, 'Princeton Mind,' 21.

[30] W. R. Hutchison, *The Modernist Impulse in American Protestantism* [1976] (Oxford: OUP, 1982 reprint), 267f; Hart, 'Princeton Mind,' 20f.

[31] J. G. Machen, *What Is Faith?* [1925] (Grand Rapids: Eerdmans, 1962 reprint), 135, 133.

instinct with light. But it is God alone who can produce the change.

Machen thus pleaded with his readers: "let us not try to do without the Spirit of God."[32]

Christianity and Liberalism (1923)

In 1923, the year following Fosdick's call for liberals to take up arms against fundamentalism, Machen published his definitive attack on the liberal system, *Christianity and Liberalism*. By this point in time, Machen was conscious that liberalism had moved far beyond the halls of academia, where he had first encountered its destructive force. Its withering effects could now be seen in the everyday life of the church, its "attack upon the fundamentals of the Christian faith...carried on vigorously by Sunday-School 'lesson-helps,' by the pulpit, and by the religious press."[33] *Christianity and Liberalism* thus sought to engage liberalism at a popular level.

Now, it is noteworthy, as John Piper has pointed out, that Machen did not entitle his book *Fundamentalism and Liberalism*.[34] In his mind

---

[32] J. G. Machen, *Christianity and Liberalism* [1923] (Grand Rapids: Eerdmans, 1956 reprint), 67.

[33] Machen, *Christianity and Liberalism*, 17.

[34] J. Piper, 'Machen's Response,' 6. Machen, it should be noted, rejected the term 'fundamentalist' as an adequate description of his theological position. As he once remarked: "The term fundamentalism is distasteful to the present writer and to many persons who hold views similar to his. It seems to suggest that we are adherents of some strange new sect, whereas in point of fact we are conscious of maintaining the historic Christian faith and of moving in the great central current of Christian life" (cited Stonehouse, *Machen*, 337). On another occasion he explained his perspective on this term thus: "Thoroughly consistent Christianity, to my mind, is found only in the Reformed or Calvinistic Faith; and consistent Christianity, I think, is the Christianity easiest to defend. Hence I never call myself a 'Fundamentalist.' There is, indeed, no inherent objection to the term; and if the disjunction is between 'Fundamentalism' and 'Modernism,' then I am willing to call myself a Fundamentalist of the most pronounced type. But after all, what I prefer to call myself is not a 'Fundamentalist' but a 'Calvinist'—that is, an adherent of the Reformed Faith. As such I regard myself as standing in the great central current of the Church's life—the current which flows down from the word of God through Augustine and Calvin, and which has found noteworthy expression in America in the great tradition

liberalism and fundamentalism were not "two varieties of the same religion." Rather, they were "two distinct religions proceeding from altogether separate roots."[35] Possibly the most powerful of the seven chapters in the book is that entitled *Doctrine*. In it, Machen tackles the liberal assertion that experience is the bedrock of the Christian faith and that in its essence "Christianity is a life," not a system of doctrinal truth.[36]

As Machen points out first of all, when one reads the letters of the Apostle Paul it is obvious that he was not "indifferent to doctrine; on the contrary, doctrine was the very basis of his life." His was no "undogmatic religion." He was deeply concerned about the truth of his message and the need to get it exactly right. On the manner of its presentation, though, he could show "magnificent tolerance." For example, in Philippians he was tolerant of those who with bad motives preached to make his imprisonment worse. Why? Because they were declaring what was objectively true about Christ (Philippians 1:15-18).[37]

"But the tolerance of Paul," Machen was quick to point out, "was not indiscriminate." In Galatia, he went so far as to pronounce a curse on his opponents because they were getting the message objectively wrong. They were telling Gentiles that "the believer's own effort to keep the Law" was necessary to complete the saving work that God had begun in their lives by faith and by the Spirit. To twentieth-century liberals Paul's action may appear to be fighting over utter trivialities since both he and the Judaizers would have agreed on dozens of precious things, including the necessity of faith for salvation. But it was hardly trivial.

---

represented by Charles Hodge, and Benjamin Breckinridge Warfield and the other representatives of the 'Princeton School'" (cited Stonehouse, *Machen*, 428). Darryl Hart, *Defending the Faith*, x, rightly sees Machen as a "Presbyterian traditionalist who championed Calvinistic creeds and Reformed patterns of church government against the innovations of fundamentalists and modernists alike."
[35] Cited A. D. MacLeod, *Stanford Reid: An Evangelical Calvinist in the Academy* (Montreal & Kingston: MQUP, 2004), 331, n.8. This statement was part of an advertising blurb for *Christianity and Liberalism*.
[36] Machen, *Christianity and Liberalism*, 18-20.
[37] Machen, *Christianity and Liberalism*, 21f, 25.

The difference which divided him from the Judaizers was no mere theological subtlety, but concerned the very heart and core of the religion of Christ. "Just as I am without one plea, But that thy blood was shed for me"—that was what Paul was contending for in Galatia; that hymn would never have been written if the Judaizers had won. And without the thing which that hymn expresses there is no Christianity at all.[38]

Again, if one looks at the first missionaries of the apostolic church, one does not find them exhorting their hearers with such words as the following: "Jesus of Nazareth lived a wonderful life of filial piety, and we call upon you our hearers to yield yourselves, as we have done, to the spell of that life." The great message with which these early disciples were armed was a historical message: Christ died for our sins and he is risen. Their witnessing was not about what "Jesus was doing within the inner recesses of the individual life," but to what he had done once for all in his death and resurrection. Without history and the doctrinal explanation of that history "joined in an absolutely indissoluble union," Machen forthrightly declared, "there is no Christianity."[39] As he wrote two years later:

We believers in historic Christianity maintain the objectivity of truth.... Theology, we hold, is not an attempt to express in merely symbolic terms an inner experience which must be expressed in different terms in subsequent generations; but it is a setting forth of those facts upon which experience is based.[40]

Some liberals, though, were quite prepared to admit that Paul and the apostolic church misunderstood the true nature of Christianity. Thus, they appealed to Jesus as one who taught a "simple, non-doctrinal religion." Again, Machen shows how such an appeal flies in the face of the historical facts about Christ's life and ministry. The teaching of Christ was rooted in doctrine since "it depended upon a stupendous

---

[38] Machen, *Christianity and Liberalism*, 24f.
[39] Machen, *Christianity and Liberalism*, 27, 52f.
[40] Machen, *What Is Faith?*, 32.

presentation of Jesus' own Person:" his messianic consciousness, his placing "his own words on an equality with what he certainly regarded as the divine words of Scripture," his claiming of "the right to legislate for the kingdom of God."[41]

The liberal desire, then, for "a non-doctrinal religion" is in reality a giving up not only of Paul and the apostolic church, but also of Jesus himself. "The liberal preacher is really rejecting the whole basis of Christianity, which is a religion founded…on facts."[42] It is for this reason that Machen can affirm that naturalistic liberalism is not simply a different kind of Christianity. It is not Christianity at all.[43]

Conclusion

In conclusion, Machen's defence of Christianity as a historically verifiable, doctrinally-rooted faith reminds us of a number of vital truths that are inextricably interwoven: God has revealed himself in history—primarily in the incarnation, death, and resurrection of Christ; men and women have access to this revelation in the Scriptures, and the Christian faith is rooted in these specific historical events. As Paul said in 1 Corinthians 15:17, "if Christ has not been raised, your faith is futile." Machen well knew that Christianity is more than history—as he told the Scottish Free Church Assembly in 1927, "we must know Christianity in our inner lives"—but if the historical affirmations of the Bible are not true, if they are errant accounts clothing inerrant truth, or if, as is commonly affirmed by radical deconstructionists today, we have no access to these historical events, then Christianity is sunk.[44]

It is vital to recognise that this issue is not merely of antiquarian interest. Some contemporary evangelicals seem bent on reproducing the errors of those whom Machen so ably opposed. John Goldingay, principal of St. John's Theological College in Nottingham, England, and a professing evangelical, has critiqued the high doctrine of Scripture evidenced in the Princeton tradition. Warfield, in particular,

---

[41] Machen, *Christianity and Liberalism*, 33-36.
[42] Machen, *Christianity and Liberalism*, 45, 47.
[43] Machen, *Christianity and Liberalism*, 52.
[44] Hart, 'Princeton Mind,' 23-25; Marsden, 'Understanding Gresham Machen,' 58.

is taken to task for affirming the factual and historical inerrancy of Scripture.[45] Goldingay believes that while the Bible is errant in some of its historical and scientific details, on the whole it is quite reliable. The assertion that the Bible is inerrant is only accurate when it comes to matters dealing with salvation.[46] To be sure, Goldingay's position is not that of Herrmann or Harnack, who regarded much of the historical narrative of Scripture as riddled with myth and error. But the difference appears to be simply one of degree, and not of kind.[47]

As Machen reflected on the way that the liberalism of his day was obscuring the gospel, he longed for a "new Reformation," a time when the gospel would "come forth again to bring light and liberty to mankind;" a time when "those upon whom God has laid His hand, to whom the gospel has become a burning fire within them...speak the word that God has given them and trust for the results to Him alone." When such a time came it would "not be the work of men but the work of the Spirit of God." Nevertheless, he was convinced that the coming of this time "will be prepared for...not by the concealment of issues, but by clear presentation of them; not by peace in the Church between Christian and anti-Christian forces, but by earnest discussion; not by darkness, but by the light."[48]

May we, by God's grace, share both this longing and this conviction.

---

[45] J. E. Goldingay, *Models for Scripture* (Grand Rapids: Eerdmans; Carlisle: Paternoster, 1994).

[46] Goldingay, 212f, 272.

[47] For two significant critiques of Goldingay's book, see P. Copan, '*John Goldingay. Models for Scripture,*' in *Trinity Journal*, NS 16, No. 2 (Fall, 1995), 255-259, and D. Carson, 'Slippery slope for Scripture,' in *Evangelicals Now* 11, No. 4 (April 1996), 20f.

[48] Machen, *What Is Faith?*, 103f.

Charles Tupper

Perry Edwards

Rev. Charles Tupper, a second-generation Regular Baptist, was arguably the most influential Maritime Christian leader of the nineteenth century, and yet he is virtually unknown in the Christian world. Many people know of Tupper's son, Sir Charles Tupper, who was an early prime minister of Canada and a father of Confederation, but few know his father, who perhaps had a greater influence on Canada, particularly the Maritime Provinces, than his son did. As a theologian and a pastor, he devoted considerable time developing resources to help people understand and apply the Bible. He provided intellectual, theological, and emotional stability for the growing Regular Baptist denomination in the Maritime provinces, ensuring the denomination's future growth.

His childhood

Charles Tupper was born in Cornwallis, Nova Scotia, on August 6th, 1794, just a few years before the 'Great Reformation' (1806-08), which was part of a broader movement known as the 'Second Great Awakening' (1790-1810). The 'Great Reformation' infused new life into many churches in Nova Scotia, leading to hundreds of conversions to Christ. Although Tupper's parents were Presbyterians, his mother was baptised and joined the Regular Baptist church when Charles was only five years old. Nine years later, near the end of the 'Great Reformation,' Charles' father was also baptised and joined the Regular Baptists.

Charles' parents were a godly couple who faithfully taught their children the Scriptures. Tupper later acknowledged this when he wrote:

> It becomes me gratefully to acknowledge the divine goodness toward me, that my parents were truly pious people. Prayer was

constantly offered, both morning and evening, in my father's house accompanied with the reading of the Holy Scriptures.[1]

Although Tupper's family became Baptists, his religious instruction in the home was still influenced by the family's Presbyterian roots. Tupper was required to learn the Westminster Assembly's Shorter Catechism when he was growing up.[2] The teaching of the Westminster Catechism was not contrary to the teaching of the Baptist Church which they joined, where the pastor, Edward Manny, was a Calvinist preacher. By this means, Tupper was immersed in Calvinistic theology from childhood, and he was thoroughly convinced of Calvinism for his entire life. His early childhood training in the Westminster Confession and his attendance at a Calvinistic Baptist Church contributed to his eventual acceptance of the Calvinist Baptist faith.

Not only did he remain faithful to his theological roots, but as he matured into manhood he grew in his appreciation for the catechetical training he received as a child. When he was sixty-nine years old he said that learning the Westminster Shorter Catechism had been "serviceable."[3] He didn't say how it was serviceable, but the mention of his early instruction at such an old age demonstrated that its influence ran deep in his life. His appreciation for his early catechetical instruction is also seen in the fact that he encouraged the use of a catechism within Baptist circles to help train young people in the basic tenets of the Christian faith.[4]

Tupper's parents not only immersed him in Reformed theology but also taught him to shun what they considered to be worldly and destructive activities. These included horse racing, card playing, stage plays, alcohol, and the reading of novels. Tupper learned this lesson well and managed to avoid the common pitfalls of the youth in his

---

[1] *The Christian Messenger*, March 18th, 1863, 85.
[2] I. E. Bill, *Fifty Years with the Baptist Ministers and Churches of the Maritime Provinces of Canada* (St. John: Barnes, 1880), 682.
[3] *Christian Messenger*, April 22nd, 1863, 125.
[4] *Christian Messenger*, February 17th, 1869, 53.

day. He called horse racing and card playing "nefarious and vicious practices."[5] Concerning stage plays he wrote,

> all who wish well to their country and the rising generation ought, in my opinion, to set their faces against everything of this nature, as well as against all theatrical amusements.

He believed that most novels were of little value. He continued,

> the infatuated readers of novels can not ordinarily bring themselves down to the perusal of true history, geography, or any scientific, philosophic, or religious treatise, which might inform the mind, improve the morals, or benefit the soul.[6]

Whether or not Tupper was right in his assessment of these 'worldly activities,' his convictions did enable him from an early age to focus his reading and study on those things that would help him to understand the Bible more clearly. His *Autobiographical Sketch* reveals that he wasted little time on matters he considered frivolous, focusing instead on the study of language, the Bible, and historical works.

His education

Educational opportunities were limited in nineteenth-century Nova Scotia. Many children did not learn to read or write, and only had a few short years of formal schooling, and Tupper was no exception. Certainly, part of the problem was the poor quality of teachers available in the early nineteenth century.[7] It was not until the mid-eighteenth century that any teachers can be found working in any communities of Nova Scotia. In fact, by 1759 only Halifax and Lunenburg were seeking out teachers to educate their children.[8]

---

[5] *Christian Messenger*, May 13th, 1863, 149.
[6] *Christian Messenger*, June 24th, 1863, 177.
[7] *Christian Messenger*, March 18th, 1863, 85.
[8] J. E. Crockett, *Origin and Establishment of Free Schools in Nova Scotia* (M.A. thesis, Dalhousie University, 1940), 3.

But, with the arrival of the New England Planters in the 1760's, there was an increased demand for better education. The New Englanders were accustomed to a higher level of education than was available in Nova Scotia, and so they sought to make changes. Often these communities would seek out their own teachers and pay them as best they could, but with each family being personally responsible to pay for their children's education, many were not sent to school. The result was a large number of illiterate children who grew up with little or no formal education. It was not until 1780 that the government of Nova Scotia put forward legislation for the establishment of a public school.[9]

The first public school supported by government funds was established in the city of Halifax in 1811, and marks the beginning of government-funded schools. Even before the establishment of a public school, many private schools were flourishing in the city at this time.[10] Although educational opportunities were growing in the larger city centres, many rural communities were unable to benefit from them. The following description of a Nova Scotia school teacher in the second half of the eighteenth century gives an idea of the quality of education in rural communities:

> With the coming of English settlers to Nova Scotia, the itinerant school master appeared on the scene. Often a broken down soldier or a man otherwise incapacitated from the hard work of frontier life, the itinerant school master set up his school in the house of a settler who had a room to spare and who was willing to give it.... Ill-educated and knowing no more of the technique of teaching than to require memorization of material, the itinerant schoolmaster nevertheless filled an important need. In many parts of the province, he was the only source of education.[11]

---

[9] Crockett, 4-7.
[10] Crockett, 9.
[11] D. Hilchey & B. Robinson, *Nova Scotia: Three Hundred Years in Education* (A centennial Project of the Nova Scotia Teachers Union, 1981), 3.

This was the educational environment in which Tupper grew up and learned to read and write.

Although Charles Tupper was a brilliant man, his high level of intelligence had yet to blossom and was not recognised in his early educational experience. He wrote,

> I remember to have heard it remarked that 'I learned quickly, but forgot as quickly.' This was true. What had been learned in the summer season, was nearly all forgotten in the course of the winter following.

He went on to attribute his lack of progress to two factors. First, he did not have the books as a child to stimulate his interest in education, and second, like many children, he did not recognise the inherent value of education.[12]

He only went to school for twelve weeks after the age of ten,[13] but this did not prevent him from accumulating an extraordinary amount of secular and biblical knowledge throughout his life. In 1811, when Tupper reached seventeen years of age, his mind was opened up more fully to the world of knowledge and he developed an insatiable desire to learn. He began by studying the English grammar book of his youth. Six months after this intellectual awakening he wanted to learn Latin, so he asked Rev. William Forsyth, a local Presbyterian Minister, to teach him, and he graciously agreed. Tupper wasted no time, and used every spare minute to feed his new hunger for knowledge.[14] He was gifted by God with intelligence bordering on genius, and proficiency in languages beyond most men of his age, or any age. On December 22nd, 1859, at the age of sixty-five, he wrote in his diary,

> finished the perusal of Luther's German version of the Bible. I have now perused the whole of the sacred volume in eight languages; these are, Hebrew, Syriac, Greek, Latin, Italian,

---

[12] *Christian Messenger*, March 18th, 1863, 85.
[13] *Christian Messenger*, April, 29th, 1863, 133.
[14] *Christian Messenger*, August 19th, 1863, 245.

French, German, and English, besides the New Testament in Spanish and Portuguese.[15]

It is an amazing fact that he learned all of these languages with little assistance from others. One source indicates that he mastered thirteen languages.[16] He attributed his success in language study to God's blessing, his own efforts, and the occasional help from friends.[17]

His conversion

During the latter part of the eighteenth century and the beginning of the nineteenth century, the new birth experience was the central focus of what has been called, 'Canadian radical evangelicalism.'[18] The man who was most influential in making the new birth experience central in the Maritime Provinces was Henry Alline. Alline was born on June 14th, 1748, at New Port, Rhode Island, and his parents emigrated to Nova Scotia in 1760. At twenty-seven years of age, following a great spiritual struggle, Alline trusted in Christ on March 26th, 1775. So dramatic was his conversion experience that Alline made it the standard by which all conversions should be judged. He "expected his followers and all true Christians to share his unique version of the New Birth, which he regarded as the only satisfactory means of regeneration."[19] Those who were converted under his ministry longed to know the same intense experience that he enjoyed.[20]

Immediately after his conversion, Alline began to tell other people about the change in his life. This was the beginning of a preaching ministry that would last only a few short years, but had a profound impact on the religious life of Nova Scotia and New

---

[15] *Christian Messenger*, December 23rd, 1868, 421.
[16] T. D. Denham, D. Hunt & T. H. Belyea, *The History of Germain Street Baptist Church, St. John N.B., for its First One Hundred Years, 1810-1910* (St. John: Saint John Globe, 1920).
[17] Bill, 683.
[18] G. A Rawlyk, *The Canada Fire: Radical Evangelicalism in British America, 1775-1812* (Montreal & Kingston: MQUP, 1994), xv.
[19] Rawlyk, 12.
[20] Rawlyk, 17.

Brunswick. Although he was not a Baptist, Alline contributed greatly to the defection from old allegiances and to the adoption of Baptist principles. His influence was so vast that one contemporary wrote that Alline "was to the Baptists of these Provinces what John the Baptist was in his day to the coming kingdom of Christ." [21] Rawlyk commented, "his contemporaries regarded him as Nova Scotia's George Whitefield," [22] and "the charismatic Alline helped trigger Nova Scotia's so-called First Great Awakening."[23] Bell wrote,

> Henry Alline stands unrivaled as the greatest 'Canadian' of the eighteenth century, the greatest Maritimer of any age and the most significant religious figure this country has yet produced.[24]

Whether one views him as the "greatest Maritimer of any age" or not, it cannot be denied that his influence was widely felt throughout the Maritime Provinces, and shaped the region's religious culture.

Those converted under Alline's ministry included Congregationalists, Methodists, and Presbyterians, as well as many from smaller religious sects. This diversity makes it difficult to determine the basic theological beliefs of the movement, which has been rightly described as a group of "unclassifiable enthusiasts."[25] Their origin can be traced back to what is known as the 'First Great Awakening' in America, which took place under the ministries of Jonathan Edwards, George Whitefield, and other lesser-known figures.

The awakening took place at a time when "formality and deadness characterised many of the churches" of New England. This spiritual deadness was, in part, a result of the half-way covenant of 1662, which allowed those who were baptised as infants, but had not undergone an experience of conversion, to become church members. The awakening produced large numbers of conversions and a renewed

---

[21] Bill, 13.
[22] G. A. Rawlyk, *The New Light Letters and Spiritual Songs, 1778-1793* (Hantsport: Lancelot, 1983), 4.
[23] G. A. Rawlyk (ed.), *The Sermons of Henry Alline* (Hantsport: Lancelot, 1986), 8.
[24] D. G. Bell (ed.), *The Newlight Baptist Journals of James Manning and James Innis* (Hantsport: Lancelot, 1984), xiii.
[25] Bell, 4.

desire to return to New Testament principles, particularly that of a regenerate church membership. Many of those converted at this time became known as 'New Lights' because of their belief that they had had a "new light experience."[26]

Although it is difficult to define the basic tenets of the 'New Lights,' the one unifying factor in the movement was its emphasis on the need for a recognisable new birth experience. The conversion experience was of central importance for the New Lights and many original leaders of the movement underwent dramatic conversions and expected others to experience the same.[27]

Charles Tupper was deeply impacted by this religious revival even from a young age. He wrote about his childhood spiritual struggles:

> At the close of the last century [eighteenth] and the beginning of the present [nineteenth], there was an extensive revival of religion in King's County and adjacent places. My eldest brother and two sisters professed faith in Christ, and were baptized by the late Rev. Theodore S. Harding [an early Baptist father in the Maritimes], of Horton. Though I was then only six years old, my attention was seriously called to the subject of vital godliness.[28]

Although Tupper was affected by the revival, it would still be several years before he experienced conversion in his own life.

When he was nineteen years old he accepted an offer to teach at a school in the western part of Cornwallis, Nova Scotia. Although he lacked formal training (as many teachers did in the early nineteenth century), he was a good teacher, who established reasonable rules for the children. He would not allow profane language, and showed a personal interest in each of his students' lives.[29] At the end of the school year, he went back to his former occupation, which was

---

[26] H. A. Renfree, *Heritage and Horizon: The Baptist Story in Canada* (Mississauge: Canadian Baptist Federation, 1988), 10.

[27] Bell, 4.

[28] Bill, 682f.

[29] *Christian Messenger*, August 19th, 1863, 261.

farming. When he was twenty years old, his father gave him the freedom to choose his own course in life.

At first, Tupper desired to be a farmer, but when he was offered another teaching position he accepted it and completed all the necessary requirements to obtain a school licence. He began this second stint as a school teacher in October, 1814, in Lower Aylesford, but was forced to set aside his work as a teacher due to a prolonged illness. During his illness, he searched his heart, as he was prone to do in times of critical trouble, and he concluded that he was not a Christian. However, after he got well he went back to teaching, and again neglected the question of his eternal destiny.[30]

On December 31st, 1814, while in New Canaan, Horton, Tupper was invited by a friend to attend a 'New Light' prayer meeting. He went to the meeting, but initially was not impressed with what he considered to be confusion. He was not accustomed to the highly emotional nature of the meeting, and he reacted against it. Nevertheless, at one point during the meeting, he entered into a time of deep thought. He wrote:

> I thought within myself, I have noticed some extravagances among these people. They seem at times to be transported beyond reason. But am I acting a more reasonable part? I acknowledge myself to be a guilty sinner, under the curse of God's law, exposed every moment to death, and to an eternity of woe. Is it not, then, more consistent in them to be strongly moved with reference to matters of infinite moment, than it is in me to remain unmoved while in a state of such imminent danger? Under a consciousness of my sinfulness, and the madness of my course, I turned my face toward the wall, to conceal my emotions, and wept profusely.[31]

At the end of the meeting, Tupper concluded that this was just another emotional experience, and that it would have no lasting effect on his life. He was naturally inclined to hide his emotions from other people, and he determined never to reveal his emotions to anyone, but to

---

[30] *Christian Messenger*, September, 23rd, 1863, 301.
[31] *Christian Messenger*, October 7th, 1863, 317.

continue seeking God in secret. This determination, however, did not last very long. The next day, which was the Lord's Day, he went with his sister to a 'New Light' prayer meeting at New Minas. He knew that the meeting would be similar to the one the night before, but he had promised his sister that he would go, and he was unwilling to break that promise. He was firm in his resolve to avoid any emotional excitement, so as not to disgrace himself publicly.

When he arrived at the meeting he found a seat in the corner so that he could avoid being too close to those who were leading the service. While he sat in the corner he noticed a man smiling, and he found this very distasteful. He had been taught that a man should have a solemn expression on his face when worshipping God, and he felt that this man was guilty of irreverence, and concluded that he was not in good company. Those attitudes changed after he heard several prayers offered and listened to multiple men speak. He found his heart and conscience under conviction of sin, but still resisted giving in to his convictions. After the final speaker was finished, Tupper was convinced that he needed to seek God for mercy or he would be lost forever. He later wrote that, after an intense internal struggle, "all thought of concealment was now abandoned. I requested prayer to be offered for me, as for 'the vilest of the vile.'" Near the end of the meeting, what he feared the most took place. He gave outward public expression of his emotion. He described it as follows:

> I therefore fell upon my knees in the presence of all the people, and engaged in fervent prayer. When I had become nearly exhausted, I heard one person saying to another, 'See the work of God on this stranger!' Someone remarked, 'it is Charales Tupper.' The mention of my name seemed to affect me like electricity. I immediately arose, and walked out of the house saying to myself, 'The thing I feared has come upon me.' My strong resolution had been broken: and I should now be a laughing stock for the world, and a reproach to religion, but could never be a Christian.[32]

---

[32] *Christian Messenger*, October 21st, 1863, 333.

Despite this intense religious experience, Tupper still experienced no peace. The burden of sin still weighed heavily upon him, and he was often in a state of despair. He did, however, have a 'gleam of hope,' and began to believe that there was a possibility that he might eventually be saved.

Tupper revealed to his parents the struggle that he was having, and his father gave him Joseph Alleine's book *Alarm to the Unconverted*,[33] which he read with great profit. Joseph Alleine was a seventeenth-century Puritan, whose understanding of conversion was thoroughly Reformed/Calvinistic. At this time, Tupper was imbibing a Reformed understanding of faith and conversion, even while he was undergoing a spiritual transformation in a New Light meeting.

On February 17th, 1815, Tupper finally experienced the spiritual breakthrough which he was looking for. At the end of the school day, he was so exercised in mind and spirit that he stayed at the schoolhouse for the entire night. He read the Scriptures as well as Joseph Alleine's *Alarm to the Unconverted*. He prayed through the night without relief. But, as the morning approached, there was a definite change in his condition. It was evident that God had done a work of grace in his heart.[34] His heart was finally regenerated, and he was filled with a new joy.

One of the issues that immediately confronted Tupper after his conversion was baptism. Before his conversion, Tupper described himself as 'theoretically a Baptist;' that is, he accepted the Baptist teaching on baptism intellectually, but after becoming a Christian he believed that it was necessary to study the issue of baptism more closely to determine what the Bible taught. Tupper was not so much interested in what different groups believed about baptism, but what the Bible taught concerning this doctrine. He did not want to join any denomination of Christians until he had examined the Bible. After examining the Scriptures, he concluded that the Bible did indeed teach that believers are the only proper subjects for baptism, and that immersion was the biblical mode. He did read the books from a variety of denominations, such as the Church of England and the

---

[33] J. Alleine, *Alarm to the Unconverted* [1671] (http://gracegems.org/28/alarm_to_the_unconverted2.htm).
[34] *Christian Messenger*, December, 16th, 1863, 397.

Presbyterians, but concluded that the Baptists held most closely to the Bible. He was baptised by Edward Manning in Cornwallis on Sunday, May 14th, 1815, and became a member of the Cornwallis Baptist Church.[35]

His ministry

Shortly after his conversion, he began to give short messages to the congregation following the regular sermon. His love for the unconverted was seen early on, and is graphically displayed in an address that he gave at the beginning of his preaching ministry. He wrote,

> At the close of the sermon I addressed the congregation. It was my intention to speak to the Christians; but when I looked around upon unconverted sinners, in the broad road to unending woe, my bowels yearned over them, and I immediately proceeded to exhort them very earnestly to flee from the wrath to come, and to embrace the glorious Redeemer.[36]

He never lost his love and concern for spiritually lost people. The importance of the new birth remained the central theme of his preaching throughout his life and ministry.

Charles Tupper was ordained to the Christian ministry on July 17th, 1817, and served several congregations in Nova Scotia, New Brunswick, and Prince Edward Island. His public ministry lasted for fifty-five years and during those years he preached 8,191 sermons and visited 16,585 families.[37]

As a minister, Tupper did not pursue his studies at the expense of his evangelistic and pastoral duties. He often studied while journeying by horseback so as to avoid neglecting his preaching

---

[35] *Christian Messenger*, April 6th, 1864, 109.

[36] *Christian Messenger*, January 20th, 1864, 21.

[37] B. M. Moody, 'Charles Tupper,' in F. G. Halpenny & J. Hamelin (eds.), *Dictionary of Canadian Biography, Vol. XI: 1881-1890* (http://www.biographi.ca/en/bio/tupper _charles_11E.html).

ministry in favour of academic pursuits. In July of 1818, when he began to study the Greek language, he wrote, "Strong fears frequently assailed me lest my studies should divert my attention from the momentous work of winning souls to Christ."[38] This was a common fear in the early nineteenth century, especially amongst those who were influenced by Newlightism. Henry Alline warned of the danger of learning becoming a substitute for divine assistance. As a result of this emphasis, his followers cultivated a low view of education, considering it to be a hindrance to true preaching. Anti-intellectualism was a problem in many Baptist churches, and it would not be until 1828 that an institution of higher learning was established in Nova Scotia to educate Baptist ministers.[39]

Although he supported the establishment of this institution, Tupper lived with a constant tension between learning and a passion for souls. He did not believe in an unlearned ministry, but he did see the danger inherent in focusing too much on academic studies. In his early twenties, while Tupper was contemplating the possibility of entering ministry, this tension had been intense:

> Strong fears assailed me, lest I should confide in human learning rather than in the Lord who only could make me a good and useful minister of the gospel. Some pious friends expressed similar fears: and constrained me against making efforts for the attainment of education. They suggested that such a course would be likely to render me lifeless and inefficient.

Tupper was influenced by many people who did not have a very high view of education, and their discouragement certainly contributed to Tupper's struggle. But despite this lack of encouragement, Tupper, still looking back to his early twenties, continued:

---

[38] *Christian Messenger*, July 5th, 1865, 213.
[39] B. M. Moody, 'The Maritime Baptist and Higher Education in the Early Nineteenth Century,' in B. M. Moody (ed.), *Repent and Believe: The Baptist Experience in Maritime Canada* (Hantsport: Lancelot, 1980), 90. The school was originally an extension of Horton Academy, and was designed to provide training for men called to Christian ministry. Its name was later changed to Acadia University, and it was relocated to Wolfville, Nova Scotia.

It was, however, evident to me, that one whose duty it would be to expound the sacred Scriptures, was under indispensable obligation to employ all available means in order to make himself thoroughly acquainted with their exact meaning; and that to this end he ought to study diligently, as well as to pray earnestly for divine assistance.[40]

He concluded that it was right to study Latin, and any other language that would help him to understand the word of God more clearly. This tension between academics and soul-winning was helpful in his development, and likely kept him from becoming either too intellectual or too emotionally charged in his approach to ministry.

Tupper was held in high regard, and his intellectual and teaching gifts were recognised by the leadership of the Regular Baptist Churches. The elevated level of respect for Tupper is seen in his appointment as the first editor of the newly formed *Baptist Missionary Magazine* in 1827. I. E. Bill wrote concerning this appointment:

In this arrangement regarding the new Magazine the providence of God is most distinctly seen. There was no high institution of learning open to the Baptists in those days for training their young men for the ministry, or for editorial life; but Jehovah had given them a young man, who by self-culture had placed himself in a position which so commanded the respect and confidence of the Fathers, that they cordially united in appointing him to the editor's chair of the first magazine published either by them or any other denomination in these Provinces. In the prosecution of this mission Elder Tupper showed himself in all respects worthy of the important trust committed to his care.[41]

---

[40] C. Tupper, 'Autobiographical Sketch,' in *Christian Messenger*, April 20th, 1864, 122.

[41] Bill, 710.

The foundation of the ministry

The ministry of Charles Tupper was built upon five pillars: sound theology, balanced enthusiasm, church organisation, baptism, and abstinence.

Sound theology

This first pillar, was, for Tupper, Calvinistic theology. This was emphasised in the articles he wrote, and those he allowed to be published, in the *Baptist Missionary Magazine*. As chief editor of the magazine from 1827-33, he had great influence over the choice of articles that were printed. The inclusion of a letter written by 'Philalethes' in the July issue of 1827 indicates that Tupper, from the beginning of the magazine's publication, intended to promote and reinforce Calvinistic belief in the Regular Baptist Churches. The letter strongly condemned Arminianism as a dangerous heresy that was corrupting the churches.

> But to what place of worship shall we go, to what Preacher shall we repair, to hear the sweet sound of free grace and a finished salvation? Has not Arminianism, that religious Proteus, crept into all our churches and does she not mingle a little of her leaven in almost every address from the pulpit? Is not Christ dethroned from the seat of his Omnipotence, stripped of his all perfect Righteousness, and his all sin-cleansing blood, by this Goddess, which all the world worshippeth, and rendered merely her servant or assistant?[42]

This emphasis on Calvinism and critique of Arminian theology was, in part, a response to the ongoing influence of the Arminian theology of Henry Alline that permeated the churches throughout Nova Scotia and New Brunswick. Alline's theology was a mishmash of disconnected theological ideas which were bound to lead people in all

---

[42] C. Tupper, 'An Essay, on the cause of the obscurity of Scripture to us,' in *Baptist Missionary Magazine* (July 1827), 73.

sorts of theological directions and create disunity in the church. Rawlyk wrote,

> there was also, of course, as has already been noted, an important heterodox element in the volatile mixture making up Alline's theology.... In a particularly discerning critique, Reverend Matthew Richey pointed out that the Falmouth preacher's theology was a strange mixture of undigested, often conflicting points of view.[43]

The anti-Calvinist slant of Alline's writings, and the lingering influence of his preaching, continued to shape the theological understanding of many Christians. Tupper's main concern was to protect the Regular Baptists by providing a defence of the true faith. Utilising the *Baptist Missionary Magazine*, he promoted an organised Calvinistic system of theology in order to provide theological stability in the Baptist churches.

Balanced enthusiasm

Tupper was not 'a highly charged, emotional' preacher, but one who spoke to the heart through the mind. He despised the use of rhetorical devices designed to manipulate the emotional state of the audience. He may have possessed the ability to use these devices, but his desire to be understood in a very direct and frank manner kept him from employing them very often, if at all.[44] Wilson described Tupper as

> a quiet and shy preacher who traveled on horseback reading theological and grammatical texts. From the pulpit he stressed the importance of biblical Christianity and Calvinism.[45]

---

[43] G. A. Rawlyk, *Ravished by the Spirit: Religious Revivals, Baptists, and Henry Alline* (Montreal & Kingston: MQUP, 1984), 74.

[44] C. Tupper, 'Domestic Missions,' in *Baptist Missionary Magazine* (October 1827), 118.

[45] J. Wilson, *Leading a 'New Epoch:' Charles Tupper, Ingram Bill, Richard Burpe and the Regular Baptists of New Brunswick, Nova Scotia, and Prince Edward Island, 1800-1850* (M.A. Thesis, Queens University, 1995), 17.

He also avoided the use of flowery language in his preaching because he was most concerned with being understood by the common man.[46] Indeed, his preaching style was more suited to his intellectual disposition than the fiery rhetoric of Henry Alline. His method was also influenced by his belief that God speaks to the heart through the mind, not the emotions. This does not mean that Tupper did not believe in passionate preaching. He included an article in the *Baptist Missionary Magazine* that provided the following counsel to young preachers:

> There is, perhaps, no complaint about preaching more common, than that ministers do not feel what they say. The sermon was good it is said; the sentiments correct, neatly arranged, and happily expressed. But there was nothing to give it life, and vigour and animation. The preacher, instead of entering into the spirit of his sermon, and preaching, 'as though he ne'er should preach again, as dying unto dying men,' is dull and lifeless; showing that he believes little, and feels nothing of what he utters.[47]

In light of his inclusion of this article, one could argue that Tupper's own preaching was more than simply a presentation of intellectual ruminations, but also involved passionate proclamation of gospel truth.

Tupper also sought to avoid the misuse of impressions and impulses, which were prominent in the ministry of Alline, as well as many Regular Baptists and other 'New Lights.' When Tupper published the article *On Impressions* in 1827, it was still believed by many that a person only had to obey the commands of Scripture if they under were under a strong compulsion to do so. Tupper wrote,

---

[46] Tupper, 'Domestic Missions,' 118.
[47] "Timotheus," 'On the Connections Between a Preacher's Private Life, and his Official Ministrations,' in *Baptist Missionary Magazine* (April 1827), 38.

> it has been, and still is, thought by some, that what is strongly impressed upon their minds is their duty, and they are not bound to do what is not so suggested to them.[48]

In this article he called his readers back to Scripture, arguing that all impressions that are contrary to the Bible should be disregarded. Whereas in the ministry of Alline, impressions were in some cases considered to be above Scripture, for Tupper the Scriptures were above impressions. Tupper was not against impressions; he just believed that all impressions should be interpreted in the light of the Bible's teaching.

Tupper believed that the Bible was the final source for faith and practice. He believed that "intellectual familiarity with Christian doctrine" was important, in fact essential, if one was faithfully to live the Christian life. While not downplaying the reality and need of personal experiences, he held to a high view of Scripture and agreed with the first lines of the *1689 Baptist Confession of Faith* which says, "the Holy Scripture is the only sufficient, certain, and infallible rule of all saving knowledge, faith, and obedience." [49]

In *On Impressions* Tupper encouraged people to seek the help of the Holy Spirit when studying the Scriptures, reminding readers that there would be no further revelation from God, whether in the form of prophecy or an oracle, and that one should not seek for any. He went on to say that "the Scriptures must determine the path of duty."[50] In an article on the qualifications of deacons he wrote,

> Let us carefully search them [the Scriptures], and endeavour, in this as well as every other point of duty, implicitly and strictly, to follow their dictates.[51]

Furthermore, he wrote,

---

[48] C. Tupper, 'On Impressions,' in *Baptist Missionary Magazine* (April 1829), 296.
[49] *The Baptist Confession of Faith* (*1689*), 1.1.
[50] Tupper, 'Impressions,' 297f.
[51] C. Tupper, 'An Essay on the Office, Works, and Qualifications of Deacons,' in *Baptist Missionary Magazine* (October 1827), 110.

The Baptists generally, regarding the sacred Scriptures as a full and explicit rule of faith and practice, deem the instructions contained in them quite sufficient to guide the sincere inquirer, whose mind is free from prepossession, to the right discharge of this duty.[52]

These and similar statements on the authority and sufficiency of Scripture are scattered throughout the writings of Tupper.

Church organisation

Tupper emphasised the need for a church to be well organised. In the *Baptist Missionary Magazine* he published articles on the role of deacons, and on the private and public life of the pastor. In his latter years, he wrote a series of articles for *the Christian Messenger* entitled, 'Letters to a Young Preacher.' In these articles, he covered such topics as the public reading of Scripture, public prayer, sermon preparation, administration of the ordinances, performing marriage ceremonies, and visiting the sick, aged, and families. He even gave counsel on when to leave a church. The inclusion of these articles and many others of a practical nature were intended to help the churches function in an organised, efficient, and yet moral and spiritual manner.

Baptism

Tupper believed that baptism by immersion after conversion was biblical, and that all who profess faith in Christ should publicly declare their faith in the waters of baptism. Between the years 1811 and 1848, a controversy over the mode and subjects of baptism took place in the Maritime Provinces. The Regular Baptists were effective evangelists, and in the early nineteenth century they were making inroads into Maritime communities that were predominately Anglican, Methodist, and Presbyterian. As a result of their preaching, many people were leaving these denominations, rejecting infant baptism, and joining Baptist congregations. The more established

---

[52] C. Tupper, *Baptist Principles Vindicated: In Reply to the Revd. J. W. D. Gray's Work on Baptism* (Amherst: Christian Messenger Office, 1844), 9.

denominations responded to this disconcerting situation by attacking the Baptist understanding of the mode and subject of baptism. Goodwin wrote:

> The aggressive evangelistic efforts of the Maritime Regular Baptists during the first half of the nineteenth century created a sense of panic among the region's paedobaptists. Whether or not the immersionists posed as great a threat to the Anglicans, Methodists, and Presbyterians as they believed is not clear. However, the perception of Baptist advance sparked a debate over baptism, its mode, and suitable candidates, which had a profound impact upon the Regular Baptist community.[53]

Tupper played a leading role in this controversy, producing some of his best polemical works during this period. Probably his most important work was entitled, *Baptist Principles Vindicated: In Reply to the Revd. J. W. D. Gray's Work on Baptism*, in which he defended the Baptist position against paedobaptism. Tupper believed that baptism was not a side issue, but a central command that should be obeyed by all professing believers.[54]

Abstinence

Tupper despised the use of alcohol and the negative impact it had on people's lives. He attributes his attitude towards alcohol to an earnest prayer offered by his mother to God on behalf of her brother, who had begun to indulge in strong drink. He wrote that his mother's prayer,

> led me to regard drunkenness with abhorrence, as a fruitful source of misery, and a thing to be greatly dreaded, and cautiously avoided. Through the period of youth, and peculiar

---

[53] D. C. Goodwin, *"The Faith of the Fathers:" Evangelical Piety of Maritime Regular Baptist Patriarchs and Preachers, 1790-1855* (Ph.D. Thesis, Queens University, 1997), 226.
[54] For a full outline of the baptismal controversy, see Goodwin, *Faith of the Fathers*, chapter 6.

exposure to this temptation, my pious mother's fervent prayer exerted a salutary influence upon me.[55]

While his mother had an impact on his attitude toward alcohol, he was probably more influenced by the general spirit of evangelicalism in his day. There was a growing rejection, not only of the abuse, but even the occasional consumption, of alcoholic beverages in the early nineteenth century. The temperance movement was just getting underway and like so many other people, Tupper was swept up in the movement.

Tupper began his ministry at the beginning of what John Merrill called, "the longest continuous reform movement in American history." Before the temperance movement began in the 1820s, most people (including evangelicals) considered alcohol to be a blessing from God for the enjoyment of mankind. Drinking habits in the early nineteenth century were different from drinking habits today. Many people consumed alcohol daily as a medicine or tonic. Merrill notes that it was used to sterilise unclean drinking water, and that travellers drank it to combat fatigue.[56]

This was also true of the Maritime Provinces. Charles Tupper, referring to the year 1815, wrote:

> In accordance with the erroneous views then prevalent—not yet wholly exploded—alcoholic liquor was regarded by many as a panacea or remedy for all diseases.

By the 1820s, alcohol use had reached an all time high in North America, giving rise to significant social issues. In many cases not only did a man drink, but his wife and children drank as well. Inebriated husbands would abuse their wives and children, and squander what little money they had. As a result, many children were not properly cared for, and went into a life of crime and prostitution.[57]

---

[55] *Christian Messenger*, March 18th, 1863, 85.
[56] J. Merrill, 'The Bible and the American Temperance Movement,' in *The Harvard Theological Review* 81, No. 2 (April 1988), 145.
[57] J. Noel, *Canada Dry: Temperance Crusades Before Confederation* (Toronto: Toronto UP, 1995), 6.

The Temperance movement sought to address and solve these problems.

In the early 1820's the temperance movement did not promote total abstinence, but moderate consumption of alcohol to avoid drunkenness.[58] This is also what Tupper believed at the time. Over time the movement grew more rigid until alcohol consumption was condemned outright. Tupper's views evolved along the same line. Around 1829 he formed the temperance society in Amherst, Nova Scotia, and began to preach against the use of any form of intoxicating drink. He wrote in 1866:

> In my view intemperance is so great an obstacle to the interests of vital religion, by holding the unregenerate in the chain of Satan, and by drawing professors of faith into gross impiety, that a minister of Christ is well employed, in his appropriate work, when putting forth zealous and continuous efforts for its suppression.[59]

Although Tupper's convictions on alcohol consumption were influenced by the growing rejection of alcohol in North America, he did believe that he had biblical support for his position. In October 1829 he wrote an article on intemperance for the *Baptist Missionary Magazine*. He quoted liberally from the Scriptures[60] to support his stance on alcohol consumption.[61] So while Tupper was influenced and shaped by contemporary views, he believed he was acting in accordance with the word of God.

Conclusion

Charles Tupper was one of the greatest and most influential Maritime Baptist leaders of the nineteenth century. His long ministry helped to stabilise the young and growing Regular Baptist denomination. In the

---

[58] Noel, 17.
[59] *Christian Messenger*, December 12th, 1866.
[60] Prov. 23:21; 20:1; 10:21; 23:29-35; 1 Cor. 6:9f; Gal. 5:18-21; Isa. 5:11, 14, 22, 24.
[61] C. Tupper, 'Intemperance,' in *Baptist Missionary Magazine* (October 1829), 361-364.

year of his conversion (1815), there were 12 Pastors, 26 churches, and 1,207 members. When Tupper died in 1881, there were 195 pastors, 348 churches, and approximately 39,000 members.[62] The ministry of Charles Tupper left its mark on the denomination and only God knows how much of the blessing Eastern Canadians enjoy to this day can be directly linked to that faithful man of God.

---

[62] Moody, 'Tupper.'

Pastoral and Practical Papers

Ministerial Burnout

Carl Muller

It is not uncommon for ministers of the gospel that they should consider the finest and inevitable expression of their overwhelming zeal for the kingdom to be going full bore into their work, with little or no consideration given to their physical and emotional limitations. I would rather *"burn out than rust out,"*[1] they say, in a misapplication of that famous statement. Too often the result of such an approach to the service of God is that these Christians find themselves weighed down and worn out. Their usefulness is, for a time, hindered, and they end up padding the statistics of those whose ministries have brought them to the point of what is nowadays called 'burnout.'

As one who has, over the course of forty plus years of ministry, experienced 'burnout' on two occasions, I want to say that there is a better way. Burnout is not the inevitable consequence for one who wishes to take his calling to ministry seriously.

Winston Churchill points us in the right direction. Paul Johnson relates the following:

> In 1946, when I was seventeen, I had the good fortune to ask him a question: 'Mr. Churchill, sir, to what do you attribute your success in life?' Without pause or hesitation, he replied: 'Conservation of energy. Never stand up when you can sit down, and never sit down when you can lie down.' He then got into his limo.[2]

Johnson observes:

> Churchill's great strength was his power of relaxation…. The balance he maintained between flat-out work and creative and

---

[1] I have seen this attributed to Amy Carmichael and George Whitefield; even Neil Young sang: "It's better to burn out than to fade away," in his, 'My, My, Hey, Hey (Out of the Blue).'

[2] P. Johnson, *Churchill* (New York: Penguin, 2009), 5.

restorative leisure is worth study by anyone holding a top position.[3]

There is hope, then, that those who serve the king can burn with zeal and not burn out. Let us explore this subject in honour of one whose zeal for the kingdom is boundless, and whose compassion for those who suffer in service is immeasurable.

Acknowledging burnout

Let us begin by acknowledging that burnout is, as they say, 'a thing.' Unfortunately, many Christians, and not a few Christian traditions, would affirm that there is no such thing as 'burnout,' at least not for Christian ministers. One pastor told me that he was profoundly thankful for the illness that landed him in hospital. Finally, he could get some rest without guilt. I have myself been accused of playing the 'mental health' card. However, though understanding and sympathy is not always forthcoming from Christians, both inside and outside the church there is growing acknowledgement of the reality and dangers of burnout.

On our way to a routine pastoral visit, my fellow elder casually asked me how I was doing. I dissolved into tears. Knowing me to be, for the most part, emotionally stable, alarm bells rang in his head. Thus began my first experience of burnout.

Dr. David Murray helpfully defines burnout as "physical, emotional, mental, and spiritual exhaustion and breakdown." He comments: "It is usually caused by living at too fast a pace, for too long, doing too much." When you come face to face with a bear, he writes, "you go into fight or flight mode." The pastor who is burning out is in *constant* 'fight or flight mode.' As Murray continues,

> We're living as if we're in that heightened state all the time. The body then produces chemicals and reactions…. This constant inflammation and chemical imbalance that is occurring in our bodies is affecting not only our bodies. It is

---

[3] Johnson, 128, 163.

affecting our emotions, our thinking, and ultimately our spiritual lives.[4]

We need to exercise caution when it comes to statistics.[5] The helpful John Mark Ministries warns that often the truth behind the statistics is hard to ascertain, as the sources of those statistics are often not given.[6] Nonetheless there is enough reliable information that indicates that burnout is a significant problem in pastoral ranks. Christopher Ash cites George Barna, who informs us that some 1500 people leave pastoral ministry each month due to burnout, conflict or moral failure, and that a third of pastors feel burned out within just five years of entering the ministry.[7]

The Mayo Clinic identified burnout as

> a special type of work-related stress—a state of physical or emotional exhaustion that also involves a sense of reduced accomplishment and loss of personal identity.[8]

Paul Vitello, religion editor for the New York Times, states:

> Members of the clergy now suffer from obesity, hypertension and depression at rates higher than most Americans. In the last decade, their use of antidepressants has risen, while their life expectancy has fallen. Many would change jobs if they could.[9]

Christopher Ash notes that

---

[4] D. Murray, 'What is Burnout and Why is it so Dangerous?' (http://www.crossway. org/articles/what-is-burnout-and-why-is-it-so-dangerous/).
[5] Mark Twain wrote: "There are three kinds of lies: lies, damned lies, and statistics." Twain wrongly attributed the quote to Benjamin Disraeli. Its origin is uncertain.
[6] 'Pastor Burnout Statistics' (http://www.jmm.org.au/articles/27347.htm).
[7] C. Ash, *Zeal Without Burnout* (Epsom: Good Book Company, 2016), 16.
[8] 'Job burnout: How to spot it and take action' (https://www.mayoclinic.org/healthy-lifestyle/adult-health/in-depth/burnout/art-20046642).
[9] P. Vitello, 'Taking a Break from the Lord's Work' (https://www.nytimes.com/2010/ 08/02/nyregion/02burnout.html). In an NPR interview, Vitello shows that burnout and its impact on overall health is a problem in all faith groups (https://www.npr.org/ templates/story/story.php?storyId=128957149).

almost half of pastors *and their wives* say they have experienced depression or burnout to the extent that they needed to take a leave of absence from the ministry.[10]

On the pages of Holy Scripture, Elijah stands before us as one whose

encounter with the prophets of Baal left him burned out and fearful of the threatenings of Jezebel. He speaks as one who has lost perspective. *I've had enough; take away my life; I might as well be dead.*

On the pages of Christian history, we discover that Martin Luther knew what it meant to be overwhelmed, and

although he would have been unfamiliar with the terminology of burnout, his tendency to bouts of melancholy would seem to fit the pattern.[11]

It should be noted that burnout is not the same as self-denial. The latter is something to which our Lord Jesus calls us (Luke 9:23-24); the former is something that "damages strength and life to no good effect," to quote Ash, who finds the analogy with firefighting helpful for clarifying the difference. He records the words of a pastor who wrote to him:

It's been very helpful to me to contemplate the difference between burnout and sacrificial living for the Lord. Your reflections...really helped me to understand the difference. I put it into terms of fighting a fire as I'm a volunteer firefighter as well as being a pastor. Obviously you have to push yourself physically when fighting a fire. It's a stretching experience that is uncomfortable and physically difficult. You have to know

---

[10] Ash, 16 [italics original]. The World Health Organisation includes burnout in its International Classification of Diseases (ICD 11), defining it as "a syndrome conceptualized as resulting from chronic workplace stress that has not been successfully managed" (https://www.who.int/news/item/28-05-2019-burn-out-an-occupational-phenomenon-international-classification-of-diseases).

[11] A. Begg, 'Foreword' to Ash, 10.

your limitations while making the sacrifices needed to get the tasks done that must be done.

It's foolish to ignore your limitations, try to be the hero, and cramp up, pass out, or have a heart attack while in a burning structure because you're beyond the limits of what God has supplied you with the capability of doing. It's a form of heroic suicide that is counterproductive because you're now no longer effective in fighting fire and the resources that were dedicated to fighting the fire are now dedicated to saving you.[12]

It seems to me that many pastors practise the "heroic suicide" about which this brother wrote, and in doing so hinder their usefulness. The idea of 'burning out rather than rusting out' calls for heroic *service*, not heroic *suicide*.

Understanding burnout

The warning signs are usually there: sleeplessness; emotional instability; reduced productivity; a heavy spirit; exhaustion; "persistent feelings of nervousness, sometimes escalating into full-blown panic."[13] I did not notice any of these signs. It was not until that night when I dissolved into tears in response to a simple question, that I realised that something was wrong, and began to wonder what had happened. How did I get to this point?

The simple answer is that we just have too much going on. When I burned out the first time, life was overwhelming: there were problems in the church, I saw no need to rest, a close family member was dying, I was too busy for devotions, I never said 'no' to any work, and so on. When my daughter burned out, we wrote down a list of everything she was involved in, and all the responsibilities on her plate. The list was staggering, and I was rather astonished that she had not crashed sooner. So yes, the simple answer is that we have too much going on. But now we have to probe a little deeper: how does a

---

[12] Ash, 24.
[13] Ash, 121f. See also D. Murray, *Reset: Living a grace-paced life in a burnout culture* (Wheaton: Crossway, 2017), 25-31, for physical, mental, emotional, relational, vocational, moral, spiritual, and pastoral warning lights.

pastor get to the point where he has been (as Murray says) "living at too fast a pace, for too long, doing too much"? What drives a minister to "heroic suicide"?

Ministry is difficult

As Spurgeon said:

> our work, when earnestly undertaken, lays us open to attacks in the direction of depression. Who can bear the weight of souls without sometimes sinking to the dust? … All mental work tends to weary and to depress, for much study is a weariness of the flesh; but ours is more than mental work – it is heart work, the labour of our inmost soul…. Such soul-travail will bring on occasional seasons of exhaustion, when heart and flesh will fail.[14]

Life in general is difficult, and the Christian ministry especially so. Pastor Andrew Roycroft writes:

> No therapy, no planning, no good intention, no resistance or defiance, can change the fact that ministry is hard, and that it often entails a seemingly disproportionate amount of suffering and pressure.[15]

Given that, how unwise for ministers of the gospel not to realise that

> in the midst of a long stretch of unbroken labour, the same affliction may be looked for. The bow cannot always be bent without fear of breaking.[16]

To avoid breaking the bow, let us heed the words of our Lord: "Come away by yourselves to a desolate place and rest a while" (Mark 6:31).

---

[14] C. H. Spurgeon, *Lectures to My Students* (London: Marshall, Morgan & Scott, 1954), 156.
[15] A. Roycroft, 'A Pastor in Therapy, (https://thinkingpastorally.com/2019/11/18/a-pastor-in-therapy/). Pastor Roycroft writes about his own burnout in 2019.
[16] Spurgeon, 160.

Success is dangerous

Sometimes what drives a pastor to superhuman efforts is an ignoble desire for success. In his heart there lives a concern for the glory of God as well as, to a lesser degree, a desire for ministerial success! I have been to enough fraternals to know that a pastor loves to tell the story of how he 'built up the church.' A desire for that kind of 'success' can drive him to a work rate that sacrifices his health, and perhaps even the welfare of his family. I would add that whilst a desire for 'success' can be dangerous, 'success' itself can also be perilous.

> The very hearts that are depressed when all things seem against them, are often unduly exalted in the day of prosperity. Few men are like Samson, and can kill a lion without telling others of it.... Most of Christ's labourers probably have as much success as their souls can bear.[17]

Pride is pervasive

It accompanies us to seminary, it sidles up into the pulpit with us, and it encourages us to let people know regularly that we are working very, very hard, much harder than lesser mortals. It is at the root of what Ash calls "ministry machismo". Should you encounter that seemingly indefatigable pastor who never needs time off, Ash's counsel is that you find a loving way to tell him, "you are behaving like an arrogant fool."[18]

Pride will make you unwilling to admit that you cannot cope anymore, and will drive you on well past the point of breaking. Pride will prevent you from seeking help. Pride will move you to resent those who try to help. Pride will hinder you from coming before God in weakness and crying out fervently to him for strength. Dr. Lloyd-Jones said somewhere that the besetting sin of the church in the twentieth century was self-sufficiency. So it still is. Pride and self-

---

[17] J. C. Ryle, *Expository Thoughts on the Gospels: Luke* [1879] (Welwyn: EP, 1985 reprint), 171.
[18] Ash, 79.

sufficiency have a causative role in the lifestyle that leads to burnout, and it hinders the soul that is struggling to cope with burnout.

Delusion is rampant

A quite common ministerial delusion is a 'messiah complex.' Take zeal for the glory of God, a love for preaching the truth, a passion for souls, a desire to edify saints, sprinkle in a touch of male ego, a dash of arrogance, a dollop of success, and you have the perfect recipe for a 'messiah complex.' The little man with the big 'M' on his chest now feels himself absolutely indispensable to the church, and quite enjoys his role. Humility prevents him from saying it, but he does feel that the church cannot get along without him. And so, with no regard for his limitations, he will give himself to the work.

Life is complicated

There are times in your life when you feel the way the Israelites did:

> Moses spoke thus to the people of Israel, but they did not listen to Moses, because of their broken spirit and harsh slavery.[19]

Sometimes the circumstances God sets before us inevitably result in a heavy heart and a shattered spirit. We can still rejoice. We can

> trace the rainbow through the rain,
> And feel the promise is not vain
> That morn shall tearless be,[20]

but we are weighed down by grief and sadness. A very dear family member had died, and the profound sadness of such a heavy loss, added to a variety of other issues, led to my first burnout. Life is hard and complicated.

---

[19] Ex. 6:9.
[20] From the hymn, *O Love that wilt not let me go* (George Matheson, 1842-1906).

Providence is mysterious

Sometimes a burnout will happen even when you have everything in place to prevent it. The simple fact is that, in the providence of God, life becomes overwhelming. The burnout happens, then, for the purpose of glorifying God, for the purpose of your growth and sanctification, or perhaps to allow other saints to grow, and other lessons to be taught. I learned from my first burnout, and put into practice the lessons I learned: exercise; regular devotions; saying 'no' when I had enough on my plate, and so on.

But then, twenty years later, it happened again. The reason it happened was simply that there was a confluence of life circumstances which were out of my control, and which together were quite overwhelming. All of these factors put me on the floor again. And it happened, not because of an unwise lifestyle, not because of any particular sin, but simply in the wise and mysterious providence of God. God had purposes in bringing this about—to humble, to teach, to renew, to stir. Ray Ortlund explains why you, through no fault of your own, might burn out:

> if a faithful pastor experiences burnout, it isn't necessarily evidence against him. It's God turning that pastor into living proof that 'God raises the dead' (2 Corinthians 1:9). It's what the pastor's people need to see in him—not only the power of God sustaining him in the normal flow of ministry, but also the power of God resurrecting him from the extreme moments of defeat.[21]

Paul Johnson writes about Dwight Eisenhower:

> So far as I can see, he had only three days' leave in total from September 1939 to the spring of 1945, during which he normally worked a day lasting from 6 am to 11 pm.

---

[21] R. Ortlund, 'Waiting on the Lord to Renew our Strength: Reflections on Pastoral Burnout,' (https://www.9marks.org/article/waiting-on-the-lord-to-renew-our-strength-reflections-on-pastoral-burnout/).

In March 1945, he and his staff went to Cannes and stayed four days. Eisenhower spent the first two days sleeping. Afterward, he even refused to play bridge: "I can't keep my mind on cards. All I want to do is sit here and not think." He would later say that he had "never been so tired, mind and body, in his entire life. He was fifty-five."[22]

You and I will never have to lead the allied forces into battle, but, in the mysterious providence of God, we may well have days that put us on our backs, and bring us to an end of ourselves. We will submit to our Father's inscrutable wisdom and lean on his omnipotent arm.

Escaping burnout

Rest

Andrew Roycroft writes:

> One of my grandest mistakes in the lead up to burn out was my rejection of rest as a vital part of my work. I was staying up late, rising early, and very seldom ever switching off to my work. I wore this as a badge of honour (which, admittedly, I only showed to myself), and felt it to be a reassurance that I was 'doing enough'. Unknown to me, this behaviour was reinforcing my pride and self-sufficiency, while making ruin of the sabbath principle that God has built into our nature as human beings.[23]

Rest, then, is the first order of business in escaping burnout. The Lord Jesus says to us, as he did to his disciples so many years ago: "Come away by yourselves to a desolate place and rest awhile" (Mark 6:31).

Let your rest be thorough

I took roughly three months off work. Others have taken more. I would strongly urge a complete break from work. Now in some cases this is impossible. In a small church, the pastor simply cannot be away

---

[22] P. Johnson, *Eisenhower* (New York: Penguin, 2014), 53.
[23] Roycroft.

for several months. However, if you understand that a complete break is optimal, then perhaps you will do your best to get as much rest as you can in a difficult work context. You will also be more careful to avoid unnecessarily taking on extra work.

It is to be hoped that the burned-out pastor is working alongside elders who are men of wisdom, compassion, and grace. They will see that he is burning out. They will understand this to be a legitimate concern. They will realise that, should time off be given, this faithful servant will struggle with guilt. So they will take the initiative, insist that he take a break, assure him of their support, and that they will take care of things in his absence. The burned-out brother will receive kindness from their hands and encouragement from their lips. This will help enable a thorough rest. A kind elder said to me years ago: "We want you back when you are better. No sooner. And when you are back, we will adjust your workload and schedule so that this doesn't happen again." Thank God for such men!

Let your rest be spiritual

As with Eisenhower, what is usually needed is sleep, and time to sit and not think. However, the sweetest element of time off work is the opportunity to seek the Lord, to read his word in unhurried fashion, to think and pray, to ponder and meditate, to dive deep into the word and soar to the heights of fellowship with God. The soul-refreshing experience of which Isaiah speaks is what you are after:

> but they who wait for the LORD shall renew their strength;
> they shall mount up with wings like eagles;
> they shall run and not be weary;
> they shall walk and not faint.[24]

During my time off I embarked upon two studies that proved of immense benefit: a study of the names of God, and a study of the beauty of Christ. My burnout came during the tumultuous days of the Covid pandemic. When I returned to work I was convinced that the

---

[24] Isa. 40:31.

exploration of these themes which had so refreshed my soul would be of great benefit to my congregation as well.

Let your rest be enjoyable

Christopher Ash writes:

> Times of quiet, enjoyment of beauty, the experience of refreshing exercise, stimulating sport, wonderful music, wholesome reading and conversation, can at their best be God's handmaidens to spiritual refreshment, as they are combined with hearing afresh the promises of God in the gospel.[25]

Idyllic afternoons in my backyard, reading beneath the shade of a tree, did me immeasurable good!

Along with David Murray, I would recommend reading for pleasure, not simply for study and learning. Dr. Murray quotes an author whose reading of *War and Peace* "put me back in control of my life"! Murray goes on to document the health-giving benefits of pleasure reading.[26] I found the reading of seven of Paul Johnson's excellent biographies quite exhilarating.[27] They took me to a world not my own, and that was refreshing.

Let your rest be sufficient

Once again, this is difficult, depending on one's circumstances. But my fellow elder's words were wise: "come back when you are ready." Too often I hear people say that when they return from time off, they are still exhausted, and dread taking up their responsibilities again. Sometimes you do more by doing less. To return refreshed and eager to work will, in the long run, benefit the church as well as the patient!

---

[25] Ash, 74f.
[26] Murray, *Reset*, 97f.
[27] For those who need unimportant details, those biographies were: *Darwin, Napoleon, Socrates, George Washington, Mozart, Churchill,* and *Eisenhower*. Highly recommended!

Let your rest be guilt free

Spurgeon counsels his students thus:

On, on, on for ever, without recreation, may suit spirits emancipated from this 'heavy clay,' but while we are in this tabernacle, we must every now and then cry halt and serve the Lord by holy inaction and consecrated leisure. Let no tender conscience doubt the lawfulness of going out of harness for awhile, but learn from the experience of others the necessity and duty of taking timely rest.[28]

We do not abdicate our responsibility by rest, but rather we "serve the Lord by holy inaction and consecrated leisure." Spurgeon adds:

I do not call the *dolce far niente*[29] laziness; there is a sweet doing of nothing which is just the finest medicine in the world for a jaded mind.[30]

Rather than feeling guilty about it, we should understand rest and recuperation as one way in which we serve the Lord, benefit the church, and prolong our ministries.

Let your rest be regular

I am not sure why pastors, when counselling congregants who work 24/7, can refer to those Christians as 'workaholics,' when they themselves do precisely the same thing. The inconsistency seems lost on them. It seems to me, however, that regular rest might save one from emergency rest. One day off a week, a few weeks off a year, can do body and soul a world of good and will contribute towards a lifestyle that does not rush headlong towards burnout.

---

[28] Spurgeon, 161.
[29] Italian: pleasant idleness; sweet doing nothing.
[30] Spurgeon, 168.

Kindness

Lady Macbeth might have no appreciation for the "milk of human kindness" that flows through her husband's veins, but kindness is like lifeblood for the burned-out pastor. In Psalm 142:4 David, who found himself "in the cave", wrote:

> no refuge remains to me;
> no one cares for my soul.

When you find yourself in that same cave, experiencing those same feelings, how the kindness of others will bless your soul. Like mercy, that kindness seems to drop as 'the gentle rain from heaven.' Kindness is one aspect of the fruit of the Spirit (Galatians 5:22, 23), and may be defined as follows:

> the inner disposition, created by the Holy Spirit, that causes us to be sensitive to the needs of others, whether physical, emotional, or spiritual. Goodness is kindness in action—words or deed.[31]

Some Christians are so wonderfully creative and find such novel and inventive ways of expressing Christian love and demonstrating Spirit-born kindness. And how that buoys the spirit of a downcast and bone-weary servant. It may be as simple and powerful as the tender and encouraging phone messages I received during my burnout, left by the one whom we honour in this volume, messages accompanied by the sensitive comment that a reply would not be looked for. Kindness may come in the form of a card. As Dr. Sam Sheppard, wrongly convicted of the murder of his wife, languished in prison, he was buoyed by letters from his family: "Sam depended on the letters. They were 'like a shot of epinephrine' or a half time pep talk...only better."[32] A few lines written on a simple card can be a 'shot of epinephrine' to a struggling saint! Perhaps you don't know what to say? A pastor friend

---

[31] J. Bridges, *The Practice of Godliness*, (Cedar Springs: Navpress, 1983), 231.
[32] J. Neff, *The Wrong Man: The Final Verdict on the Dr. Sam Sheppard Murder Case* (New York: Open Road Media, 2015), 243.

told me that one of the most encouraging notes he ever received said simply: "I understand." Kindness does not require verbosity.

Doctors

The first thing we did when our daughter began to show signs of burnout was to take her to hospital and have a battery of tests run, to ascertain whether there was any serious medical issue at the root of her symptoms. When those tests came back negative, we set about addressing the issue we suspected: burnout. Sometimes general practitioners will be the first to identify the problem of burnout. Andrew Roycroft writes:

> when I landed in my GP surgery…my only complaint was some pain in my foot. I left his office in the knowledge that my blood pressure was sky high, that I had to take two weeks enforced leave, and that some major changes would need to take place in my work patterns.[33]

The medical establishment informs us about the physiological reactions to stress, and how exhaustion and sickness can result from the unrelenting pressure of being in constant 'fight or flight' mode.[34] Such a patient can benefit from being under the care of a faithful osteopath. Such was my experience, for which I will always be grateful.

All that is to say that it is important to seek the help of the medical practitioners who are available to you.

Avoiding burnout

Fair warning

Perhaps it would be best to start at the beginning. Seminaries should include, as part of their pastoral theology classes, a warning against the almost irresistible lure of the superhuman pastor. The would-be

---

[33] Roycroft.

[34] S. I. Fox, *Human Physiology* (Dubuque: Brown, 1984), 197.

pastor should be counselled about the reality and the dangers of burnout. If, as we are told, a third of pastors say they feel burned out "within just five years of starting,"[35] such an education would seem to be essential. If my experience is anything to go by, young men will find these warnings hard to believe. But try we must! Let seminaries imitate Christopher Ash, who writes:

> I have been keen to help [young men] see that the best kinds of ministry are, more often than not, long term and low key. I have tried to prepare them for a marathon, not a short, energetic sprint. In other words, to help them have a lifetime of sustainable sacrifice, rather than an energetic but brief ministry that quickly fades in exhaustion.[36]

'Know thyself'

This sage advice dates back to the ancient Greeks, who knew a thing or two, but self knowledge and self-awareness is, sadly, a rare thing amongst Christians, and even amongst ministers. During my first burnout I discovered, while reading Ed Welch's book, *When People are Big and God is Small*, that I liked to please people, and that this contributed to my burn out. The fear of man was a snare.[37] How important it is to know yourself and your weaknesses! The merry-go-round of trying to please everybody is absolutely exhausting, and you will be flung from it in no time!

Know yourself. Does pride energise you? Does fear paralyse you? Does personal glory motivate you? Does the need to control drive you? Do past hurts embitter you?

Know yourself—and accept who you are. You are not required to work at the same rate as others. You are required to work as hard as *you* can:

> Love so amazing, so divine,

---

[35] Ash, 16.
[36] Ash, 20.
[37] Cf. Prov. 29:25.

Demands my soul, my life, my all,[38]

but *your* 'all' is different from your brother's. People are different, and what energises one drains another. Social interaction exhausts me, while brothers in the ministry come alive in a crowd. Know yourself, and construct your lifestyle and your ministry accordingly.

Build a manageable schedule

Do this in consultation with your wife or a faithful friend, since you can probably not be trusted rightly to define 'manageable.' Essential to creating and maintaining such a schedule is the invaluable ability to say 'no.' Knowing your limitations and saying 'no' to opportunities which will take you beyond them is necessary to survival in the ministry. The tyranny of the urgent should not drive us to make commitments that are delusional. Saying 'no' does not mean that you don't care, but simply that you know your limitations. It is an acknowledgement that 'we are but dust and shadow.' God "remembers that we are dust" (Psalm 103:14); we would do well to do the same.

Building a manageable schedule will require the fine art of delegation. Charles Simeon sets a good example. The minister of Holy Trinity Church, Cambridge (from 1783 until his death in 1836), "faced severe opposition in his early ministry" as well as the "routine challenges of shepherding the congregation," and found out soon enough that "his candle was in danger of burning out". He decided to delegate. He

> established a 'Visiting Society' and appointed a man and a woman church member to be responsible for the pastoral care of homes in their particular district.[39]

Simeon did not have a father-in-law, for he never married, but perhaps he learned from Moses' father-in-law, who in Exodus 18:17-23 counsels Moses that to try and do it all yourself is "not good," that the

---

[38] From the hymn, *When I survey the wondrous cross* (Isaac Watts, 1674-1748).
[39] Begg, 11.

burden is "too heavy for you," that he is "not able to do it alone," and that he should find others to bear the burden with him. That way, "you will be able to endure". Delegating might wound your pride, but your way will be easier.

Just relax

Build enjoyable times into your schedule. Paul Johnson writes:

> Churchill's great strength was his power of relaxation. Sometimes he painted.... He loved having his womenfolk with him—Clemmie and his daughters.... He liked action movies, such as *Stagecoach* and *Destry Rides Again*.[40]

And, of course, he took naps.[41]

Find a hobby. Perhaps chess will help—though not many will find the rigours of that game relaxing. At the very least, don't spend all your time dashing down the information highway. Stop neurotically checking your email. Don't carry your phone about as if it were attached to your hand. Fast from social media for a week, advises Doug Groothuis. He requires this of his students at Denver Seminary, and says that "the results have been nothing less than profound for the majority of the students:"

> they find more silence, time for reflection, and prayer, and more opportunities to engage family and friends thoughtfully. They become more peaceful and contemplative—and begin to notice how media-saturated most of our culture has become.[42]

So, yes, learn to relax.

---

[40] Johnson, *Churchill*, 128f.
[41] A. Soojung-Kim Pang, 'Winston Churchill's Secret Productivity Weapon, (https://michaelhyatt.com/naps/).
[42] Quoted in Murray, *Reset*, 94f.

Conclusion

Recommendations

First, I recommend that you be wary. "Therefore let anyone who thinks that he stands take heed lest he fall" (I Corinthians 10:12). This can happen to you.

Second, I recommend that you be ready. Be ready in case it happens to you, and in case you are called upon to minister to someone to whom this has happened. The best way to be ready is by reading the following books: Christopher Ash's *Zeal Without Burnout*, David Murray's *Reset*, Brian Croft and Jim Savastio's *The Pastor's Soul*, and Martyn Lloyd-Jones' *Spiritual Depression: Its Causes and Cure*.

Reminders

The ministry can lay a man low.

> Ten years of toil do not take so much life out of us as we lose in a few hours by Ahithophel the traitor, or Demas the apostate. Strife, also, and division, and slander, and foolish censures, have often laid holy men prostrate, and made them go 'as with a sword in their bones.'[43]

And sometimes, in the service of our God, we will burn out. But I want to remind you that God knows: "God saw the people of Israel— and God knew" (Exodus 2:25). And I want to assure you that God helps:

> let us then with confidence draw near to the throne of grace, that we may receive mercy and find grace to help in time of need.[44]

And I want to tell you that God restores:

---

[43] Spurgeon, 161.
[44] Heb. 4:16

But we have this treasure in jars of clay, to show that the surpassing power belongs to God and not to us. We are afflicted in every way, but not crushed; perplexed, but not driven to despair; persecuted, but not forsaken; struck down, but not destroyed; always carrying in the body the death of Jesus, so that the life of Jesus may also be manifested in our bodies. For we who live are always being given over to death for Jesus' sake, so that the life of Jesus also may be manifested in our mortal flesh.[45]

Burnout will strike you down, but by God's grace it will not destroy you. You will stand again, and serve again, and be useful again.

Peter Adam is vicar emeritus of St. Jude's Church in Carlton, Australia, and formerly principal of Ridley College in Melbourne. He has had a wonderfully useful Christian life, but has lived and served Christ in the shadow of a breakdown which he had early in his ministry. Without warning, one Monday morning, "he awoke and began spontaneously to cry, and found himself unable to stop weeping." He recovered and went on to serve the Lord, but he says that "he has never, since then, been able to work more than 50 hours in a week." However, he learned to "trust God more, and also realised that God can use our weaknesses as well as our strengths".[46] He was struck down but not crushed, and God has used a weak servant to magnify his strength (cf. 2 Corinthians 12:7-10). He can do the same for, in, and through you.

---

[45] 2 Cor. 4:7-11.
[46] Ash, 17.

Has the Era of Preaching from Scripture Come to a Boring End?

Paul Engle

Another Sunday service has concluded. The pastor feels discouraged, and worries that his sermon was not well received. People in the third row on the left kept whispering to each other and passing notes during most of the message. It appeared that others were texting, or updating their email inbox, or checking in on Facebook. A man on the right side of the sanctuary was asleep until the third main point of the sermon when something inexplicably jarred him back to alertness. Others looked plain bored as they checked their watches wondering, 'When will this ever end?' Is it any wonder the pastor finds it hard to conjure up the energy to begin to work on next Sunday's sermon?

"Don't they appreciate all the hours I invest in doing a careful exegesis of the text, consulting multiple commentaries, and selecting some timely illustrations that provide a window into the text? Maybe I should drastically cut the length of my sermons, or occasionally come up with substitutes actually to replace the sermon. Why are the people finding it harder and harder to listen to sustained exposition? For that matter, why do some appear to be disengaged even during the public reading of Scripture? Or might the seeming loss of interest in sermons in our generation also be related to larger cultural shifts? Has the era of preaching and exposition come to a boring end? Is it really worth it to invest hours in sermon preparation? Does Jesus' parable of the soils have anything to say about what I see happening in my congregation? Does it all boil down to a matter of the heart?[1]"

Here's the reason why I'm posing these questions: unless one is living in a cave on an isolated ocean island, you can't help but notice the sweeping changes in communication which have engulfed us in recent decades. We've witnessed the advent of television, computers, cell phones, and then the internet, readily accessible on our choice of screens. All of these changes have shaped how we communicate and

---

[1] Cf. Lk. 8:1-15.

receive information, with spill-over implications for preaching in Christian worship services.

Screen-time increasing

In the developed world, and to some extent in the two-thirds world, we are now living our lives in a screen-dominated culture. Many of us regularly view monitors or screens in our homes, at gas station pumps, sports bars, restaurants, classrooms, on the exterior walls of urban buildings for advertising purposes, and now in our churches. It's no secret that this explosion of new technology has had a shaping influence on all but a small tribe of Luddites who prefer to live cloistered lives, removed from current culture and civilisation.

Neil Postman, the noted professor of communication from New York University, chronicled and memorialised this shift in his landmark book *Amusing Ourselves to Death: Public Discourse in the Age of Show Business*.[2] Although the book was written decades ago, Postman was prescient in recognising shifts that are still occurring today. The questions he raised are now being asked of new technologies that have emerged since the writing of his book. This has led some to observe that he actually wrote a twenty-first-century book that was published in the twentieth century. Postman talked about the shift in our culture from a word-centred into an image-centred culture, what might be called the decline of the age of typography, and the ascendency of the age of television, and now the internet. The shift has happened relentlessly, though some individuals and groups have not taken the time to ponder the impact this has had on our daily lives, including what occurs in churches on Sundays.

Postman references and draws on two earlier seminal books— *Brave New World* by Aldous Huxley, and *1984* by George Orwell— recognising that their prognostications, especially Huxley's, have turned out to be prescient. He suggests that we have arrived at Huxley and Orwell's future vision in which

---

[2] N. Postman, *Amusing Ourselves to Death: Public Discourse in the Age of Show Business* (New York: Penguin, 1985, 2005).

a population becomes distracted by trivia, when cultural life is redefined as a perpetual round of entertainments, when serious public conversation becomes a form of baby-talk, when, in short, a people become an audience and their public business a vaudeville act.[3]

George Orwell feared that books would be banned in the future, whereas Huxley feared that there would be no reason to write and produce books, because no one would want to read them. Having worked for a number of years as publisher in a major global book publishing company, I can attest that what has kept many publishers and editors awake at night is wondering if anyone in the future would purchase our books, in effect making our jobs obsolete. Postman sagely observed that maybe Huxley was right, that we have changed from perhaps the most print-oriented culture ever to have existed, into a culture whose ideas, information, and epistemology are derived from television (and now the ubiquitous internet), not the printed word. Written words are seen to have moved to the periphery, while images have moved to centre screen.

Is this ascendency of the visual harmful?

Some might wonder if this ascendency of the visual is really that harmful, or is this concern much ado about nothing? After all isn't a picture worth a thousand words, and don't those of us who are primarily visual learners retain more when communications include visual elements? True on both counts! Postman suggests, however, that this triumph of the visual actually frees us from the obligation to think. Everything becomes image, meaning that nothing has substance. The age of exposition has become the age of entertainment. Let me remind you of what has occurred in recent years:

- verbal messages have become short Twitter 280-character bursts, often accompanied by a photo or video clip;

---

[3] Quoted in J. Yardley, 'The Vacuum at the End of the Tube' (Review of Postman), in *Washington Post,* November 3rd, 1985.

- Facebook posts require images if they are to garner 'likes;'
- Instagram scanning replaces book reading, to say nothing of the eyeballs focused on YouTube or Vimeo videos rather than printed exposition in thoughtful books.

Images, whether still or moving, seem designed to elicit an immediate emotional response. Dare we ask, 'are words dead?' Will they be replaced by the billions of photos uploaded every single day, including emoji's, GIFS, and memes?

So what's the problem accompanying these trends? Think for a minute, how on a daily, if not hourly, basis, most of us are spoon-fed bits of information which often are context-less, sequence-less, unedited, unverified, sometimes leading to a diet of fake news and conspiracy theories, designed to take captive our time and thought processes. Gradually our culture sees less need for reasoned, logical argument, discussion, reflection, and any other reasoned discourse. Imagery has become more than a supplement to language. Postman suggested imagery began

> to replace it as our dominant means for constraining understanding and testing reality…. The new focus on the image undermined traditional definitions of information, of news, and to a large extent of reality itself.[4]

No wonder some have said that the future belongs to the visually literate. Is there any room left for worship services in which leaders actually read words and thoughts from a printed book, while listeners follow along in their 'book,' as the up-front person gives a verbal exposition of the ideas in that timeless, divinely inspired text?

I'm far from wanting to surrender or abandon the pulpit. Rather than walking away in defeat, I'm more convinced than ever that a case needs to be made for retaining and strengthening the place of Scripture reading and preaching in our worship assemblies. Let's see how we can build a case—a case that needs to reach today's Christians,

---

[4] Postman, 74.

especially young, upcoming church leaders. So let's begin with Scripture narratives.

A historical survey of the Bible's place in worship assemblies

When we study the history of God's people in biblical times we learn that reading and preaching from Scripture were central in the worship assemblies of believers from the earliest of times. Consider four examples:[5]

The Sinai assembly of God's people (Exodus 19:1-8; 24:1-7)

A prototype assembly of God's people gathered at Mount Sinai following their exodus from centuries of slavery in Egypt. As six hundred thousand men, plus women and children, camped at the base of the mountain in the Sinai Peninsula (traditionally identified as Jubal Musa), Moses several times ascended the mountain, where God made himself known, and communicated to his prophet. On one of these mountaintop visits Moses received two stone tablets, on which the finger of God had inscribed the words of the Decalogue—the ten commandments that revealed God's moral law.[6]

As God's people assembled at the base of the mountain, Moses, as God's appointed leader, spoke the words of God to the people:

> Thus you shall say to the house of Jacob, and tell the people of Israel....
> So Moses came and called the elders of the people and set before them all these words that the LORD had commanded him.[7]

---

[5] A case for the importance of reading and preaching from Scripture could be made from a theological perspective rooted in the unique authoritative nature of infallible, inerrant Scripture. Or a case could be made on the basis of historical precedent beginning with the early post-apostolic era down through the Reformation, and extending into more modern times. But in this chapter we will limit our argument to drawing from biblical examples.

[6] Ex. 31:18.

[7] Ex. 19:3, 7.

On another occasion, after spending time on the mountain, Moses descended, built an altar, offered sacrifices, and in this context of worship

> he took the Book of the Covenant and read it in the hearing of the people…and said, 'Behold the blood of the covenant that the LORD has made with you in accordance with all these words.'[8]

What was this Book of the Covenant? It likely refers to the words of God recorded in Exodus chapters 20-23, which include the Decalogue and other divine laws. Some commentators, however, have suggested that it may refer to a book with God's words that has been lost. Later in the Old Testament we see references that may allude to the same Book of the Covenant:

- he [King Josiah] read in their hearing all the words of the Book of the Covenant that had been found in the house of the LORD (2 Kings 23:2);
- keep the Passover to the LORD your God, as it is written in this Book of the Covenant (2 Kings 23:21);
- the Book of Moses (2 Chronicles 25:4) [in the days of King Amaziah, he had access to what's called the Book of Moses, which some suggest may be the same Book of the Covenant referenced at the Mount Sinai assembly].

How did the people at Mount Sinai respond to this public, corporate hearing of God's words? "All the people answered together and said, 'All that the LORD has spoken we will do.'"[9] Later, Scripture reports, "they said, 'All that the LORD has spoken we will do, and we will be obedient.'" [10] This Sinai assembly set a precedent for future assemblies of worship in which the public reading of God's word is a vital essential.

---

[8] Ex. 24:7f.
[9] Ex. 19:8
[10] Ex. 24:7

The Water Gate assembly (Nehemiah 8:1-18)

Generations later, crowds of God's people gathered in the city of Jerusalem around a raised wooden platform. It was now the seventh month, the New Year's Day in the civil calendar. The project of rebuilding the wall of Jerusalem, after its earlier destruction by the Babylonians, had already been completed under the leadership of Nehemiah. Now a large assembly of God's people convened. A platform had been erected in advance in the square near the Water Gate along the walls of ancient Jerusalem on the east side of the city. As God's people stood attentively, Ezra read the Book of the Law of Moses to a spiritually hungry crowd. How appropriate that he be the man in charge, since he was a priest, scribe, and descendent of Aaron, and it was who had led a contingent of Jews back to Jerusalem from their seventy-year Babylonian captivity in a foreign land.

What sets apart this occasion is that for years the practice of public reading of Scripture had been neglected. God's people had ignored the generations-old instructions Moses gave the people earlier:

> At the Feast of Booths, when all Israel comes to appear before the LORD your God at the place that he will choose, you shall read this law before all Israel in their hearing.[11]

Now, years later, God's law was once again read before the assembled Jerusalem crowd. It is likely that the scroll from which Ezra read contained either portions of the Pentateuch or the entire Pentateuch. Since neither the codex nor what we identify as books today had been developed at this early time in history, the "Book of the Law of Moses" from which Ezra read would have been a scroll. Williamson cites Wilhelm In der Smitten, who argues that we have here almost the same formal elements as in a typical synagogue service:

> assembly; request for a reading from the Torah; opening of the Torah-scroll; standing by the people; blessing of the community; response by the community; prostration (?);

---

[11] Deut. 31:10f.

sermon; reading of the Torah; oral Targum with exhortation; departure (for an *agape* meal?).[12]

How did the people receive the word of God?

A careful examination of the text in Nehemiah 8 yields three answers to this question:

They listened with attentiveness

This applies equally to men, women, and children. This reading in Jerusalem was not completed in a jiffy. Daily readings lasted five to six hours. Ezra "read from it facing the square before the Water Gate from early morning until midday."[13] This continued on as "day by day, from the first day to the last day, he read from the Book of the Law of God."[14] One wonders how today's congregations would handle this.

They listened with reverence

They recognised that the LORD God himself was speaking through this reading. The gathered crowd outwardly demonstrated a spirit of reverence by standing during the lengthy readings, raising hands, chanting "Amen, Amen," and even by falling prostrate on the ground in worship.[15] Certainly, external gestures are no automatic guarantee of inner sincerity; however, outward actions, then and now, can be a true expression of the heart-felt reverence that God's people experience when hearing God's word read publicly.

---

[12] H. G. M. Williamson, *Ezra, Nehemiah* (Dallas: Word, 1985), 281, referencing W. T. In der Smitten, *Esra: Quellen, Uberleieferung und Geschichte* (Assen: van Gorcum, 1973), 40-44. Williamson notes that, while this is intriguing, it's a supposition without definitive proof.

[13] Neh. 8:3

[14] Neh. 8:18

[15] Neh. 8:5f.

They also listened with understanding

The crowd included both women and men, but also others "who could understand."[16] The implication seems to be that children who were old enough to comprehend what was happening were also in attendance. The reading was also accompanied with a paraphrased explanation and application of the Scripture to the lives of the hearers. Sounds familiar? Our practice of including biblical sermons in worship services finds a precedent from the earliest history of God's people. We've long been considered a people of the book. It has been suggested, though some commentators question this interpretation, that Ezra may have read the law in Hebrew, and that the Levites then translated it sentence by sentence into the vernacular Chaldean dialect for those unfamiliar with Hebrew. This need for translation comes because the Jews during the captivity spoke Aramaic rather than Hebrew. However, according to Keil, "it is more correct to suppose a paraphrastic exposition and application of the law."[17] This seems to anticipate what we might call expositional preaching, in which a unit of text forms the basis for the sermon.[18]

How did God's people respond to what they received?

They responded with conviction and weeping

During the reading of the word they shed tears of remorse,[19] because the word, serving as a mirror, reflected their failure to measure up to

---

[16] Neh. 8:3

[17] C.F. Keil, *Biblical Commentary on the Books of Ezra, Nehemiah and Esther* (Edinburgh: T. & T. Clark, 1873), 230.

[18] Matthew Henry (in an updated version by M. H. Manser called *The New Matthew Henry Commentary* (Grand Rapids: Zondervan, 2010), makes this application from this text: "It is therefore necessary that those whose role is teaching should explain the word and make it clear. Understandest thou what thou readest? (Ac 8:30) and Have you understood all these things? (Mt 13:51) are good questions to put to listeners, and How should we except someone guide us? is a proper question for them to ask their teachers (Ac 8:31). Reading is good, and preaching good, but explaining brings the reading and preaching together, and so makes the reading more intelligible and the preaching more persuasive."

[19] Neh. 8:9

God's expectations. It was true then, and it is true now, that the words of Scripture are not only designed to comfort the afflicted, but also to afflict the comfortable, pricking the conscience to make one uneasy about sin.

They responded with joy[20]

In keeping with the observance of the Feast of Tabernacles, Nehemiah reminded the people that, once they had grieved, it was not to continue as the prolonged response to what they heard. Yes, it could have helped prepare for joy. Now the desired response was that this be an occasion for eating, drinking, and celebrating. "The joy of the LORD is your strength."[21] Bottom line:

> All the people went on their way to eat and drink and to send portions and to make great rejoicing, because they had understood the words that were declared to them.[22]

They responded with obedience [23]

The people saw their sin revealed in the full light of God's word. The ceremonial law required the regular observance of the Feast of Tabernacles during the seventh month, when they were to construct wooden booths in which they would live for seven days to commemorate their deliverance from Egypt. God's people had disobeyed this command for hundreds of years, but now the public reading and exposition of the word provoked the immediate response of obedience to correct this long-standing neglect. With enthusiasm and haste the people gathered wood to erect the necessary booths.

> And all the assembly of those who had returned from the captivity made booths and lived in the booths, for from the

---

[20] Neh. 8:10-12
[21] Neh. 8:10
[22] Neh. 8:12
[23] Neh. 8:13-17

days of Jeshua the son of Nun to that day the people of Israel had not done so. And there was very great rejoicing.[24]

The people also responded with stimulated appetite

Not only did they listen attentively the first day, but they returned for more the following day. The chapter ends by recording that

> day by day, from the first day to the last day, he [Ezra] read from the Book of the Law of God. They kept the feast seven days, and on the eighth day there was a solemn assembly, according to the rule.[25]

Commentator G. Coleman Luck observes:

> It is an almost invariable rule that earnest listening to the clear teaching of God's word whets the spiritual appetite for more.[26]

How's our appetite?

Nazareth Synagogue assembly (Luke 4:16-30)

We've looked at some Old Testament assemblies. But now we turn to what happened in the New Testament. Did the coming of Christ result in any changes to the worship structure?

Throughout his public ministry Christ followed the same pattern as the Old Testament, demonstrating the ongoing need for public reading and exposition of Scripture. Luke gives an example of one of the times when Christ attended a synagogue service—this time in his home town of Nazareth, where he had spent more than two decades of his youth.

Notice several ways in which that Nazareth service demonstrates the central place of Scripture-reading and teaching in this New Testament assembly of worship:

---

[24] Neh. 8:17
[25] Neh. 8:18
[26] G. Coleman Luck, *Ezra and Nehemiah* (Chicago: Moody, 1961), 113.

- Scripture's centrality was physically evident by the inclusion of a small chest containing scrolls of the Old Testament as the main article of furniture in the synagogue;
- Scripture's priority was also evident in the use of seven readings of Scripture in each service;
- the importance of Scripture was also evident in the appointment of a synagogue official called a chazzan, who was given the responsibility of caring for the scrolls of Scripture (cf. "attendant" in 4:20);
- the centrality of Scripture was also evident in that readers always stood for the public reading of Scripture texts (4:16);
- each service also included an exposition of Scripture following its reading.

Christ himself followed this synagogue pattern, endorsing the emphasis on the reading and exposition of Scripture. This synagogue practice would eventually have a strong influence on the practices of the Christian church.

Early church worship assemblies:

Let's look at several examples of how the precedents from Sinai, the Water Gate, and the synagogue carried over into the life of the early church.

1. When the Apostle Paul started a new church in Ephesus he secured the lecture hall of Tyrannus, where he taught the people daily over a two-year period. Scripture was the source of his teaching (Acts 19:9-10).

2. The Apostle Paul also counselled the young pastor Timothy to "devote yourself to the public reading of Scripture, to exhortation, to teaching" (1 Timothy 4:13). Why? Because Paul was convinced that God chose to use preaching as the means to bring people to Christ: "it pleased God through the folly of what we preach to save those who believe" (1 Corinthians 1:21).

3. When inspired New Testament apostolic letters were first delivered to the early churches, they were read publicly in services:

- when this letter has been read among you, have it also read in the church of the Laodiceans; and see that you also read the letter from Laodicea (Colossians 4:16);
- I put you under oath before the Lord to have this letter read to all the brothers (1 Thessalonians 5:27).

4. The early church recognised leaders whose primary responsibility was to engage in preaching and teaching.

Let the elders who rule well be considered worthy of double honour, especially those who labour in preaching and teaching.[27]

This undoubtedly helped guarantee that preaching remained a central part of weekly gatherings.

This practice continued in the post-apostolic era. In the second century Justin Martyr explained what was then the practice of the church:

On the day called Sunday all who live in cities or in the country gather together in one place, and the memoirs of the apostles or the writings of the prophets are read, as long as time permits. Then, when the reader has finished, the president in a discourse instructs and exhorts to the imitation of these good things.[28]

So if we had visited a church in that era we would have expected to hear the reading and preaching of Scripture in every service of worship.

How to give the Bible the proper place in worship services

In light of all that we find in Scripture, it's not surprising that the Westminster divines, who met in London in the 1640's to develop a

---

[27] 1 Tim. 5:17
[28] Justin Martyr, *First Apology*, 67.3f.

confession, catechism, and directory of worship, stressed the critical place of Scripture in worship assemblies. Here are two examples:

> The essential elements of the congregation's worship of God include the reading of Scripture with godly awe; exegetical preaching with a conscientious hearing of the word reflected in obedience to God, with understanding, faith and reverence.[29]

> Reading of the word in the congregation, being part of the publick worship of God, (wherein we acknowledge our dependence upon him, and subjection to him) and one means sanctified by him for the edifying of his people, is to be performed by the pastors and teachers....
>
> All the canonical books of the Old and New Testament (but none of those which are commonly called *Apocrypha*) shall be publickly read in the vulgar tongue, out of the best allowed translation, distinctly, that all may hear and understand.[30]

Two suggestions

Remember Scripture's unique role

The Bible has a unique, divine origin from God himself, setting it apart from all other books. It doesn't surprise us that, as far back as we can trace the beginnings of the Christian community, the reading and preaching of Scripture occupied an important and essential place. Those who may be quick to predict the demise of sermons would do well to reflect on the chain of historical examples.

From the point at which Jesus began his public ministry by preaching (Mark 1:14-15) and until he returns for his bride, he continues to speak through the means of biblical preaching. It's only right that church leaders should become alarmed and stand their ground when anyone suggests replacing the weekly Sunday worship service sermon with a media production, a musical performance, or other up-dated substitutes.

---

[29] *Westminster Confession of Faith*, 21.5.
[30] *The Directory for the Publick Worship of God*, section 2, paragraphs 1 & 3.

The former President of Covenant Theological Seminary, Bryan Chapell, wrote in the *Covenant Seminary Review*:

While the church's liturgy, theology and history all confirm the public reading of Scripture to be the touchstone of authentic worship, the touchstone is growing increasingly remote and small in some traditions. Often considered mundane—if not superfluous—in many entertainment oriented churches today, the reading of Scripture has been reduced to being a mere introduction to the sermon; an epigram to get the congregation in the mood for the preacher's message. Such trends ultimately will set the church adrift from its biblical distinctives and theocentric moorings. So critical is the reading of Scripture to the mission of the church, that it cannot be regarded lightly in the worship, or training of church leaders.

Recognise preaching as a means of grace

Traditionally Reformed believers have referred not only to the sacraments as 'means of grace,' but also to preaching as an essential means of grace. The *Westminster Shorter Catechism* asks, "How is the word made effectual to salvation?" The answer reads:

The Spirit of God maketh the reading, but especially the preaching of the word an effectual means of convincing and converting sinners, and of building them up in holiness and comfort through faith unto salvation.[31]

If we look at preaching in this light we appreciate why it's so necessary as an ordained means of grace.

The *British Weekly* several years ago printed a letter to the editor:

Dear Editor: I notice that ministers seem to set a great deal of importance on their sermons and spend a great deal of time in preparing them. I have been attending church services quite regularly for the past thirty years and during that time, if I

---

[31] *Westminster Shorter Catechism, Q. 89.*

estimate correctly, I have listened to no less than three thousand sermons. But to my consternation I discover I cannot remember a single one of them. I wonder if a minister's time might be more profitably spent on something else?

That letter caused a flurry of angry responses for weeks. But eventually a single letter closed the debate:

My Dear Sir: I have been married for thirty years. During that time I have eaten 32,850 meals—mostly of my wife's cooking. Suddenly I have discovered that I cannot remember the mention of a single meal. And yet, I received nourishment from every one of them. I have the distinct impression that without them, I would have starved to death long ago.[32]

This letter to the editor may make us smile, but illustrates the point well. Exposure to the public preaching of Scripture and preaching of the word is a means of grace, which is as essential to the nourishment of our souls as regular meals are to the nourishment of our bodies. Reading and preaching from Scripture is part of the dialogue of worship, or what some call the rhythm of revelation/response. Through the reading and preaching of Scripture God speaks to us, in order that we might in turn respond with praise, song, prayer, and offerings.

Final challenge

In the early church the Apostle Paul confessed that he came preaching, not with eloquence or superior wisdom, but

in weakness and in fear and much trembling, and my speech and my message were not in plausible words of wisdom, but in demonstration of the Spirit and of power, that your faith might not rest in the wisdom of men but in the power of God.[33]

---

[32] Cited by S. Heitzig, *Homeland Security: Protecting your Faith, Family, &Future* (Alachua: Bridge-Logos, 2010), 149.
[33] 1 Cor. 2:3-5

For those of us who are called to pulpit ministry, it behoves us to remember that we, like the Apostle Paul are charged with the proclamation of the gospel fearlessly, not in our own strength, but in our weakness. The pull of the world's cultural shifts (from word-based to image-based, from exposition to entertainment) should not detract us from our mission. The reading and preaching from God's word must always remain the hallmark of biblical worship. On this, we must not cave in. God has promised that his word will not return void. Preach it!

Preaching the Prophets: Zechariah[1]

Glendon Thompson

Introduction

"The past is like a foreign country and its texts are written in a foreign language;" so observes Jason Scott-Warren.[2] Although his declaration concerns 'secular' history, in some sense it applies to Scripture generally and the prophetic literature in particular. Of the three divisions of the Old Testament (law, prophets, and writings), none appears more foreign, and consequently suffers greater neglect, than the prophets. Yet inattentiveness to these prophets scarcely portends incipient Marcionism—at least, not among evangelicals. Marcion (died c. AD 160), earned the unenviable distinction of being the first person condemned as a heretic by the church, partly because he repudiated the entire Old Testament—and the Lord it describes—as inferior to the New Testament. Evangelicals, however, bear no resemblance to Marcion. The apparent reticence of some evangelicals to seriously engage the biblical prophets arises, most likely, from complexities in the prophets' messages and not from aberrant views of God. The vast historical, cultural, political, and linguistic differences between ancient and contemporary settings, along with unfamiliar images in the prophets, pose several interpretative challenges for present-day believers. Yet, we approach Scripture with a set of non-negotiable presuppositions, among them the inspiration, authority, and perspicuity of God's word. Since the prophetic corpus belongs to the warp and woof of Christian Scriptures, church members and pastors may not sidestep these biblical books without greatly impoverishing themselves and the congregations they lead.

---

[1] I have known Bob Penhearow for some thirty years, and consider him a valued friend and fellow pilgrim on the road to glory. Many know of his keen interest in the Old Testament and the proclamation of God's word. This contribution straddles both disciplines, and I dedicate it to him, knowing full well that he could have said everything I have written, with even greater precision and insight.

[2] J. Scott-Warren, *Early Modern English Literature* (Cambridge: Polity, 2005), 2.

The divine inspiration of the prophetic books, therefore, renders them essential for Christian reflection and proclamation. But affirming the authority of these inspired books is one thing; proclaiming them is quite another. The subsequent discourse aims to accomplish two modest objectives to encourage even more pulpit exposition of the prophetic literature: (1) to suggest five principles vis-à-vis the proclamation of the prophets, and (2) to provide an example of a sermon one may formulate from a selected text in the book of Zechariah.

Five principles for the proclamation of prophetic texts

The historical-cultural context

First, before attempting to expound the prophets, familiarise yourself with their historical and cultural contexts. The prophets ($n^eb\hat{i}$'$\hat{i}m$), first and foremost, functioned as mouthpieces or spokesmen for God. The Lord chose these servants with, *inter alia*, the following features: membership in the covenant community, an understanding of the spiritual landscape, and inflexible loyalty to the God of Israel. Like the 'judges' before them, the prophets were charismatic, Spirit-filled (Micah 3:8) leaders;[3] as such, they solemnly declared, "Thus says the LORD!"

Further, the biblical prophets received divine communication through various means—dreams, visions, angelic intermediaries, and oracles from God. Additionally, their task involved both 'forthtelling' (exhortation, reproof, correction, and instruction) and 'foretelling' (prediction of events—some immediate and others distant). Although the prophets interpreted God's dealings with his people and predicted future events, they sought chiefly to persuade the community to pursue holiness, love, and obedience to the divine will.[4]

---

[3] Cf. B. W. Anderson, *The Eighth Century Prophets: Amos, Hosea, Isaiah, Micah* (Philadelphia: Fortress, 1978), 1.

[4] A. B. Mickelsen, *Interpreting the Bible* (Grand Rapids: Eerdmans, 1991), 288; cf. M. A. Sweeney, 'The Latter Prophets and Prophecy,' in S. B. Chapman & M. A. Sweeney (eds.), *The Cambridge Companion to the Hebrew Bible/Old Testament* (Cambridge: CUP, 2016), 233.

As a result, the prophetic messages are not abstract, arcane theological treatises reserved for gifted academics. Instead, they are divine missives for the 'cure of souls'—to borrow the language of the Old Testament scholar, Von Rad.[5]

The prophetic work at the heart of this discussion, Zechariah (which serves as an overture to the prophetic literature), is one of the longest books among the twelve Minor Prophets (Hosea, Joel, Amos, Obadiah, Jonah, Micah, Nahum, Habakkuk, Zephaniah, Haggai, Zechariah, and Malachi). Like the Major Prophets (Isaiah, Jeremiah, Ezekiel, and Daniel)—so distinguished because of their larger size— the Minor Prophets share common tropes, such as repentance, covenant fidelity,[6] judgment, the hope of future resurrection and restoration, and the coming of the messianic king. Despite these shared themes, Zechariah resists all attempts to subject his message to a Procrustean bed, making him say the same thing in the same way as all the other prophets.[7] The seer, like his colleagues, addresses 'concrete life situations,' and contributes distinctively to the larger body of prophetic corpus.

Zechariah 1:1 dates the call of the prophet to the second year of the reign of the Persian king, Darius I (522-486 BC). The superscriptions of Haggai and Zechariah reveal that Zechariah began prophesying two months after Haggai (Haggai 1:1; Zechariah 1:1).[8] Accordingly, both men prophesied in the early years after the return of Jews from the Babylonian exile. Cyrus the Great issued an edict in 538 BC, permitting exilic Jews to repopulate Yehud (the Persian name

---

[5] G. Von Rad, *Old Testament Theology, Vol. 2* [English translation by D. M. G. Stalker] (New York: Harper & Row, 1965), 231.

[6] V. H. Matthews, 'Prophetic Literature,' in C. Carmichael (ed.), *The Cambridge Companion to the Bible and Literature*, (Cambridge: CUP, 2020), 105.

[7] Cf. Anderson, 2; D. E. Gowan, *Theology of the Prophetic Books: The Death and Resurrection of Israel* (Louisville: Westminster John Knox, 1998). For an excellent discussion of many of these prophetic themes, see S. Dempster, 'The Tri-Partite Old Testament Canon and the Theology of the Prophetic Word,' in A. T. Abernethy (ed.), *Interpreting the Old Testament Theologically* (Grand Rapids: Zondervan, 2018), 82-94.

[8] R. Lux, 'Zechariah in the Books of Twelve,' in L.-S. Tiemeyer & J. Wöhrle (eds.), *The Book of the Twelve: Composition, Reception, and Interpretation*, Supplements to Vetus Testamentum 184 (Leiden: Brill, 2020), 239, labels these 'partial superscriptions,' but this distinction makes little material difference.

for the sub-province of Judah),[9] rebuild the temple, and restore its furnishings. [10] Approximately fifty thousand Jews accompanied Zerubbabel, the governor, and Joshua, the high priest, to Jerusalem in the initial wave of returnees (Ezra 2, Nehemiah 7). They set about enthusiastically rebuilding the temple, but after erecting its foundation, opposition from the surrounding Gentile population (Ezra 4-5), aided by economic and material hardships,[11] resulted in an eighteen-year hiatus in the temple restoration project. Consequently, the LORD raised Haggai to spur on the people to complete the construction of the temple. He then called Zechariah to complement Haggai's work. J. G. McConville insightfully captures the key difference between these two prophets: Haggai rebuked the spiritual declension of the returnees and exhorted them to rebuild the temple, while Zechariah majored on "the glorious future that awaited Judah."[12] Although Zechariah's prophecy vibrates with irrepressible hope, the seer also points "the community to repentance and spiritual renewal,"[13] and labours "to reorient the postexilic community toward the expectation of the promised restoration."[14] Perhaps Andrew Hill best sums up the prophet's mission:

> Zechariah's message was one of rebuke, exhortation, and encouragement—a tract for troubled times.[15]

Hermeneutical and exegetical considerations

Recognising the historical-cultural setting, though unequivocally important, marks only the preliminary step in the proclamation of prophetic texts. Second, then, biblical exposition should seek to

---

[9] B. E. Kelle, 'Israelite History,' in M. J. Boda & J. G. McConville (eds.), *Dictionary of the Old Testament Prophets* (Downers Grove: IVP, 2012), 415.
[10] Gowan, 162.
[11] Cf. Kelle, 415.
[12] J. G. McConville, *Ezra Nehemiah, and Esther* (Philadelphia: Westminster, 1985), 32.
[13] A. E. Hill, *Haggai, Zechariah, Malachi* (Downers Grove: IVP, 2012), 106.
[14] J. D. Hays, *The Message of the Prophets: A survey of the Prophetic and Apocalyptic Books of the Old Testament* (Grand Rapids: Zondervan, 2010), 346.
[15] Hill, 103.

master the 'rules of engagement,' or the constitutive elements of prophetic interpretation. More particularly, before commencing exegesis, interpreters do well to identify the genre of the text: for example, Hebrew narrative, poetry, wisdom, prophecy, gospel, epistle, or apocalyptic material. Genre contributes variety and, utilising Paul Ricoeur's expression, "a surplus of meaning," to enrich understanding.[16] In this vein, Old Testament narratives encourage readers to view their lives as part of God's grand, unfolding story of covenantal faithfulness to his people. [17] Correspondingly, poetry imparts divine truth aesthetically and often astonishingly, disrupting spiritual sedimentation and complacency, and opening new dimensions of knowing God.[18] Prophecy reminds readers that there is more going on than meets the eye. God works invisibly and ineluctably to fulfill his plans. Even this perfunctory description of how some genres contribute to meaning should convey the significance of 'genre-sensitive reading.'

No doubt, the stock recommendation to consider the genre of texts may exasperate some, but the importance of genre for interpretation calls for repeated, even exaggerated emphasis, like that of E. D. Hirsch: "All understanding of verbal meaning is necessarily genre-bound." [19] Just as the rules of hockey vary from those of basketball, so the rules governing prophecy vary from those governing other biblical genres. So what rules or distinguishing features of prophetic literature should one know to interpret this genre? Peter Gentry lists seven characteristics of prophetic books: they

(1) call people back to the covenant;
(2) announce the themes of judgment and restoration;
(3) employ repetition, a standard feature of Hebrew literature;
(4) contain oracles of divine judgment against the nations;

---

[16] P. Ricoeur, *Interpretation Theory: Discourse and the Surplus of Meaning* (Fort Worth: TCU Press, 1976).
[17] A. T. Abernethy, 'Genre and Theological Vision,' in Abernethy (ed.), 48.
[18] Cf. Abernethy, 56.
[19] E. D. Hirsch, Jr., *Validity in Interpretation* (New Haven: Yale UP, 1967), 76.

(5) describe the future through the use of typology and the new exodus;
(6) use apocalyptic language;
(7) refer to the now and the not yet.[20]

All these constitutive elements of prophetic texts crop up in Zechariah. But a brief comment on two crucial aspects of Zechariah—apocalyptic language and prophetic foreshortening—seems warranted.

The term 'apocalyptic' derives from the word 'apocalypse' in Revelation 1:1. John Collins' most cited definition states that apocalypse is

> a genre of revelatory literature with a narrative framework, in which a revelation is mediated by an otherworldly being to a human recipient, disclosing a transcendent reality which is both temporal, insofar as it envisages eschatological salvation, and spatial insofar as it involves another supernatural world.[21]

A more lucid description of apocalyptic literature depicts it as an intensification of prophecy that employs highly graphic or pictorial images, divides the future into periods, emphasises divine sovereignty, uses angels and visions to disclose the future, and proclaims the ultimate victory of God.[22] A cursory reading of Zechariah reveals the apocalyptic nature of chapters 9-14. The pervasive use of figurative language and symbolic images cautions against an overly literal interpretative approach. One unpacks Zechariah's symbolisms by reading the book alongside other prophetic works and the wider biblical canon.

At the same time, the book of Zechariah evidences 'prophetic foreshortening.' Just as one surveys distant mountain peaks which appear closely grouped, but upon closer inspection vast distances

---

[20] P. J. Gentry, *How to Read and Understand the Biblical Prophets* (Wheaton: Crossway, 2017).
[21] J. J. Collins, 'What is Apocalyptic Literature?' in J. J. Collins (ed.), *The Oxford Handbook of Apocalyptic Literature* (Oxford: OUP, 2014), 2.
[22] See Hays, 54.

separate them, so the prophets tended to perceive future events as occurring within a relatively short period, but in reality, they often await fulfillment in the distant future.[23] The recognition of symbols and foreshortening in Zechariah and the prophets enables one to distinguish between the descriptive (for the original audience) and prescriptive (for later Christians).[24]

The structure of Zechariah

Third, and equally integral, an exposition of the prophets requires some understanding of the structure of the book and the selected passage. Zechariah divides into two main parts: chapters 1-8 (a series of eight visions), and chapters 9-14 (oracles of God's reign over his kingdom). A more detailed outline, like the one proposed below, exposes the major units and themes of Zechariah.

I. The Temple (1:1-8:23)

A. The Prologue and Call to Repentance (1:1-6)

B. Eight Night Visions (1:7-6:15)
1. The Vision of the Multicoloured Horses (1:7-17)
2. The Vision of Horns and Skilled Workers (1:18-21)
3. The Vision of the Measuring Line for Jerusalem (2:1-13)
4. The Vision of the High Priest Joshua in Dirty Clothes (3:1-10)
5. The Vision of the Golden Lampstand (4:1-14)
6. The Vision of the Flying Scroll (5:1-4)
7. The Vision of a Woman inside a Basket Bound for Babylonia (5:5-11)
8. The Vision of Four Chariots and the Crowning of Joshua (6:1-15)

---

[23] Cf. Gentry, 120-122.
[24] Cf. J. D. Nogalski, 'Reading the Book of the Twelve Theologically,' in *Interpretation* 61, No. 2 (April 2007), 115.

C. Fasting and Future Restoration (7:1-8:23)
1. Inquiry about Fasting and the Call for Justice (7:1-14)
2. The Promise of Future Restoration and Joy (8:1-23)

II. The Shepherd-King (9:1-14:21)

A. First Oracle: The Rejected Shepherd (9:1-11:17)
1. The Judgment of Nations (9:1-8)
2. The Coming King on a Donkey and Victory (9:9-10:1)
3. Blessing and Restoration of God's People (10:2-11:3)
4. The Foolish and Worthless Shepherd (11:4-17)

B. Second Oracle: The Shepherd and the Coming King (12:1-14:15)
1. The Deliverance of Jerusalem from the Nations (12:1-9)
2. Mourning for the Pierced One and Sin Cleansed (12:10-13:9)
3. The Universal Reign and Worship of the LORD, the King (14:1-21).[25]

Armed with an outline of the prophetic book and selected passage, and keenly attuned to its literary features (such as keywords and repetitive patterns),[26] the interpreter will extract the 'big ideas' of the passage, which, in all likelihood, will prevent his personal agenda from driving the sermon.

The theological imperative

The pastor and hymn-writer, Isaac Watts (1674-1748), counsels,

---

[25] Adapted from R. S. Hess, *The Old Testament: A Historical, Theological, and Critical introduction* (Grand Rapids: Baker, 2016), 690-691.

[26] See the useful discussion of 'repetition in Hebrew Literature,' in Gentry, 41-58.

When you retire to compose a sermon, let your great end be ever kept in view, i.e., to say something *for the honour of God, for the glory of Christ, for the salvation of the souls of men.*[27]

Watts' interest in theology hardly surprises, given his rich seventeenth-century heritage of biblical exposition. Currently, a growing number of biblical scholars appeal for a return to theological interpretation,[28] which Kevin Vanhoozer defines as

characterized by a governing interest in God, the word and works of God, and by a governing intention to engage in what we might call 'theological criticism.'[29]

Vanhoozer further clarifies that "God must not be an afterthought" in biblical interpretation, and "a properly theological criticism will therefore seek to do justice to the priority of God."[30] Given the foregoing discussion, consider a fourth suggestion for proclaiming the prophets: focus acutely on theology proper, or God. The 'grand subject' of Scripture is the triune Lord: his character, kingdom, purposes, promises, and demands.[31] The prophetic passages, strange as they may appear at times, reveal the glorious God. Berkeley Mickelsen articulates affirmatively:

---

[27] I. Watts, 'An Exhortation to Ministers,' in G. Burder (ed.), *The Works of the Reverend and Learned Isaac Watts*, (London: Barfield, 1810), 11 (https://books. google.ca/books?id=qaYTAAAAYAAJ) [italics original].
[28] See for instance, D. Treier, *Introducing Theological Interpretation of Scripture: Recovering a Christian Practice* (Grand Rapids: Baker, 2008); K. J. Vanhoozer et. al., *Dictionary for Theological Interpretation of the Bible* (Grand Rapids: Baker, 2005); H. Thomas & C. Bartholomew, *A Manifesto for Theological interpretation* (Grand Rapids: Baker, 2016); *Journal of Theological Interpretation* (2007-).
[29] K. J. Vanhoozer, 'What is Theological Interpretation of the Bible?' in *Vanhoozer et al.,* 22.
[30] Vanhoozer, 22.
[31] See M. Williams, *The Doctrine of Salvation in the First Letter of Peter*, Society for New Testament Studies Monograph Series 149 (Cambridge: CUP, 2011), 274.

Whether he is discussing the past, present, or future, the prophet is seeking to make God the most genuine reality that men can know and experience.[32]

For this reason, the door into the theology of Zechariah hinges on facing this question squarely: what does the text say about God?

The name Zechariah means 'the LORD remembers' and it stands as the theme of the book.[33] Each time a person meets Zechariah his name announces that the LORD has not forgotten his people! His message also promises the coming of God's eternal kingdom and his restoration of Israel,[34] not only from physical exile but also from metaphorical exile, or spiritual estrangement in the promised land.[35] Moreover, the prophet makes divine sovereignty over the world, including Persia (chapters 1-2, 6), and the nations surrounding Judea (chapters 9-11), a central plank in his theology. Zechariah develops the motif of divine sovereignty, primarily through the ubiquitous divine title, *Yahweh ṣᵉḇā'ôt*—the LORD of hosts/heavenly armies. The epithet surfaces forty-five times in Zechariah (more than any other minor prophet); eighteen of these appear in chapter 8, ostensibly to guarantee God's pledge of future restoration. The designation "LORD of hosts" alludes to God as the divine warrior.[36] He possesses invincible power to fulfil all his promises. Zechariah also portrays the righteous God, who (in keeping with the wider prophetic literature) demands justice for the poor, aliens, and orphans (cf. Zechariah 7:8-10).[37]

But if proclaiming Zechariah and the prophetic literature requires concentration on theology, it must also zero in on Christology. As a result, a second vital question one should pose to the text is: how does this passage find its fulfillment in the eschatological prophet, Jesus

---

[32] Mickelsen, 287.

[33] Hays, 345.

[34] B. T. Arnold & B. E. Beyer, *Encountering the Old Testament* (Grand Rapids: Baker, 2015), 458.

[35] Cf. M. A. Halvorson-Taylor, *Enduring Exile: The Metaphorization of Exile in the Hebrew Bible,* Supplements to Vetus Testamentum 141 (Leiden: Brill, 2011), 198.

[36] Cf. Ex. 15:3; Ps. 24:8; Isa. 43:13; Zeph. 3:17.

[37] R. L. Foster, *The Theology of the Books of Haggai and Zechariah* (Cambridge: CUP, 2020), 200.

Christ? When one reads texts in Zechariah with this question in mind, they offer up a wealth of allusions to Christ. Alberto Ferreiro identifies Zechariah among the most quoted or alluded to books in the New Testament. Revelation contains twenty-three allusions to Zechariah, the Gospels, twelve, along with additional allusions in other books, among them, Jude 9.[38] More specifically, only Isaiah refers to Christ more than Zechariah.[39] Mark Black catalogues seven Zecharian allusions to Christ that the Gospels cite:

(1) the king who enters Jerusalem on a donkey [9:9; cf. Matthew 21:5; Mark 11:7-10];
(2) the one whose blood re-establishes the covenant [9:11; Matthew 26:28; Mark 14:24];
(3) the shepherd valued at thirty silver pieces [11:13; Matthew 27:9-10];
(4) the one who is pierced and mourned [12:10; Matthew 24:30; Mark 14:62; John 19:37];
(5) the rejected shepherd whose sheep scatter [13:7-9; Matthew 26:31; Mark 14:27];
(6) the one who ushers in the resurrection age [14:5; Matthew 25:31; 27:51-53];
(7) the one who brings about the purified temple [14:21; Matthew 21:12-13; Mark 11:15-17].[40]

Whether or not one agrees with all the allusions to Christ Black adduces, this much seems clear: Zechariah is 'a little Isaiah.' Consequently, one ought to read Zechariah Christologically and expound the Christ foretold by the prophet and later manifested in history.

---

[38] A. Ferreiro, ed. 'The Twelve Prophets,' in T. C. Oden (ed.), *Ancient Christian Commentary on Scripture: Old Testament*, Vol. XIV (Downers Grove: IVP, 2003), 230.
[39] Hill, 103.
[40] M. Black, 'The Messianic Use of Zechariah 9-14 in Matthew, Mark, and the Pre-Markan Tradition,' in P. Gray & G. R. O'Day (eds.), *Scripture and Traditions: Essays on Early Judaism and Christianity in Honor of Carl R. Holladay*, Supplements to Novum Testamentum 129 (Leiden: Brill, 2008), 97-98; cf. A. R. Petterson, 'Messianic Expectations in Zechariah and Theological Interpretation,' in Abernethy (ed.), 203-214.

Homiletical reflections

After completing the heavy lifting of exegesis and theological reflection, the question of *how* to declare the biblical prophets becomes the most pressing issue. Today, pastors may not encounter God in the burning bush, experience his terrifying theophanic descent on Mount Sinai, or hear his withering roar from Zion (cf. Amos 1:2), but somewhat analogous to the prophets of old, we also occupy a 'prophetic' ministry, in the sense of a divine call to proclaim the revealed word. In this regard, a fifth principle governs biblical proclamation: divide Zechariah into large, but manageable units and expound them with an eye to the contemporary audience, always preaching for a verdict in reliance upon the Holy Spirit.

Picking up on the suggestion to unpack larger units of Zechariah, a sermon on chapter 1, entitled, for example, 'the Lord who remembers,' could divide into three parts: the divine summons to repentance (verses 1-6), the divine assurance of zeal for his people (verses 7-17), and the divine pledge to vanquish his enemies (verses 18-21).

Chapter 2 narrates the vision of 'the man with the measuring line,' and the text breaks helpfully into three sections: God's children protected by divine fire (verses 1-5), God's children precious in God's sight (verses 6-9), and God's children promised God's presence (verses 10-13).

Chapter 3 revolves around the cleansing of Joshua, the high priest. The passage encapsulates 'the gospel according to Zechariah.' The replacement of Joshua's dirty laundry with clean clothing resonates in the New Testament theme of justification (alien righteousness) and the attendant freedom from condemnation (Romans 8:31-34).[41] How about a sermon that explores the Lord as our defence counsel (verses 1-2), the cleansing from sin (verses 3-5), and the promised redeemer-king (verses 6-10)?

The signally important vision of the lampstand in chapter 4 centres on the indispensable role of the Holy Spirit in reviving

---

[41] R. B. Dillard and T. Longman III, *An Introduction to the Old Testament* (Grand Rapids: Zondervan, 1994), 434.

Jerusalem and rebuilding the temple. The key idea of the passage surfaces in verse 6: "Not by might nor by power, but by my Spirit, says the LORD of hosts." A sermon under the following rubrics— God's work is accomplished by God's Spirit (verses 1-6), God's work depends upon God's grace (verse 7), and God's work should not be despised in the day of small things (verses 8-10), may assist in unlocking the theological significance of the passage.

The visions of 'the flying scroll' and 'the woman in a flying basket' (chapter 5), add high drama—even tension—to the seer's nightly visions. What do they mean? The massive scroll, approximately ten feet by thirty feet (similar to a gigantic advertisement banner trailed by a light aircraft) represents the "divine word in a special edition for the spiritually blind."[42] These two visions dwell on God's determination to remove unrepentant sinners (verses 1-4) and sin *itself* from among the redeemed (verses 5-11).[43]

Chapters 7-8, the literary bridge between the two divisions of Zechariah (1-6 and 9-14) comprise a large, unified block of material that spells out how the people of God should live awaiting the messianic king. The passage teaches that the Lord requires God-centredness (7:1-7), God-likeness (7:8-14), and God-produced joyfulness (8:1-23).

On one level, the final division of Zechariah (chapters 9-14) poses a greater challenge to interpreters than chapters 1-8 because of its sustained apocalypticism. Yet, on another level, chapters 9-14 offer fruitful avenues for gospel proclamation due to the recurring references to the coming messianic king. Consequently, the portrayal of 'the king on a donkey' (chapter 9) lends itself to a discourse on the humility, righteousness (verse 9), and victory of the redeemer-king (verses 10-17).[44]

Further, the shepherd motif in the interpretatively challenging chapters 10-11 provides a *via media* between the extremes of a superficial reading of the text, or an excessively detailed study that severely tests the limits of a congregation's patience. Teasing out the

---

[42] Gentry, 98.
[43] For comments on chapter 6, see below.
[44] See, G. Van Groningen, *Messianic Revelation in the Old Testament*, (Grand Rapids: Baker, 1990), 899.

shepherd motif against the backdrop of false shepherds (10:1-3a), the good shepherd (10:3b-12), the rejected shepherd (11:4-17), and the stricken shepherd (13:7-9) finds suggestive resonances in Christ, the good (John 10:11), great (Hebrews 13:20) and chief shepherd (1 Peter 5:4). Similarly, the notion of a crucified Messiah emerges in chapters 12-13. One option is to develop the themes of the pierced one (12:10-14), the fountain opened for cleansing (13:1), and the effects of cleansing (13:2-9).

Finally, Zechariah 14 warrants a presentation that takes into account the coming Day of the LORD (verses 1-2), the LORD, the warrior-king (verses 3-15), and the worship of the sovereign king (verses 16-21).

Also, proclaiming Zechariah (or any biblical text for that matter) involves awareness of the three R's of biblical exposition—relevance, response, and reliance. The temptation in any biblical oration is to expend considerable energy on deciphering 'the world behind the text' (historical-cultural setting) and the 'world within the text' (historical-grammatical exegesis), but give relatively scant attention to 'the world before the text' (the contemporary setting). Admittedly, the hard part of preaching entails bridging the gaping chasm between the ancient text and the contemporary audience. But if a sermon on an Old Testament text is to 'live,' to resonate in the twenty-first century, the communicator must translate the biblical message so that his audience comprehends and internalises it. Making the sermon richly meaningful requires, among other things, identifying the trans-temporal concerns, truths, and spiritual needs a biblical passage addresses and then applying, what Nicholas Wolterstorff felicitously labels, "the divine discourse" to the present situation,[45] employing current idioms and suitable illustrations.

Yet, even if one sensitively relates the message of Zechariah to twenty-first-century hearers, the duty of proclaiming the prophetic word remains incomplete without a conscious appeal for a response.

---

[45] N. Wolterstorff, *Divine Discourse: Philosophical Reflections on the Claim that God Speaks* (Cambridge: CUP, 1995). For a pointed, howbeit, critique of Wolterstorff, see, H. A. Blocher 'God and the Scripture Writers: The Question of Double Authorship,' in D. A. Carson (ed.), *The Enduring Authority of the Christian Scriptures* (Grand Rapids: Eerdmans, 2016), 519-521.

Preaching is fundamentally paraenetic or hortatory, imparting truth, but also demanding a heart-response to God. Here, of course, the servant of the Lord should exercise due care when pressing the claims of the Old Testament, since believers are members of the new, not the old, covenant. Still, the ethical injunctions of the old covenant continue in the new covenant, pedagogically informing its higher moral obligations,[46] summed up in the love command (cf. Romans 13:9-10; Galatians 5:14). Thus, preaching the prophetic word entails preaching for a verdict.

Admittedly, no speaker can autonomously foster even one godly thought in another person's heart. Precisely for this reason, proclaiming prophetic texts like Zechariah demands complete reliance upon the one who alone changes lives—the Holy Spirit. In this regard, "one great and general rule," according to Isaac Watts,

> is, ask advice of heaven by prayer about every part of your preparatory studies; seek the direction and assistance of the Spirit of God, for inclining your thoughts to proper subjects, for guiding you to proper Scriptures, and framing your whole sermon both as to the matter and manner, that it may attain the divine and sacred ends proposed.[47]

Such dependence upon the Spirit certainly includes sermon delivery. Nothing else but the Spirit's help will do. To reiterate, Zechariah himself encourages dependence upon the Spirit in doing God's work: "Not by might, nor by power, but by my Spirit, says the LORD of hosts" (Zechariah 4:6).

It may be worthwhile to conclude the discourse on preaching prophetic texts with a practical demonstration; hence, the subsequent

---

[46] G. J. Wenham, *Story as Torah: Reading the Old Testament Ethically* (Edinburgh: T. & T. Clark, 2000), 132, for example, convincingly demonstrates the relevance of the Old Testament for New Testament ethics by indicating Paul's usage of four lessons from Exodus and Numbers in 1 Corinthians 10 to enjoin ethical demands: "'Do not be idolaters as some of them were' (1 Cor. 10:7; cf. Ex. 32); 'We must not indulge in immorality as some of them did' (1 Cor. 10:8; cf. Num. 25); 'We must not put the Lord to the test, as some of them did' (1 Cor. 10:9; cf. Num. 21:4-9); 'Nor grumble as some of them did' (1 Cor. 10:10; cf. Num. 16)."
[47] Watts, 11.

material assimilates in a sermonic form (and for illustrative purposes) some of the suggested proposals to explicate the biblical prophets.

A little exercise in expounding prophetic texts: Zechariah 6:1-15

The chariots of the LORD and the Branch.[48]

In the novel *1984,* George Orwell envisions a future despotic state— "Ingsoc." The ubiquitous slogan, "Big Brother is watching you," summarises the absolute control the state would exercise—even over the beliefs of its citizens. The 'Ministry of Truth,' for Orwell, dictates beliefs, and the 'thought police' enforce compliance. Today, some Christians consider life under a pandemic as surviving a mild version of 'Big Brother,' a secular society, ignorant and antagonistic to biblical truths and priorities. Such thinking can easily result in a sense of utter powerlessness and despair. Thankfully, Zechariah 6:1-15 provides enduring lessons for living in this peculiar hour.

The post-exilic prophet, Zechariah, addressed Jews who had recently returned from exile under an ancient and violent 'Big Brother,' the Babylonians. They besieged Jerusalem in 586 BC, looted and burnt its temple, captured King Zedekiah, and callously slaughtered his sons before his eyes, before blinding him and hauling him off, unceremoniously, with the children of Judah, to exile in Babylon. But after approximately seventy years, Jews reoccupied Jerusalem and began rebuilding the temple; however, local hostilities forced the abandonment of temple reconstruction for eighteen years. Nevertheless, the LORD sent Zechariah to encourage his people through a series of visions and oracles. In the final vision (6:1-8), the prophet perceives four chariots, drawn by four horses, coming from between two bronze mountains and galloping off to the four corners of the earth. Verses 9-15 consist of a prophecy regarding the future Branch, who will build the temple of God. The two divisions of chapter 6 (at places, an exegetical obstacle course)[49] relate one basic

---

[48] A sermon preached at Jarvis Street Baptist Church, Toronto, 7th February, 2021.
[49] The comments on some textual issues in Zechariah 6 serve only to justify the author's exegetical choices and neither suggests nor commends burdening sermons with discussions of disputed textual matters.

message: God's absolute sovereignty over history.[50] Some posit that the ruling or sovereign Lord is the main theme of Scripture; everything flows from it; everything is subordinate to it.[51] Be that as it may, Zechariah 6 underlines three advantageous aspects of divine sovereignty.

The powerful sovereignty of God

First, the text stresses the sovereign power of God (1-4). Travis 'the Beast' Bagent is a world champion arm-wrestler. He overpowers most opponents with consummate ease, and wears down tenacious ones with persistent strength. To all comers, he declares 'resistance is futile.' But in the contest of strength, God brooks no rival. Zechariah underscores the absolute power of God to a dispirited people likely questioning: 'Is our God stronger than pagan gods?' The opening scene of the night vision responds with an emphatic, 'yes!' Zechariah states,

> Again I lifted my eyes and saw, and behold, four chariots came out from between two mountains. And the mountains were mountains of bronze (verse 1).

While many of the details in the vision function as props, the "bronze" mountains seemingly symbolise the gateway of heaven.[52] Zechariah observes four chariots emerging from God's impregnable dwelling place that none can take by storm.[53] The vision revolves around these four chariots—later described as the "four winds of heaven" (verse 5). In the ancient world, chariots operated similarly to our limousines. They transported high-ranking officials and wealthy people. More

---

[50] Cf. P. C. Craigie, *Twelve Prophets, Vol. 2* (Philadelphia: Westminster, 1985), 186; C. L. Meyers & E. Meyers, *Haggai, Zechariah 1-8* (Garden City: Doubleday, 1987), 318.
[51] L. Köhler, *Old Testament Theology* [English translation by A. S. Todd] (Philadelphia: Westminster, 1957), 30.
[52] J. G. Baldwin, *Haggai, Zechariah, Malachi* (Downers Grove: IVP, 1972), 131; cf. Craigie, 186; T. McComiskey, 'Zechariah,' in T. McComiskey (ed.), *The Minor Prophets* (Grand Rapids: Baker, 1998), 1106.
[53] Baldwin, 131.

significantly, chariots in the Old Testament also epitomised military power, the equivalent of today's battle tanks. The prophet Isaiah employs the imagery of chariots in this sense, to depict divine strength:

> For behold, the LORD will come in fire,
> and his chariots like the whirlwind,
> to render his anger in fury,
> and his rebuke with flames of fire.[54]

Thus, the chariots in Zechariah's vision signify the 'divine omnipotence' going forth to intervene in human affairs,[55] to wage war, and to judge. The postexilic community sorely needed such a message—just as we do today.

The vision also highlights God's sovereign power through the description of the horses accompanying the chariots:

> The first chariot had red horses, the second black horses, the third white horses, and the fourth chariot dappled horses—all of them strong (verses 2-3).

Since horses appear in the first and eighth visions (1:7-17; 6:1-8), they bookend the entire night-visions.[56] Nonetheless, critical differences exist between these visions. For instance, the first vision excludes chariots, the colours of the horses in both visions differ, and the visions serve different purposes.[57] According to Mark Boda,

> Whereas the first vision depicted horses fresh from a reconnaissance mission for which speed was essential, this

---

[54] Isa. 66:15.
[55] Meyers & Meyers, 318; Hill, 171.
[56] Cf. Hill, 174.
[57] Despite speculations over the significance of the horses' colours (especially in light of Rev. 6:1-8), Zechariah offers no explanation; therefore, it may be safer to refrain from reading too much into the various colours; cf. R. L. Smith, *Micah-Malachi* (Waco: Word, 1984), 214.

final vision pictures horses embarking on a retribution campaign for which power is crucial.[58]

Boda rightly views the horses as emblems of power because Zechariah depicts the red, black, white, and dappled horses as "strong" (verse 3). He reiterates the might of the horses in verse 7, leaving little doubt that they project irresistible power to conquer: "When the strong horses came out, they were impatient to go and patrol the earth" (verse 7a). Thus, for Zechariah, God rules supremely.

Furthermore, the recurring verb, "come/go [out]" (*yāṣā'*), points to God's powerful rule. The verb *yāṣā'* occurs seven times (verses 1, 5, 6 [thrice], 7, 8) and frames the vision.[59] Why the sustained insistence that horses were 'going out?' To draw attention to *motion* in the vision.[60] Zechariah's vision bristles with activity. The prophet perceives horses coming forth from between two mountains (verse 1), having earlier presented themselves before the LORD (verse 5). They are chomping at the bits, so to speak, "impatient to go and patrol the earth" (verse 7). Clearly, 'things are happening' in the eighth vision— as in the preceding visions. (For instance, artisans advance to destroy the nations that destroyed Judah, an individual surveys Jerusalem, the high priest receives divine cleansing, and a scroll and basket fly through the air).[61] The vision of chariots depicts movement, and dispels any notion that God's power is static. Seventeenth and eighteenth-century deists posited a disengaged, inactive God. Like a clockmaker, he winds up the world and leaves it to unravel autonomously. Some CEO's adopt a hands-off management style— not so the LORD. Zechariah conceives divine power as dynamic. The LORD is actively involved in the world. With unceasing strength and vigour, he enters the fray to gather his children and scatter his foes. He will not cease until he vanquishes all his enemies.

Verse 8 describes the unqualified victory of the LORD over his adversaries:

---

[58] M. J. Boda, *Haggai, Zechariah*, (Grand Rapids: Zondervan, 2004), 319,
[59] Baldwin, 8.
[60] D. L. Petersen, 'Zechariah's Visions: A Theological Perspective,' in *Vetus Testamentum* XXXIV, 2 (April 1984), 199.
[61] See Peterson, 199f.

Then he cried to me, 'Behold, those who go towards the north country have set my Spirit at rest in the north country.'

Baldwin sums up the thoroughness of the divine conquest: "No more remains to be done."[62] Zechariah perceives the LORD carrying the day. Neither human ingenuity, nor political machination, nor demonic influence will succeed against the LORD.

The prophet thus presents a tantalising vignette of the invisible power of Israel's God. He exercises incomparable and indefeasible strength to uphold the stars, so that "by the greatness of his might, and because he is strong in power not one is missing" (Isaiah 40:26). By that same power, he strengthens his people to prevail against overwhelming odds. 2 Chronicles 13 is a case in point. The chronicler narrates how Israel's army 'outnumbered and outmaneuvered' the forces of Judah, but "Judah prevailed, because they relied on the LORD" (verse 18). In sum, Zechariah's vision heralds God's ability to sustain and empower a weak and subordinate postexilic community. Know that the same Lord also bears you up in all your trials and temptations by his phenomenal strength:

Once God has spoken;
twice have I heard this:
that power belongs to God.[63]

The universal sovereignty of God

Second, the text shines the spotlight on the sovereign dominion of God. Most nations have abolished monarchical rule, although some nations still preserve a royal head of state, such as King Salman of Saudi Arabia. While these royal personages usually possess enormous wealth and influence, they rule over a markedly delineated and limited sphere. Conversely, the Lord exercises worldwide rule. Zechariah dwells on the cosmic reign of God, first, through the designation, "the LORD of all the earth." The prophet enquires about the four horses

---

[62] Baldwin, 140.
[63] Ps. 62:11.

(verse 4), and the angel replies, "These are going out to the four winds of heaven, after presenting themselves before the LORD of all the earth" (verse 5). The title, "the Lord of the whole earth" appeared previously in the fifth vision. There, Zechariah perceived a lampstand with seven lamps and two olive trees beside it. The angel clarified that the two olive trees are the "two anointed ones [Joshua and Zerubbabel] who stand beside the Lord of the whole earth" (4:14). Zechariah thus uses the expression, "the LORD of all the earth" to portray the sovereign rule of God over creation. The Lord announces, "all the earth is mine" (Exodus 19:5): mankind and beast (Exodus 13:2), the land (Leviticus 25:23), the beast of the forest, the cattle on a thousand hills (Psalm 50:10), indeed, the world and its fullness (Psalm 50:12). Every microbe, then, and every blade of grass, belongs to the "LORD of all the earth" (6:5). And since he rules the world not as its titulary head, but its rightful king, he is the universal Lord.

Aside from the designation, "the LORD of all the earth," Zechariah demonstrates God's worldwide reign by tracking the directions of the horses' travel: "The chariot with the black horses goes towards the north country, the white ones go after them, and the dappled ones go towards the south country" (verse 6). The black and white horses dash towards the north, in the vicinity of Babylon, while the dappled horses depart for the south, perhaps in the vicinity of Egypt. Strikingly, the passage passes silently over the direction of the red horses. But the presence of four teams of horses intimates that they hasten to the four points of the compass. Verse 7 further supports the idea that the horses range throughout the world:

When the strong horses came out, they were impatient to go and patrol the earth. And he said, 'Go, patrol the earth.' So they patrolled the earth.

At the same time, verse 6 concentrates on the northern route of the black and white horses because this region

had painful associations for the postexilic community, for it
was the direction from which their former enemies had entered
the land to take the earlier generations into captivity.[64]

On this reading, the northern direction of the horses drives home
God's universal sovereignty over Israel's and Judah's enemies. The
Babylonians, followed by the Medes and Persians, ostensibly had no
qualms declaring themselves 'masters and commanders' of the
ancient world. But the LORD declares, 'Not so fast!' His 'chariots of
wrath' head unimpeded into the supposed territory of the pagan gods,
because, as the Puritan theologian, William Ames (1576-1633)
observes, the God of the whole earth can neither be excluded from
any place nor be confined to any place.[65]

Such is the reassuring nature of the vision. The little community
in Zechariah's day need not assimilate into the pagan culture,
succumb to the counsel of despair, or take matters into their own
hands and lash out against the powerful, like amateur investors in
Gamestop (the videogame retail chain) did recently. Upon learning
that Wall Street investors were betting against Gamestop shares,
hoping the stock price would fall, these untrained investors decided to
fight back against big business, and strike a blow for the 'little man.'
They snapped up Gamestop shares, causing the stock price to rise
meteorically (at one point, to a thousand percent!), in the process
wiping out millions of dollars belonging to wealthy investors. God's
people though pressured by the world neither cower nor rage; things
are under control; the chariots of God are everywhere.

The gracious sovereignty of God

Third, the text throws into relief the sovereign grace of God (6:9-15).
'Grace?' you say? Where is grace in the passage? While the term
'grace' surfaces only once (in verse 14 as "Hen," another name for
Josiah), the concept permeates the entire chapter. Consider that in
verses 1-8, the horses dash forth to judge sinful nations, especially

---

[64] McComiskey, 1109.
[65] W. Ames, *The Marrow of Theology* [1639] (Grand Rapids: Baker, 1968 reprint),
86.

Babylon. Judgment against this ancient foe conversely results in liberation for Israel—a gracious act of God in itself. Although Cyrus the Great commissioned the repatriation of exilic Jews to Jerusalem, ultimately, the post-exilic community owed its deliverance to the indomitable grace of God, in fulfillment of Jeremiah's prophecy (Jeremiah 29:10). The motif of sovereign grace reaches the high-water mark in the second—and climactic—section of the chapter (verses 9-15). It contains the divine promise of a greater blessing than the second temple: the coming kingdom of the Lord Jesus Christ.[66]

The oracle in verses 9-15 commences with the divine command for Zechariah to visit the house of Josiah and receive silver and gold from recent Jewish returnees, Heldai, Tobijah, and Jedaiah (verses 9-10). The Lord also instructs the seer to fashion a crown[67] from the silver and gold and place it on the head of Joshua, the high priest (verse 11). The crowning of the high priest represents a decidedly unusual act since the high priest did not customarily wear a crown. Joshua's crown, therefore, arrestingly symbolises the uniting of two offices, king and priest, in one person. Although a plausible case exists for viewing Joshua or Zerubbabel as the bearer of the twin-office,[68] verse 12 seemingly militates against this interpretation:

> And say to him, 'Thus says the LORD of hosts, "Behold, the man whose name is the Branch: for he shall branch out from his place, and he shall build the temple of the LORD."'

Since the verse employs the indefinite, "Behold 'a' man,"[69] (not 'the' man), and locates the Branch in the future (cf. Zechariah 3:8), to interpret the Branch (*ṣemaḥ*) as Joshua, Zerubbabel—or anyone

---

[66] See W. C. Kaiser, Jr., 'Micah, Nahum, Habakkuk, Zephaniah, Haggai, Zechariah, Malachi,' in L. J. Ogilvie (ed.), *The Preacher's Commentary, Vol. 23* (Nashville: Nelson, 1992), 359.

[67] The text speaks of "crowns." Perhaps Joshua wore a combined crown made of gold and silver. For a discussion of the alternative explanations of "crowns," see Baldwin, 133.

[68] E.g., Sweeney, 245, contends for Joshua as the person to whom the verse refers.

[69] McComiskey, 1113.

else—seems unwarranted.[70] *Şemaḥ* denotes the Davidic Messiah.[71]
Jeremiah reinforces the idea of the messianic Branch:

> Behold, the days are coming, declares the LORD, when I will
> raise up for David a righteous Branch, and he shall reign as
> king and deal wisely, and shall execute justice and
> righteousness in the land.[72]

Verses 12b-13 manifest the sovereign grace of God in the person and
work of the Branch. First, "he shall branch out" (verse 12) or, in the
language of Isaiah, grow up before the LORD "like a young plant and
like a root out of dry ground" (Isaiah 53:2). Although unimpressive
and despised by men, the Branch is exalted in the sight of God.[73]
Second, "he shall build the temple of the LORD" (verse 12). Verse 13
emphatically restates the successful labour of the Branch: "It is he
who shall build the temple of the LORD." Not Joshua, but he, the
Branch, will build the LORD's temple. Since the construction of the
Jerusalem temple was already in progress, the future building program
of the Branch alludes to the kingdom Christ would inaugurate. Third,
the Branch "shall bear royal honour" or be exalted in splendour.
Fourth, he "shall sit and rule on his throne." Fifth, he "shall be a priest
on his throne," and sixth, "the counsel of peace shall be between them
both" (verse 13). Possibly, the latter clause treats the two roles of king
and priest as "symbolic personages" existing harmoniously in the
Lord Jesus Christ.[74] Besides, the New Testament repeatedly discloses
that the Lord Jesus Christ is both king and priest.[75]

The chapter closes with two observations. First, the crown
adorning Joshua's head will remain in the temple to remind Helem,
Tobijah, Jedaiah, and Hen (nicknames for Heldai, Tobijah, Jedaiah,

---

[70] See W. H. Rose, 'Zechariah and the Ambiguity of Kingship in Postexilic Israel,' in
I. Provan & M. J. Boda (eds.), *Let us Go up to Zion: Essays in Honour of H. G.
Williamson on the Occasion of his Sixty-Fifth Birthday* (Leiden: Brill, 2012), 221.
[71] Baldwin, 136-137.
[72] Jer. 23:5; cf. 33:15.
[73] Kaiser, 357.
[74] Cf. McComiskey, 1116; J. Calvin, *Commentaries on the Twelve Minor Prophets,
Vol. 5: Zechariah and Malachi* [1559] (Grand Rapids: Baker, 1979 reprint), 155f.
[75] Cf. 1 Tim. 6:15; Heb. 8:1; Rev. 19:16; cf. McComiskey, 'Zechariah,' 1116.

and Josiah?),[76] and future generations, of the coming Christ (verse 14). The crown thus represents the promise of redemptive grace to all God's people through the future king-priest.[77]

Next, verse 15 reveals human involvement in the future eschatological kingdom:

> And those who are far off shall come and help to build the temple of the LORD. And you shall know that the LORD of hosts has sent me to you. And this shall come to pass if you will diligently obey the voice of the LORD your God.

The reference to "those who are far off" comprises repentant (diaspora) Jews and Gentiles. Altogether, verse 15 discloses God's sovereign grace in the gift of Christ to Jews and Gentiles[78] (and when Jews and Gentiles comprise the kingdom, people will acknowledge the LORD's servant, the prophet). Nevertheless, Zechariah teaches that to participate in the reign of God, one must evince wholehearted obedience to the coming king.[79]

The message of God's sovereign power, dominion, and grace must clarify our vision. Like Zechariah's post-exilic community, we sense the acute tension of living betwixt 'present realisation' and eschatological fulfillment.[80] Nonetheless, our survival and progress ultimately depend upon God's greatness—not our abilities. Thus, we accomplish God's work in our generation not based on numerical or financial strength, but only through God's sovereign power. He uses weak and 'insignificant' people to accomplish his will (1 Corinthians 1:26-29).

Moreover, divine sovereignty invites greater trust in God. People often comment dejectedly, the more things change the more they remain the same, but the vision of chariots reinforces this fundamental

---

[76] D. L. Petersen, *Haggai and Zechariah 1-8* (Philadelphia: Westminster, 1984), 278.
[77] Cf. Craigie, 188.
[78] Cf. Zech. 2:11; 8:22; Isa. 2:2-4; 56:6f; 60:1-7.
[79] Cf. K. L. Baker, 'Zechariah,' in F. E. Gaebelein (ed.), *The Expositor's Bible Commentary, Vol. 7* (Grand Rapids: Zondervan, 1985), 641.
[80] W. A. VanGemeren, *Interpreting the Prophetic Word: An Introduction to the Prophetic Literature of the Old Testament* (Grand Rapids: Zondervan, 1990), 185.

truth: "things are on the move."[81] God is even now working invisibly, yet sovereignly judging sinners, lovingly and irresistibly drawing his elect into his kingdom, and sustaining them with all-sufficient grace. Trust the gracious Lord in all your trials and sufferings.

Once more, the Lord in his sovereign grace has sent the Branch, the Lord Jesus Christ. He is our king and great high priest, who established the reign of God on earth through his life, his ministry, and his death and resurrection. Therefore, align yourself with the crucified and risen Christ and hearken to his voice in the obedience of faith. Remember, to participate in the kingdom of God (serve its purposes and enjoy its blessings) you must submit completely to Christ. Close with him and await the future, jubilant cry: "Hallelujah! For the Lord our God the Almighty reigns" (Revelation 19:6).[82]

---

[81] Petersen, 'Zechariah's Visions,' 200.

[82] In addition to commentaries on Zechariah already cited, the following two are also recommended: M. J. Boda, *The Book of Zechariah* (Grand Rapids: Eerdmans, 2016); B. G. Webb, *The Message of Zechariah* (Downers Grove: IVP. 2003).

Biblical Support for the Practice of Biblical Meditation

Ron Barnes

Introduction

Biblical meditation is "deep thinking on the truths and spiritual realities revealed in Scripture for the purposes of understanding, application and prayer."[1] The premise of this paper is that the practice of biblical meditation is clearly commanded and encouraged in both the Old and New Testaments. This will be demonstrated by examining the various occurrences of the most common Hebrew words translated as meditation, *hāgāh* and *śîyaḥ*. An examination of the lexical definitions of these two words will help further to define and clarify the meaning of meditation. A survey of their occurrences will demonstrate how biblical meditation is practised and commanded in the Old Testament. An examination of *meletaō*, the Septuagint equivalent to *hāgāh*, will further demonstrate the consistency of the meaning of the word 'meditate' in the New Testament as well as the Old.

This paper will include an exegesis of Old Testament passages that command and describe the method and purpose of biblical meditation. An exegesis of three New Testament passages will further support the thesis that biblical meditation is commanded as a spiritual discipline in the New as well as in the Old Testament Scriptures.

Usage and definition of *hāgāh*

This Hebrew root occurs twenty-four times as a verb, twenty-two times in the common verb stem Qal, and twice in the causative stem Hiphil. The root is used also in other Semitic languages: in Aramaic

---

[1] D. S. Whitney, *Spiritual Disciplines for the Christian Life* (Colorado Springs: NavPress, 1991), 48.

it means "to think or meditate, murmur or speak," and in Syriac the noun, *heghyona,* is defined as "reading, thinking, and meditating."[2]

Hāgāh occurs primarily in poetry, especially in the Psalms and Isaiah. Its basic meaning is a low sound, characteristic of the moaning of a dove (Isaiah 38:14) or the growling of a lion over its prey (Isaiah 31:4).[3] In Job 37:2 it refers to soft thunder.[4] The word is used to refer to 'muttering' or 'whispering' as in Isaiah 8:19 where it occurs in the causative Hiphil form.[5]

Another meaning of the verb is 'to speak.' Examples of this occur in the Psalms, where it is used in synonymous parallelism with other verbs that can be translated as 'to speak,' or in connection with the lips or tongue (Psalms 37:30; 38:13). The sound of *hāgāh* comes from the palate (Proverbs 8:7), the throat (Psalm 115:7), or the tongue (Psalm 35:28).[6] It is used with reference to particular kinds of speaking, such as lament (Isaiah 16:7; Jeremiah 48:31) or praise (Psalm 35:28). Yet *hāgāh* is not the normal word for speaking in the Old Testament. It is used at times to describe the inner longings of the human soul.[7]

The word is used in nine verses with the meaning "to reflect, to think, to meditate."[8] It can be understood as "devise, plan,"[9] and is used in this way to describe the plots of wicked men or nations (Psalm 2:1; Proverbs 24:2). "The righteous can also 'devise' or 'ponder' a proper answer (Proverbs 15:28)."[10] When one begins to examine these usages together it becomes apparent that biblical meditation should be understood as the careful reflection on the meaning of Scripture, with particular attention given to devising a plan of obedience.

---

[2] *Theological Dictionary of the Old Testament: hāgāh.*
[3] *Theological Wordbook of the Old Testament,* # 467.
[4] W. Wilson, *The Bible Student's Guide* (London: Macmillan, 1870), 271.
[5] *Theological Dictionary of the Old Testament: hāgāh.*
[6] Wilson, 271.
[7] *Theological Dictionary of the Old Testament: hāgāh.*
[8] Josh. 1:8; Pss. 1:2; 2:1; 38:12 [Hebrew: 38:13]; 63:6 [Hebrew: 63:7]; 77:12 [Hebrew: 77:13]; 143:5; Prov. 15:28; 24:2.
[9] *Theological Dictionary of the Old Testament: hāgāh.*
[10] *Theological Wordbook of the Old Testament,* # 467

When one combines this meaning, 'meditation,' with the idea of audible sounds it is most probable that audible murmuring of the Torah is implied, especially in verses like Joshua 1:8. So *hāgāh* can be used of softly spoken recitation in connection with the study of God's law.[11] One need not assume, however, that all the audible sounds of meditation are exclusively from the recitation of the Scripture. Properly understood, the word "implies what we express by one talking to himself."[12] Biblical meditation then is the muttering of Scripture, as well as muttering to oneself about Scripture. When one combines this with the usage that suggests 'devise' or 'plot,' one can see that the goal of the audible self-talk is to devise a plan of obedience to Scripture.

In practical experience this is similar to the human experience of worrying. Very often, when a person worries, he may mutter to himself as he ponders the difficulties facing him and plans what actions he might take to deal with the problems. In this sense it can be argued that biblical meditation is like focused worrying about the meaning and the practical application of Scripture. While *hāgāh* is not in the imperative form, the implication of both Joshua 1:8 and Psalm 1:2 is that meditation is an expected practice for those who are serious about understanding the will of Yahweh and putting it into practice. Biblical meditation is key when trying to avoid evil (Psalm 1:1-3) and to be spiritually blessed (Joshua 1:8).

Usage and definition of *śîyaḥ*

Of this second significant word in relation to biblical meditation there are thirty-eight occurrences in the Old Testament, twenty of them verbs and eighteen nouns. The predominant use is in the Psalms, where there are twenty-one occurrences.[13] "The basic meaning of this word appears to be 'rehearse,' 'repent,' or 'go over a matter in one's mind.'" This rehearsal or meditation can take place outwardly as a verbal recitation, or inwardly. The word is best translated as 'meditation' in the Psalms, Psalm 119 being of particular importance,

---

[11] *Theological Dictionary of the Old Testament*: *hāgāh*.
[12] Wilson, 271.
[13] *Theological Dictionary of the Old Testament*: *śîyaḥ*.

as there a noun form is used to represent reverent meditation.[14] Exegesis of passages from the Psalms will therefore be given especial attention.

As with *hāgāh*, *śîyaḥ* also can be translated "to talk with oneself."[15] The two words should therefore be understood to be virtually synonymous, and this is particularly evident through the ways in which they are used in the common practice of synonymous parallelism, which is the repeating of the thought of one line of Hebrew poetry in a second line using different words. This will be examined further in the exegesis of the Psalms where these words occur together.

Usage and definition of *meletaō* in the New Testament

This, the Septuagint equivalent of *hāgāh*, can be understood as "to be concerned about, work, take great pains with, scheme, plan."[16] It can be translated as "think about, meditate on."[17] It is used on two occasions in the New Testament. The first is in Acts 4:25, which is a quotation of Psalm 1:2, speaking of how the nations devise or plot vain things. The second use is in 1 Timothy 4:15 where the Apostle Paul uses the imperative and commands Timothy to 'meditate' on, or 'take great pains' with, the tasks of reading Scripture, preaching, and teaching. The idea of this text is that Timothy must think continually about these tasks by keeping them on his mind through the act of meditating upon them.[18] So it is clear that *meletaō* has a New Testament definition which corresponds with the Old Testament usage.

---

[14] *Theological Wordbook of the Old Testament*, # 2255.
[15] Wilson, 271.
[16] *Exegetical Dictionary of the New Testament*: *meletaō*.
[17] W. Bauer, *A Greek-English Lexicon of the New Testament and Other Early Christian Literature* [English translation by W. F. Arndt & F. W. Gingrich] (Chicago: University of Chicago Press, 1979): *meletaō*.
[18] D. Guthrie, *The Pastoral Epistles* (Leicester: IVP, 1957), 98f.

Exegesis of Joshua 1:8

Meditation is declared by the LORD to be essential for the success of Joshua, the leader who would replace Moses as the one to guide Israel (Joshua 1:1-9). This first chapter of Joshua develops a series of motifs that are carried throughout the book. One of the key motifs is the theme of required covenant obedience.[19] Here in chapter 1, the means by which that obedience is brought to more exact fruition is through biblical meditation focused on the Torah.

Joshua is told to be strong and courageous as he leads the people of Israel into the promised land. Most of the book of Joshua is about Israel's military conquest of the various parts of Palestine. Yet, it is telling that the word of the LORD to Joshua in chapter 1 is not military advice, but rather spiritual direction. The keys to Joshua's success were not military might, but his faithful obedience to God. This crucial element of success for Joshua is indicative in the Old Testament, and is mentioned as pivotal for Israel's future kings (Deuteronomy 17:14-20). Joshua 1:7 includes the phrase, "being careful to do according to all the law that my servant Moses commanded you." The words 'being careful' and 'do' translate the Hebrew words *šāmar*, which means 'be careful, observe,' and *'āśāh*, which means 'to obey.' These words are paired together forty times in the Old Testament. Almost all of the occurrences correspond to keeping and obeying God's laws and commands.[20] The next verse indicates that meditation is the necessary spiritual discipline that will enable Joshua to keep God's laws and commands.

The structure of this passage makes it clear that unless Joshua makes meditation and obedience to God's law his first priority, his leadership will fail. There are three structural elements that suggest this. First, in verse 6, the command to be strong and courageous is given, and is repeated again in verse 7. Next, there are clauses of result at the end of verses 7 and 8 that promise success in his mission. This success extends to "wherever you go" and is characterised as

---

[19] M. H. Woudstra, *The Book of Joshua* (Grand Rapids: Eerdmans, 1985), 56.
[20] D. M. Howard, Jr., *Joshua* (Nashville: Broadman & Holman, 1998), 85.

'prosperous' and 'successful.' Third, there is the threefold mention of God's law in these verses.[21]

The initial phrase of verse 8 states that Joshua should not let the Book of the Law depart from his mouth, reinforcing the concept that meditation involves continual recitation and focused thinking on God's law. He is not simply to let it leave his mouth, but is to continue to consider it and repeat it throughout the day, and in the night as well. This meditation is not some sort of theoretical speculation about the law, such as some of the later Pharisees engaged in, but rather a practical study of the law. The purpose of such study was to enable the reader to observe the law in his thought life, as well as in action.[22] That Joshua is told not to allow the law to depart from his mouth, suggests that he is one who speaks God's law, and therefore is a teacher of that law. His first necessary task is to understand and obey God's law, and only then is he truly qualified to teach it.[23]

The Hebrew verbs *ṣāleaḥ* and *śākal*, that are translated respectively as "prosperous" and "have good success," are used a number of times in the Old Testament. This is the only place that the two are used together.[24] The use of almost synonymous terms in this verse emphasises how spiritual success is related directly to obedience that is enhanced through meditation on the Torah.

Ṣāleaḥ is used sixty-nine times in the Old Testament, of which fifty-nine refer to prospering and succeeding in life's endeavours, but not in reference to financial or material success. In almost all of the references, the success is the result of God's gracious and ever-present hand.[25] Two examples of this are Abraham's servant, who was given the task of searching for a wife for Isaac,[26] and Joseph's experience in Potiphar's house.[27] The Messiah himself, even when bruised, would cause God's will to prosper in his hand (Isaiah 53:10).

---

[21] R. S. Hess, *Joshua: An Introduction and Commentary* (Downers Grove: IVP, 1996), 73.
[22] Howard, 86.
[23] J. Calvin, *Commentaries on the Book of Joshua* [1564] (Grand Rapids: Baker, 1979 reprint), 32.
[24] Howard, 90.
[25] Howard, 88.
[26] Gen. 24:21, 40, 42, 56.
[27] Gen. 39:2, 3, 23.

The word *śākal* occurs seventy-eight times in the Old Testament, with the most common translation consisting of 'have insight, understanding, be wise.' In ten or eleven cases, including twice in this passage (verses 7-8), it takes the meaning 'to be successful.' In most of these cases, almost without exception, success is the result of an individual seeking the LORD with zeal, or with conscientious obedience to his commandments.[28] As well as in the present context, success is very specifically equated with the keeping of God's law in a number of other places.[29] Therefore it is clear in Joshua 1 that the key to Joshua's leadership and spiritual success is directly correlated with his careful attention and obedience to God's law. The method that is commanded by God as the way to stay focused on God's law so that Joshua might obey it and then teach it to others is through the process of meditation.

Exegesis of Psalm 1

Psalm 1 is positioned quite intentionally at the beginning of the collection of Psalms. It provides the entrance way to the rest of the book. It is the first principle, and sets the stage for the rest of the Psalms. This means that the statements contained within Psalm 1 have considerable weight and importance. This is another place where *hāgāh* is used with the meaning 'reflect, think, meditate.' Initially the psalmist declares that his intent is to show the way of the blessed, or happy, person.[30]

The word for blessed is plural which makes the statement more of an exclamation and intensive. So the psalmist is going to present the way to sheer happiness. His positive recommendation towards this happiness amounts to one thing: meditation on the LORD's Torah.[31] This corresponds closely to what has been previously considered in Joshua 1:8.

---

[28] Howard, 89.

[29] Deut. 29:9 [Hebrew: 29:8]; 1 Kgs. 2:3; 2 Kgs. 18:6f.

[30] P. C. Craigie, *Psalms 1-50* (Dallas: Word, 2004), 60.

[31] J. Eaton, *The Psalms: A Historical and Spiritual Commentary* (London: T & T Clark, 2003), 62.

However, the psalmist makes it clear that, before a person can engage in biblical meditation, it is necessary that he separate himself from the influences of the ungodly (verses 1-2).[32] The implication is that rebellion spreads like gangrene, and the one who wants blessing or happiness should avoid the thoughts, lifestyle, or advice of those who are ungodly.[33]

The three verbs translated as 'walking, standing, sitting' denote the postures of a person while he is awake and, as such, portray the entire course of life or conduct. It is also possible that these verbs represent stages of degradation, as this could represent an example of synthetic parallelism where the psalmist is repeating a similar idea but adding more description to it.[34] So walking might represent occasional conformity, then standing a more fixed association, and finally sitting might represent that one is no longer simply a companion with the wicked, but one who has become a member of those he associates with.[35] The implication is that having some evil influence can lead to a habitual pattern of life that is controlled by evil, and one that is not happy or blessed.

By contrast, in verse 2 the Psalmist speaks about what the truly happy person does. Here the Psalmist uses antithetical parallelism where he says contrasting things, with verse 1 representing the thesis and verse 2 the antithesis.[36] The happy life is not simply the avoidance of evil influences. It involves finding delight or pleasure in something entirely different. At this point one might expect that since the wicked person is identified by his associations, the godly and happy person would be described by his associations as well.[37] Certainly there is happiness found in good and godly associations, but this is not where the Psalmist says our delight is to be found. Rather, that delight is found in the Torah, the law of the LORD. The Torah provides the key

---

[32] J. Calvin, *Commentary on the Book of Psalms* [1557] (Grand Rapids: Baker, 1979 reprint), Vol. 1, 2.
[33] Craigie, 60.
[34] J. M. Boice, *Psalms* (Grand Rapids: Baker, 1994), Vol. 1, 16.
[35] J. A. Alexander, *The Psalms: Translated and Explained* [1850] (Grand Rapids: Baker, 1975 reprint), 16.
[36] C. H. Bullock, *Encountering the Book of Psalms: A Literary and Theological Introduction* (Grand Rapids: Baker, 2001), 39.
[37] Boice, 16.

source of satisfaction and pleasure for the person who is truly blessed. The key to unlocking that pleasure is meditation: careful, focused thought on this law. Thorough meditation takes time, and the blessed person will engage in it with joy, both in the day and in the night.[38]

The emphasis in this text is not meditation in and of itself. The emphasis is on the object of meditation, specifically the Torah.[39] Humanity's meaning and purpose is preserved in the Torah. The process to discover this meaning and purpose flows from continual meditation on the Torah.[40] The one who sees the Torah in this way understands it to be the intelligible expression of the will of Yahweh and, as such, an unerring compass which is sufficient to regulate all his conduct. The Torah also acts as a strong bond, which points to God's providential rule over one's life. For this reason the purpose for which one meditates upon it is not simply to become versed in the Torah, as is still practised by orthodox Jews today, but rather a yielding to the Torah so that it becomes second nature "as that which fills his life as the only meaning of that life."[41]

The person who meditates on the Torah day and night is likened to a tree that is planted by a stream of water, and, because of this water source, produces a perpetual abundance of fruit.[42] There is no sign of a lack of the life-giving water. The tree has leaves that never wither. Even times of drought have no effect on this tree and its production of fruit. The powerful implication for the practice of biblical meditation is clear: those who meditate day and night will place themselves in a position to be nourished, and the result is prosperity in all that they do. The resultant prosperity is not affected by difficult circumstances, because the source of nourishment is always present.

The statement "in all that he does, he prospers" interrupts the agricultural imagery and echoes Joshua 1:8,[43] where it is the same Hebrew word, *ṣāleaḥ*, that is used. So there is a consistent theme of spiritual prosperity that is promised for the one who will make biblical

---

[38] Calvin, *Psalms*, Vol. 1, 5.
[39] C. G. Broyles, *Psalms* (Peabody: Hendrickson, 1999), 42.
[40] Craigie, 61.
[41] A. Weiser, *The Psalms: A Commentary* (Philadelphia: Westminster, 1976), 104.
[42] Alexander, 10.
[43] Broyles, 43.

meditation a priority in his spiritual life. The image of the tree by the water and bearing fruit in season may well suggest another parallel with the man who meditates carefully on the word of the Torah. In some sense the tree is meant to take in water, sprout leaves, and produce fruit, in accordance with God's will and purpose for it. In a similar way, the blessed or godly man fulfills the purpose for which he was created when he takes in the word of God, and then obeys it in his outward actions.[44]

Exegesis of Psalm 63:6

In Psalm 63:6, we have an example of synonymous parallelism: the second line is directly related to the first, and uses different words to repeat the same idea.[45] In the first line the Psalmist David remembers God in the watches of the night. In the second line he meditates (*hāgāh*) on God. While this is not a use of *hāgāh* with a specific designation of the Bible as the locus of the meditation, it is speaking about meditation, or focused thought, on God. What motivates David to meditate on God is the reality that David owes his preservation to the providential care that God furnishes for him. So he carefully thinks about what God has done for him. Although the night was considered a dangerous time, a time when demons and evil spirits were operating, it was also considered a good time to seek God's presence in prayer and meditation.[46] So, rather than be terrified, as other men are during the night hours, David receives the comfort that comes through careful meditation on the character of God and his care.

Exegesis of Psalm 77:11-12

In Psalm 77 the Psalmist Asaph remembers some of his troubles, and is comforted and helped as he meditates (*hāgāh*) on God's work and muses (*śîyaḥ*) on his deeds (verse 12 [Hebrew: verse 13]). This verse is another example of the frequent practice in Hebrew poetry of synonymous parallelism. It appears that Asaph wants to emphasise

---

[44] Weiser, 105.
[45] Calvin, *Psalms,* Vol. 5, 439.
[46] James H. Waltner, *Psalms* (Waterloo: Herald, 2006), 306.

the importance of meditation, as he uses three verbs in close proximity which are almost synonymous. They are translated as "remember," used twice in verse 11, and then "ponder" (*hāgāh*), followed by "meditate"—or 'muse'—(*śîyaḥ*) in verse 12.[47] The focus of this meditation is the words and deeds of the LORD. This may have involved the personal experience of the Psalmist, but is also the recollection of what the LORD had done for Israel in the past. The Psalmist records what the LORD did for Israel, mentioning the specifics of Moses leading the people, and the provision of passage through the sea (verses 15-20). Considering the ways in which the LORD dealt providentially with Israel in the past is certainly an example of meditating and pondering the word of God, because it is a pondering of the record of these acts in Scripture.[48] When believers are going through times of turmoil and begin to feel desperate, they can read of what God has done for his people, meditate upon those truths, and find real comfort. So this passage is another testimony to the benefits of meditating on Scripture.

Exegesis of Psalm 119:15, 23, 48, 148

In Psalm 119:15, the Psalmist declares that he will meditate (*śîyaḥ*) on the precepts of the LORD and fix his eyes on (*nābaṭ*), or regard, the ways of the LORD. It is apparent that the first and second statements are very similar in meaning, and so we have another example of synonymous parallelism. The verb 'meditate' is parallel to, and synonymous with, the verb *nābaṭ*, meaning to 'pay attention to.'[49] The repetition of the statements and the verbs is for emphasis, and so the Psalmist is purposefully stressing the importance of meditating on the precepts of the LORD as an act of substantive personal piety. In the previous verse the Psalmist speaks of affection for the word of God, and declares that it is the treasure of treasures. Yet it is evident from verses 15-17 that while meditation on the word is delightful, the

---

[47] R. G. Bracker & W. D. Reyburn, *A Handbook on Psalms*, (New York: UBS, 1991), 675.
[48] G. W. Grogan, *Psalms* (Grand Rapids: Eerdmans, 2008), 139.
[49] Bracker & Reyburn, 1002.

purpose and learned result is the same as in Joshua 1:8 and Psalm 1—
obedience to that word.[50]

Verse 23 is another example showing the Psalmist turning to
biblical meditation in order to find comfort and help in the midst of a
vexing situation. Stylistically, in this verse the Psalmist presents
another example of Hebrew parallelism, in this instance antithetical:
the first part of the verse is contrasted with the second. The first part,
the thesis, is "even though princes sit plotting against me," and the
antithesis is "your servant will meditate (*śîyaḥ*) on your statutes."

The Psalmist finds stability in a threatening situation. Instead of
being distracted by the threatening situation of the princes talking
against him, his mind is filled with the Scriptures as he meditates.
However, one would be wrong to see this as some sort of escapism.
Rather, the truth is that the Scriptures provide the best of advice, as
the Psalmist states in verse 24 that the testimonies of the LORD are his
counsellors.[51] Once again, meditation on Scripture is encouraged by
this example, as it provides comfort and stability in a time of
challenge.

In verse 48 the Psalmist speaks of lifting his hands to the
commandments of the LORD. The lifting of the hands implies worship.
The Psalmist then specifically states that he loves the commands of
the LORD, and says that he will meditate (*śîyaḥ*) on them.[52] The proper
attitude to have as one thinks deeply on the Scripture is one of worship
and adoration. The Scriptures are worthy of that respect and attention,
and having this mindset will aid in meditation and the benefits that are
derived from it.

In verse 148 the Psalmist declares that his eyes 'meet' the
watches of the night. This means that he is awake throughout the
night. There were three periods, or watches, in the night, and the
Psalmist had his eyes open as each one approached.[53] The text states
a specific reason why the Psalmist stays awake; he explicitly says that
he is sleepless so that he might meditate (*śîyaḥ*) on God's word. When
most people are sleeping, the Psalmist stays awake, because he has

---

[50] H. C. Leupold, *Exposition of the Psalms* (Grand Rapids: Baker, 1969), 826.
[51] F. D. Kidner, *Psalms 1-72* (Leicester: IVP, 1973), 422.
[52] Kidner, 425.
[53] Bracker & Reyburn, 1039.

something more important to do, and that is to meditate on the Scriptures. The inference is clear: meditation on the word of God is of more value than sleep. The Psalmist has a wholehearted commitment to meditation on God's word, that is driving and controlling him, and is keeping him awake.[54] He intends to inspire his readers to be devoted to the word of God, by showing that his own devotion includes missing sleep so that he might meditate on it.

Exegesis of Psalm 143:5

In Psalm 143 David is under considerable duress as he calls out to the LORD. In this context he writes the words of verse 5, which speak about meditation. David again uses the literary technique of synonymous parallelism in this verse. He speaks of remembering the days of old, says that he 'meditates' (*hāgāh*) on what the LORD has done. Then, in the synonymous parallel phrase, he states that he 'ponders'—or muses on—(*śîyaḥ*) the works of the LORD. This use of parallelism is, as in other places, done for emphasis.[55]

This use of *hāgāh* and *śîyaḥ* in synonymous parallelism indicates that the words could be used interchangeably. David is emphasising once more how important meditating on the works of the LORD is. In considering these past works of the LORD, he is meditating and musing on the scriptural records of the deeds of the LORD. He therefore meditates on the Scriptures in his time of distress. Scriptural meditation appears to be an excellent way for David to get his bearings in a time of turmoil. By meditating on the deeds of the LORD which are recorded in the Scriptures, David can discover the unchangeable nature of God, and his redemptive attitude and temperament towards his people.[56] So, again, one can see that there is specific benefit in biblical meditation, and in carefully pondering the great work of God towards those who are his people.

---

[54] Grogan, 198.
[55] Calvin, *Psalms,* Vol. 5, 253.
[56] Leupold, 965.

Exegesis of Romans 12:1-2

In Romans 1-11 Paul expounds the glories of the gospel of grace. In chapter 12 there is a shift from the declaration of precious doctrine to the application of it, or from indicative to imperative. This puts Romans 12:1-2 in a very significant position within Romans, just as Joshua 1 and Psalm 1 are in key locations. As with those passages, Romans 12:1-2 has conspicuous weight, and so the believer should give these verses particular attention. In them Paul speaks about the renewing of the mind, and so this has bearing on the subject of focused thinking, which is meditation, and more specifically on the practice of biblical meditation. In verse 1 Paul describes the need to offer our bodies as living sacrifices. Verse 2 is best understood as subordinate to verse 1: it provides the means by which we carry out the comprehensive admonition presented in verse 1.[57]

In verse 2 Paul begins by describing what we are not to do, using two imperative verbs, both of which could be passive. The first is a present imperative, preceded by a negative. The force of the tense of these verbs could be translated 'stop allowing yourselves to be conformed' and 'continue to let yourself be transformed.' [58]

However, the first verb might also be middle voice, and so could be translated with a more active sense, simply as 'do not conform.' The second imperative is most definitely in the passive voice, but may also be translated more simply as 'be transformed.' This seems to be the probable meaning.[59]

Paul uses the words "this world" as essentially equivalent to 'the wicked.'[60] Thematically this gives some connection with Psalm 1, where the blessed man is not influenced by the wicked, but instead meditates on God's law. The present tense of these verbs is durative in nature, and so these processes are to be viewed as going on all the time. The believer is to engage in continual renunciation and renewal.

---

[57] D. J. Moo, *The Epistle to the Romans* (Grand Rapids: Eerdmans, 1996), 754f.
[58] C. E. B. Cranfield, *The Epistle to the Romans* (Edinburgh: T. & T. Clark, 1979), 607.
[59] Moo, 755.
[60] C. Hodge, *Romans* [1835] (Wheaton: Crossway, 1993 reprint), 344.

It is that described in the next phrase, the renewing of the mind, which aids in this process.[61]

That renewing of the mind is the means by which we are to continue to let ourselves be transformed. The mind is directly connected to our body, and is therefore included as part of 'presenting' our bodies. So the transformation that happens to us, while it begins in our inner person, works its way outward. Paul emphasises that, for our behaviour to conform to the perfect will of God, and for us truly to offer all that we are in service to God, the transformation must begin in our mind, with our thought and reason.[62] Accordingly, this passage is an exemplary text that highlights how biblical meditation is a spiritual discipline which aids in spiritual growth. The renewing of the mind can further be understood as our 'practical reason' or 'moral consciousness.' Followers of Christ are to adjust their way of thinking about every aspect of their life in conformity to the newness of life which they have in Christ. This sort of re-programming of the mind is not a sudden event, but a lifelong process in which our way of thinking slowly shifts to resemble more and more the manner in which God would have us think.[63]

However, in chapter 7 of Romans Paul has described his struggle to live according to what he knows to be right because his sin nature pulls him in a different direction. Then in chapter 8 he describes the work of the Spirit, and specifically the mind set on the Spirit (Romans 8:1-11). From these two chapters it is clear that Paul does not mean to say that the transformation of Romans 12:2 is simply a matter of changing one's thinking: it is something that requires the work of the Holy Spirit within the believer.[64] It is the Holy Spirit who both teaches, and works into a believer's mind, the commands of Christ in this process of mind renewal.[65]

At the same time, Paul certainly does not mean that the believer is a passive observer. Believers have a responsible share in the process

---

[61] E. F. Harrison, 'Romans,' in F. E. Gaebelein (ed.), *Expositors Bible Commentary, Vol. 10* (Grand Rapids: Zondervan, 1976), 28.
[62] J. D. G. Dunn, *Romans* (Dallas: Word, 1988), 714, 718.
[63] Moo, 755.
[64] Cranfield, 609.
[65] Moo, 758.

by yielding to the Holy Spirit's leading.[66] This involves resisting the pressure to adopt the customs and mindset of the prevailing culture in which one lives, while admitting that this resistance is not enough; real and lasting change must come from within.[67]

The transformation spoken about in Romans 12:2 also involves repentance. The fundamental solution to ungodly ethical behaviour is repentance, since repentance is, in essence, the renewing of the mind. Paul is emphasising that the way in which a believer's behaviour is shifted into a new and God pleasing direction is when his manner of thinking is changed.[68] So then, the renewing of the mind is the key to transformation. That renewal is the work of the Spirit, and the Spirit uses the sword that is the word of God to carry out this renewal.[69] Since it is Scripture which the Spirit uses, the spiritual discipline which is uniquely fitted to support this process is biblical meditation.

The last phrase of Romans 12:2 can be translated 'that you may prove what the will of God is.' The phrase 'that you may prove' is an infinitive preceded by the preposition *eis* and the article, a grammatical combination which expresses the purpose, or desired result, of the renewal of the mind.[70] That desired result is that one may prove what the will of God is, and that will is described as "good and acceptable and perfect." This process of proving the will of God is not the action of testing the will of God to determine whether it is good or bad. Rather, it is the process of approving the will of God by experience.[71] In this sense the one who has a renewed mind, and, as a result, carries out the will of God, has the privilege of discovering that the will of God is approved, that it is good, pleasing, and perfect.

Here is a thematic connection with Joshua 1:8 and Psalm 1. The causal result of the renewing of the mind is so that the believer might approve the will of God. Joshua 1:8 expresses a synonymous result of meditating on the Torah, which is practical obedience to it. Romans

---

[66] Cranfield, 609.

[67] R. H. Mounce, *Romans,* (Nashville: Broadman & Holman, 1995), 232.

[68] K. Barth, *The Epistle to the Romans* (London: OUP, 1933), 436.

[69] J. R. W. Stott, *Romans* (Downers Grove: IVP, 1994), 324.

[70] F. Reinecker & C. Rogers, *Linguistic Key to the Greek New Testament* (Grand Rapids: Zondervan, 1976), 375.

[71] J. Murray, *The Epistle to the Romans* (Grand Rapids: Eerdmans, 1968), 114f.

12:2 states that, as one practically follows the will of God, he discovers that it is good, pleasing, and perfect. In a similar way, in Joshua 1:8 and Psalm 1, meditating on the Torah results in obedience, which results in spiritual prosperity and fruitfulness. It is therefore easy to discern that biblical meditation is a spiritual discipline which spans both the Old and New Testaments, and the careful practice of this meditation results in a greater obedience to the Scriptures, leading to spiritual growth.

So in Romans 12:1-2 Paul lays out the sequence or pattern that God uses to continue to shape his children according to his will. It begins with the believer continuing the practice of renouncing or resisting the evil influences of the society around him. Then this believer allows himself to be transformed as his thinking is changed through the renewal of his mind. This renewal is the work of the Holy Spirit, and the Spirit uses the instrument of the word of God to do this task of mind renewal which leads to a practical change in behaviour.[72] That change in behaviour conforms to the will of God, and the believer has the delight of personally experiencing how good, pleasing, and perfect the will of God is.

Exegesis of Philippians 4:8-9

In these verses the Apostle Paul gives a final exhortation to the believers in Philippi concerning that upon which they should be focusing their thoughts. This text provides another New Testament expression of the importance of the spiritual discipline of biblical meditation. In the original text, verses 8 and 9 form one long sentence.[73] In this section Paul begins to conclude his letter, as is evident from the use of the word "finally." In this conclusion he commands the Philippian believers to "think" (*logizesthe*) on a specified list of things.

The list is distinctive, with a "strong and effective rhetorical tone."[74] This literary effect is accomplished by the six-fold repetition

---

[72] J. F. MacArthur, *The MacArthur New Testament Commentary: Romans 9-16* (Chicago: Moody Publishers, 1994), 151.
[73] W. G. Hansen, *The Letter to the Philippians* (Grand Rapids: Eerdmans, 2009), 295.
[74] M. Silva, *Philippians* (Grand Rapids: Baker, 1992), 228.

of the relative pronoun "whatever," followed by two conditional clauses. Paul achieves this strong effect through the use of these six clauses in synonymous parallelism, and by keeping them grammatically unconnected, allowing each of the listed virtues to be presented for special consideration.[75] The last two clauses are intended to bolster the sweeping character of Paul's exhortation, since there is no list that would be exhaustive.[76]

Some scholars have tried to create uncertainty as to the source of the list of virtues that the apostle gives in verse 8. Some interpreters suggest that he borrows this list from secular philosophers of his day.[77] This is because the virtues listed are not particularly Christian, and the terms are seldom used by Paul.[78] The use of such moral lists was a writing style that was employed by moral philosophers of Paul's day,[79] especially among the Stoics.[80] This evidence advances the idea that Paul may have been using a culturally relevant list and encouraging the believers in Philippi to live up to the moral excellence that they had known prior to being believers.[81] However, the means by which Paul saw these virtues practised in the believer's life was through the working of the Holy Spirit, which produces such fruit within us.[82]

Paul speaks of citizenship in 1:27 and 3:20, and so some have suggested that the list of virtues might be an encouragement to *civic duty*. Yet, this citizenship motif is very clearly used to draw the Philippians to the reality of their Christian allegiance, as their citizenship is "in heaven." When we consider the context of the letter as a whole, it is hard to consider that Paul is deliberately moving from the heights of following the example of Christ to simply being good citizens. The immediate context of verse 9 with the imperative to follow Paul's example also militates against this. Given this broader

---

[75] P. O'Brien, *Commentary on Philippians* (Grand Rapids: Eerdmans, 1991), 499.
[76] Silva, 228.
[77] G. F. Hawthorne, *Philippians* (Dallas: Word, 1983), 187.
[78] R. R. Melick, Jr., *Philippians, Colossians, Philemon* (Nashville: Broadman, 1991), 150.
[79] Silva, 229.
[80] O'Brien, 502.
[81] Hawthorne, 186.
[82] Melick, 150.

context, it is necessary that we see the virtues listed in verse 8 as distinctly Christian.[83]

Paul lists six adjectives which represent the things that are worthy of our focused thinking. He follows this up with two comprehensive nouns to finalise the list.

The list starts with "whatever is *true.*" This word is comprehensive[84] and so refers to all things that are truthful and honest.

The next virtue listed is *"honourable."* Although this word is hard to define with one term, its basic meaning is clear: "it refers to lofty things, majestic things, things that lift the mind from the cheap and tawdry to that which is noble and good and of moral worth."[85] As such, it suggests the very opposite of everything that is vulgar.[86]

The third virtue listed, "whatever is *just,*" uses another broad term that has the idea of giving justice that is due to both God and man.[87]

The fourth virtue in the list is "whatever is *pure,*" a word which suggests not simply chaste, but also the idea of being suited to worship God with a purity in motives and actions.[88]

The fifth virtue is "whatever is *lovely.*" The word which Paul uses here occurs only this once in the New Testament; it is again a broad term, communicating the basic idea of "that which calls forth love."[89]

The sixth virtue is "whatever is *commendable,*" another word used only here in the New Testament. It has the idea of being "well-spoken of" or "winning, attractive" and, as such, speaks of what is kind and likely to win people over, while avoiding what is likely to offend.[90]

Paul then uses two parallel conditional clauses, "if there is any excellence, if there is anything worthy of praise," to summarise his

---

[83] Silva, 229.
[84] O'Brien, 503.
[85] Hawthorne, 188.
[86] O'Brien, 504.
[87] Melick, 151.
[88] Hawthorne, 188 (cf. 2 Cor. 11:2; 1 Tim. 5:22; Jas. 3:17; 1 Jn. 3:3).
[89] Melick, 151.
[90] Hawthorne, 188.

list of ideals.[91] The word translated "excellence" has a broad meaning in classical Greek, where it describes excellence of any kind, including that of a person, animal, or thing, but Paul probably had a Stoic sense of moral excellence or goodness in mind, while the next word has the meaning 'praise' and something "worthy of praise." Paul uses it elsewhere to speak of the praise of God,[92] but here, when combined with "excellence," it is best understood as relating to the praise of men.[93]

The main verb of verse 8, *logizesthe*, "think" (or 'let your mind dwell'), comes at the end of the verse. The previous six adjectives and two nouns all lead up to this imperative verb and its direct object: 'let your mind dwell on these things.'[94]

This verb is strong, and is a favourite of Paul's, with thirty-four of forty New Testament occurrences being found in his epistles. It has a range of meanings such as "'to reckon, calculate, take into account' and, as a result, 'to evaluate' a person, thing, quality or event." The definition "'to ponder or let one's mind dwell on' something" is included in that range of meaning.[95] Since the tense of the verb is present, Paul is calling on the Philippian believers to let their minds continually dwell on the positive qualities that he has just articulated in the six adjectives and two nouns preceding this verb.[96]

The verb can be translated as 'meditate,' and this would be a very suitable translation in this context.[97] However, this meditation is not an end in itself, but rather, in a pattern similar to Joshua 1:8, is intended to provoke action.[98] So the purpose of such thought and evaluation is not to assess which of these qualities is good or best, but carefully to consider these traits, so that one's conduct will be transformed by them.[99] These objects of meditation are meant to guide

---

[91] Hansen, 295.
[92] Rom. 2:29; 1 Cor. 4:5.
[93] Hawthorne, 186.
[94] Hansen, 295.
[95] Hawthorne, 187.
[96] O'Brien, 507.
[97] J. B. Lightfoot, *Saint Paul's Epistle to the Philippians* (London: MacMillan, 1903), 162.
[98] Hawthorne, 188.
[99] O'Brien, 507.

the Philippian believers into good deeds.[100] In fact, these categories of quality-thoughts were meant to chart the course for their behaviour.[101]

In verse 9 Paul expands and heightens the intensity of his exhortation and he does so in three ways. First, he changes the main verb from "think" (meditate) to "practise." Second, he emphasises how correct behaviour has been modelled for them, so that they have been able to 'learn, receive, hear, and see' in Paul the manner in which they should live. Third, Paul ties his exhortation in with verse 7 and his previous promise of peace, with the words, "and the God of peace will be with you."[102] So verse 9 clearly articulates that the goal of meditating on things of good quality is for the intended result of change in behaviour, and this change will further result in God's peaceful presence with us.[103]

It is interesting to consider the context in which Paul writes this exhortation about meditation. Chapter 1 reveals that he is in prison, chained to praetorian guards (verses 13-14). The implication is that, when a follower of Christ is in the direst circumstances, the way to peace comes through meditating on things that are good and profitable.[104] This benefit of meditation is echoed in the Psalms previously considered.[105] Although, Paul does not specifically mention meditating on Scripture, the adjectives that he uses to describe the objects of proper thought can certainly be found in the highest degree in the pages of holy writ. If we examine the larger context of Philippians 4 and Paul's exhortation to "stand firm" in the Lord in verse 1, we see that the key to standing firm is dependent on how we think (verse 8), and how we act (verse 9).[106] Therefore, Paul's writings support biblical meditation as an essential element in maintaining a consistent Christian life, as well as assisting in the believer's ongoing sanctification.

---

[100] Hawthorne, 187.
[101] Melick, 150.
[102] Silva, 229.
[103] Hawthorne, 190.
[104] J. F. Walvoord, *Philippians: Triumph in Christ* (Chicago: Moody, 1971), 109.
[105] E.g., Pss. 63:6; 77:12; 119:23; 143:5.
[106] Hawthorne, 185.

Exegesis of James 1:22-25

This is another text that encourages the spiritual discipline of biblical meditation. In verse 22 James exhorts the believers to "be" (*ginesthe*) doers of the word. It is possible that he intends a more charitable understanding of this present imperative verb. It can be translated "continue being" doers of the word, rather than the ingressive present, "become" doers of the word. Regardless, the emphasis is that the hearing of the word must result in the doing of it.[107]

James uses a common literary device known as a *chiastic structure* in these verses. It is a simple chiasm where he repeats a sequence of ideas in reverse order. He begins in verse 22 with the positive command to "be doers," in order to emphasise it. Then he states that they should not be "hearers only." In verse 23, he again takes up the negative example before returning to the positive one at the end of verse 25.[108] This structure has the purpose of putting strong emphasis on the positive exhortation of being doers of the word, as contrasted with the deficiency of being only hearers. It is the positive exhortation to be doers that James wants to stand out.

James uses a parable in verses 23-24 that would be familiar to his audience. The example he uses is the practice of looking in a mirror, with the action, perhaps, of combing one's hair. The point of emphasis is not on the *manner* in which one looks, with the difference being 'glancing' in the mirror versus 'look carefully at,' since the verb used, "looks intently," commonly means 'contemplates' or 'observes carefully.'[109] The purpose is to contrast the difference between the one who is 'forgetting' the word (verse 24), and the one 'persevering,' or remaining in the word (verse 25).[110]

The main emphasis, then, is that the impression of the observation in the mirror is only temporary. So, while one is combing his hair, it might be absorbing in the moment, but in most instances would bear no practical effect as one continues on with the normal

---

[107] P. Davids, *The Epistle of James: A Commentary on the Greek Text* (Exeter: Paternoster, 1982), 96f.

[108] Davids, The Epistle of James, 97.

[109] Davids, 97 (cf. Matt. 7:3; Lk. 12:24, 27; 20:3).

[110] D. J. Moo, *The Letter of James* (Grand Rapids: Eerdmans, 2000), 83.

business of the day. The essential point is that this action of looking in the mirror is momentary and lacking result, rather than a contrast of differing mirrors or manners of seeing.[111] The doer of the word, by contrast, remains or 'perseveres,' which can mean either that he continues to 'do' the word, or that he continues to 'contemplate' it. In either case the one who remains in the word is extolled for displaying in his actions the continuing influence that the word has on his life.[112]

Basic logic dictates that for the hearer of the word to remain in the word and be a doer of it, contemplation and meditation on the word must take place so that this hearer may synthesise what practical deeds would constitute 'doing' the word. So, in a pattern distinctly similar to Joshua 1:8, we hear James calling on believers not simply to hear the word, but to meditate upon it, until the natural result is obedience.

Another way in which James 1:22-25 resembles Joshua 1:8 and Psalm 1 is in the long-term benefit that comes from meditating on the word. In verse 25 James states that the person who hears, and then eventually does, the word is a person who "will be blessed in his doing." While this benefit of blessing can have the suggestion of immediacy, the context of chapter 1 suggests a future eschatological blessing as well. The fact that the verb 'to be' is in a future tense, along with the previous reference to eschatological blessing in verse 12 of chapter 1, suggests a future orientation to this blessing. Certainly, the motif of the blessing of God on the one who hears and meditates on the word with resulting obedience, is one that resonates in both the Old and New Testaments.

Conclusion

Biblical meditation is a spiritual discipline that is of great value for the believer. In many places in the Old and New Testaments it is either commanded as a practice, or tacitly understood as a way of experiencing spiritual benefit and blessing. The most common Hebrew words for meditation, *hāgāh* and *śîyah*, demonstrate, through both definition, and the variety of occurrences, that biblical

---

[111] Davids, 98.
[112] Moo, 83.

meditation is the practice of repeating and pondering over a passage of Scripture. In many of these occurrences, like Joshua 1:8, the goal is to ponder for a sufficient duration and with a sufficiently intensive concentration that the result is a plan and a desire to obey. Several of the Psalms that speak of biblical meditation reveal that there are many benefits in doing so. These include comfort in frightening or challenging situations (Psalms 63:6; 77:13; 119:33; 143:5), and as aid in true worship (Psalm 119:48). The greatest benefit is the ongoing spiritual blessing provided by the Lord (Joshua 1:8; Psalm 1).

Biblical meditation is emphasised in a number of New Testament passages such as Romans 12:1-2, where it is understood to be a means to assist the believer in avoiding conformity to this present evil world, as one is renewed in his mind. Similarly, in Philippians 4 proper thinking is commanded, so that behaviour might reflect what Paul has modelled. The resultant benefit is the blessing of God's peace in a trying circumstance. Finally, in James 1:22-25, the practice of remaining in the word until obedience is produced is overtly commanded, and the result is again the blessing of God.

Biblical meditation is a very significant spiritual discipline, because God is rational. Jesus is described in John 1 as *the Word*, which again describes one who is rational. It follows that the great commandment includes loving God with all our heart, soul, *mind*, and strength (Mark 12:30). Believers are not to empty their minds, but to fill them with thoughts of God and with God's word, which is his rational message to us.

The practice of biblical meditation is mentioned in a sufficient number of passages throughout the Old and New Testaments to warrant the close attention of the believer. God is pleased, and we are blessed, when we make biblical meditation a consistent spiritual discipline in our lives. It is therefore beneficial that we formulate a model to do so.

CPSIA information can be obtained
at www.ICGtesting.com
Printed in the USA
JSHW051950181122
33407JS00005B/18